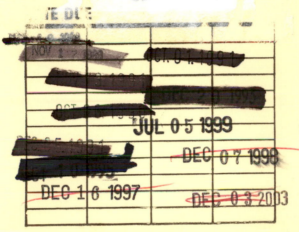

RENAISSANCE
THEATRE

Ronald W. Vince

RENAISSANCE THEATRE

A Historiographical Handbook

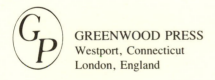

GREENWOOD PRESS
Westport, Connecticut
London, England

Library of Congress Cataloging in Publication Data

Vince, Ronald W.
  Renaissance theatre.

  Includes bibliographies and indexes.
  1. Theater—History—16th century. 2. Theater—
History—17th century. I. Title.
PN2171.V5 1984   809.2′03   83-13031
ISBN 0-313-24108-2 (lib. bdg.)

Library of Congress Catalog Card Number: 83-13031
ISBN: 0-313-24108-2

First published in 1984

Greenwood Press
A division of Congressional Information Service, Inc.
88 Post Road West, Westport, Connecticut 06881

Printed in the United States of America

10 9 8 7 6 5 4 3 2 1

For Alexandra and Jerome

CONTENTS

PREFACE

This book, like its sister volume on the ancient and medieval theatre, seeks to introduce readers to the sources of information available to the theatre historian, and to some of the methods that have been used in the interpretation of that evidence. To that end, it provides an analytical survey of the principal written and artifactual evidence for the history of the Renaissance theatres of Italy, Spain, England, and France. The writing of history itself constitutes a historical process: The methods and assumption of theatre historians change with changing intellectual fashion as well as with the discovery of fresh evidence, and history is constantly being rewritten as theories and data interact. Nevertheless, the theatre historian's task can be defined in two parts: to reconstruct and describe the theatrical forms and conventions, the audiences, and the playing spaces that have determined the dynamic and the style of past performances; and to attempt to account for particular conditions and styles as they change through time. What elements constitute style of performance and what factors govern changes in style? These questions are at the centre of theatre historiography.

There has been no attempt to discuss all the evidence available for the study of the Renaissance theatre, nor has it been possible to note all the scholarship that has contributed to our understanding of that theatre. What is offered is a compromise between theoretical historiography and a bibliography: Included is a discussion of the various kinds of evidence, with special reference to those specific sources that have proved to be of central importance, and an evaluative sketch of the most significant scholarship. The reader is referred where possible to sources that reproduce primary evidence.

During the late fifteenth and the sixteenth centuries, particularly in Italy, scholars were becoming aware of the ancient theatre, and efforts were made to recreate the theatre of Greece and, especially, of Rome. Dramatic forms and genres ostensibly based on Greek, or more often Latin, models were developed. The theoretical basis of neo-classicism was hammered out as critics translated and commented on the rediscovered Aristotle, linking him with the Roman critic Horace, and reconciling both with the moral and rhetorical traditions of the Middle Ages. The rediscovery, publication, and translation of Vitruvius' *De Re Architectura* prompted efforts to discuss and reconstruct the physical theatre of the Greeks and their stage effects as described by the Roman architect. Even that most characteristic of Italian dramatic forms, the opera, was consciously invented in an attempt to restore Greek theatre, including its use of music.

While none of this activity can be considered theatre history in a strict sense, it is history in the sense that it tells us what sixteenth-century scholars thought Greek and Roman theatre to have been. This ought to serve as a salient reminder that "history" is not the immutable past simply waiting to be discovered and recorded, but that it is what any culture believes it to be at any particular time; and this belief in turn becomes the stuff of later history. The Greek or Roman theatre of Renaissance scholarship had as much validity for that time as our Greek or Roman theatre has for us.

Thus far, any interest in the theatre of the past meant interest in the theatres of Greece and Rome. By the eighteenth century, however, not only had the medieval theatre flourished for 600 years, but England, Spain, and France had each contributed a great national theatre and drama to the yet-to-be-written history of the theatre. It is clear that Englishmen, Spaniards, and Frenchmen of the eighteenth century were becoming conscious that the previous century had produced a theatre that could stand comparison with that of antiquity and that was not altogether undeserving of scholarly attention. Most attention was directed towards the history of dramatic literature, to which was sometimes appended some consideration of theatres and actors. An equally strong tendency to biography, especially of playwrights, also developed in the eighteenth century. Finally, we find that literary history, of which theatrical or dramatic history was considered a part, began to reflect the idea of independent, individual, national theatres.

The eighteenth century, then, saw the slow gathering of materials for the writing of modern theatre history, but it also saw a continuing tendency to view theatre as dramatic literature and to emphasize biography. In England, an early effort, Gerard Langbaine's *Momus Triumphans* (1687), expanded in 1691 to *An Account of the English Dramatick Poets*, is not really a history, but rather an alphabetical list of lives. In France, *L'Histoire de théâtre français* (1734–49) by les frères Parfaict represents a large collection of material chronologically arranged, and includes long extracts from dramatic works, but it is not a history in the modern sense. The English work known as *Biographica Dramatica*, which went through various editions between 1764 and 1811, is similarly limited. Dramatic literature, biography, evaluative commentary—these rather than historical concerns of development, influence, and cause and effect were at the centre of such compilations. Moreover, without any shaping concept or purpose, the material collected is often inaccurate or irrelevant.

In some ways a more laudable attempt at a history of the French theatre was Pierre de Beauchamps' *Recherches sur les théâtres en France* (1735). Although limited by a biographical and literary bias and by a year-by-year chronological treatment, the work is marked by a real determination on Beauchamps' part to take performance into account. Clearly interested in establishing and reporting facts, he was concerned to determine whether or not a play had been performed, where, and when. Most significantly, he includes treatment of such unliterary forms as court entertainments, opera, and machine plays. Later in the century, Edmond Malone introduced serious archival research and meticulous scholarship to his investigations of the Elizabethan theatre; and Casiano Pellicer similarly explored archives and cited and quoted original documents in his study of the Spanish theatre.

In spite of this early activity, theatre history as a discipline distinct from literary history is the product of the late nineteenth century, and most of the scholarship that informs modern conceptions of the theatres of the Renaissance has been produced over the past one hundred years. The evidence collected and the theories advanced to explain it provide the substance of the present work. As a consequence, my greatest debt is to those scholars whose names are cited throughout the book.

But there are others, whose friendly encouragement and wise advice place me equally in their debt. Laurel Braswell, Richard Morton, and Chauncey Wood provided support when it was needed. Tony Hammond suffered more than friendship demands. I thank them all.

REFERENCES

Baker, David Erskine. *Biographica Dramatica, or, A Companion to the Playhouse.* Continued to 1782 by Isaac Reed and to 1811 by Stephen Jones. 3 Vols. London, 1812.

Beauchamps, Pierre-François Godard de. *Recherches sur les théâtres en France, depuis l'année onze cent soixants un jusqu'à présent.* 3 Vols. Paris, 1735.

Langbaine, Gerard. *An Account of the English Dramatick Poets.* Preface Arthur Freeman. New York, 1973.[1691]

Malone, Edmond. "An Historical Account of the Rise and Progress of the English Stage and of the Economy and Usages of Our Ancient Theatres." In *The Plays and Poems of William Shakespeare* (London, 1790), vol. I.

Parfaict, Claude and François. *L'Histoire du théâtre français depuis son origine jusqu'à présent.* Paris, 1735–49.

Pellicer, Casiano. *Tratado historico sobre el origen y progresos de la comedia y del histrionismo en España.* 2 Vols. Madrid, 1804.

Vince, R. W. "Comparative Theatre Historiography." *Essays in Theatre* I (1983), 64–72.

RENAISSANCE
THEATRE

1

ITALY AND THE RENAISSANCE THEATRE

ESTIMATES AND TREATMENTS OF THE ITALIAN RENAISSANCE THEATRE

For the most part, the history of the Italian Renaissance theatre has been written as though the period covering approximately the years 1400–1650 was a prism onto which the light of the classical theatre and drama shone to be differentiated into its component parts and diffused throughout Europe, where it fused in varying degrees with the hues of the medieval theatre to form the great national theatres of England, Spain, and France. And this has been held to be the case by historians of dramatic literature and of the theatre alike. Thus, Donald Clive Stuart in 1928 structured a major portion of *The Development of Dramatic Art* around the idea, "During the Renaissance the classical form was rediscovered and revived in Italy. Its influence then spread to France, Spain and England where it combined with the medieval form and produced drama more or less classical in proportion as its influence was operative" (p. vii). Almost half a century later, a standard introductory textbook on theatre history offers the following summary of the Italian contribution:

By 1650 Italy had evolved the dramatic types, critical principles, and theatrical practices that were to dominate the European theatre for the next 150 years. The neoclassical ideal, classically inspired comedy and tragedy, opera, *commedia dell-arte*, theatre architecture, perspective scenery, indoor lighting techniques, complex special effects and stage machinery—all of these were to find their way to other countries, where they would be assimilated and adapted to local needs. [Oscar Brockett, *History of the Theatre*, pp. 156–57]

Such a perception accords very well with notions of causality, influence, and development which historians often assume in order to impose a pattern on the sequence of chronological events. The process of historical change is traceable in these terms from Greece to Rome to Italy to the rest of Europe. The medieval theatre, which by the twentieth century had begun to be taken into account, provided an explanation for variations from the classical ideal. But the main lines of development have seemed clear.

There is, in fact, a great deal to recommend this approach to an interpretation of the Italian theatre of the Renaissance. It was to a large extent literary, elitist, and self-conscious: Literary in that experiments in dramatic form and dramatic theory were preserved in writing; elitist insofar as theatre flourished under the patronage of the academy and the court; and self-conscious in the sense that the Italian theatre represented a deliberate attempt to recreate the theatre and drama of Greece and Rome. During the fifteenth and early sixteenth centuries humanist scholars rediscovered twelve hitherto unknown plays by Plautus (1428), and between 1472 and 1518 published editions—some illustrated with woodcuts— of all the known Greek and Roman drama. Nicolas Treveth's commentary on Seneca (ca. 1300) was a prelude to the writing of new Latin plays in imitation of the Roman playwright. Albertino Mussato's *Eccerinus* (1315) has the distinction of being the earliest tragedy recorded in Italy, but it was followed by many others, all written in Latin and usually intended to be recited at ducal courts. When Greek tragedies became available in the sixteenth century, writers, although by this time composing in Italian, produced plays modelled on Sophocles and Euripides as well as on Seneca. (Indeed, during the first half of the sixteenth century there was a lively debate as to which model was preferable. Giraldi Cinthio's *Orbecche*, written in 1541, settled the issue in favour of Seneca.) At the Roman Academy founded by Julius Pomponius Laetus (1425– 98), the comedies of both Plautus and Terence were regularly performed in the Roman manner, that is, as prescribed by the only known authority, Vitruvius. By 1500 there were several such academies, all devoted to the production of plays and the reconstruction of the ancient Roman theatre. At Ferrara, between 1486 and 1505, inspired by Duke Ercole d'Este, Latin comedies were produced in Italian translation. Vitruvius' books on architecture were rediscovered in 1414 and appeared in many printed editions between 1486 and 1586: His influence on architectural treatises, theatre building, and set design was overwhelming. Finally, the habit of commenting on ancient texts combined with a renewed interest in Horace's *Ars Poetica* and, after 1536 at least, in Aristotle's *Poetics* to create a seemingly endless series of critical, theoretical, and speculative documents on the nature of literature in general and of the drama in particular.

All of this activity was experimental, in the sense that it represented attempts to define an appropriate model and then to reproduce it. The men of the Italian Renaissance were consciously planning the theatrical history of their own era in a way that would have been incomprehensible to the medieval mind (or to the modern mind as well, for that matter, although for different reasons). One of the consequences for Italy of this state of affairs was that there developed a gap between the learned theatre based on classical models and precepts, and the popular and eventually professional theatre that continued to flourish outside courtly and academic circles. This was the theatre of the *farsa rusticale*, the *mariazi*, the burlesque *frottole* (or tall tales), the *farsa cavaiole*, all performed in the rural areas around Naples, Asti, Siena, and Padua. It was the theatre of Angelo Beolco, called Ruzzante. And finally, it was certainly akin to if not the source of the *commedia dell'arte*, although the practitioners of that art readily adapted their performances to the requirements and spectacular possibilities of courtly entertainments.

A second consequence has been that the analytical attitude informing so much of the contemporary writing about the theatre has encouraged modern scholarship to proceed in a similar manner, to consider Italy's contribution to the world's theatre as separate elements that were later integrated into the theatres of other nations, rather than as a wholly integrated and unique theatrical expression whose reconstruction can inform us about ourselves as well as about sixteenth-century Italy. It is as if the Greeks' contribution consisted of the idea of tragedy as embodied in a few examples, the shape of the orchestra, the mechanics of the *ekkeklema* and the *mechané*, and Aristotle's *Poetics*. It might be argued—has been argued—that the difference lies in the generally inferior quality of Italian dramatic literature, that the dramatic theory and stage practice of Renaissance Italy get attention because the plays and their performance do not deserve it. Even if this is true, we are in no position to judge the quality of any drama until we are able to reconstruct its conditions of performance, and it has been only since World War II that theatre historians have turned their attention to those festival performances during which the *commedia erudite* was acted and have tried to see such performances as totalities.

The sumptuousness of the performances, on the other hand, has long been recognized—and deplored. John Addington Symonds, in *The Renaissance in Italy* (1881), wrote of the typical festival production:

The whole performance lasted some six hours; but the comedy itself was but a portion of the entertainment. For the majority of the audience the dances and the pageants formed the chief attraction. It is therefore no marvel if the drama, considered as a branch of high poetic art, was suffocated by the growth of its mere accessories. [II, 123–24].

George Kernodle's opinion sixty-two years later is essentially the same: "The Renaissance theatre was a theatre of spectacle and its dominating force the architect-designer" (*From Art to Theatre*, p. 15). Even in 1975, an introductory text notes that "a theatre of spectacle is seldom a theatre of literary distinction" (David Brubaker, *Court and Commedia*, p. 36). Given the traditional preference for literary values, even among theatre historians, it is not surprising that the Italian theatre has been little valued. What is somewhat surprising is to learn that the very spectacle that supposedly retarded the development of the drama is considered by many art historians as a characteristic expression of the baroque spirit, and the baroque spirit seems little valued. Even the editors of the

materials surviving from the festivities for the marriage of Cosimo I of Florence
in 1539 are moved to comment that the "ephemeral quality [of the princely
festival]—the rapid construction of flimsy, temporary decorations, even the hasty
composition of literary works—attests to an insouciance for posterity and to a
fancy for easy, shallow effect" (Andrew C. Minor and Bonner Mitchell, *A Renaissance Entertainment*, p. 78).

The value-judgments—implicit and explicit, aesthetic, moral, even political—underlying these perceptions and comments were articulated most elo-
quently in what is perhaps the most famous and influential study of the Italian
Renaissance ever written: Jacob Burckhardt's *The Civilization of the Renaissance in Italy* (1860; revised 1867). Burckhardt held that civilization is produced by individual spontaneity and consists of spontaneous human activities.
The enemy of spontaneity and therefore of civilization is power. And the creations of art and poetry and philosophy are the expressions of individual crea-
tivity, the success of which, in the perennial struggle with power, depends upon
the energy, vision, and moral character of each generation. In this realm, at
least, the individual has freedom. Burckhardt believed that the theatre is always
a late product of any civilization, and that in Italy it was diverted from true
poetical excellence by spectacle. Moreover, this was true of both the secular
and the religious drama. "We learn with astonishment," he writes,

how rich and splendid the scenes in Italy were. . . . This alone might have had no such
unfavourable effect on the drama, if the attention of the audience had not been drawn
away from the poetical conception of the play partly by the splendour of the costumes,
partly and chiefly by fantastic interludes (Intermezzi). [p. 234].

The religious drama was similarly arrested in its development by a passion for
display: Burckhardt could find in it "no trace of the grand symbolic enthusiasm
which distinguishes the 'Autos Sagramentales' of Calderon" (p. 304).

The attitude outlined in the preceding paragraphs obtained until fairly recently in studies of the period and still forms the underpinning for most introductory and popular accounts of the Italian Renaissance theatre. But there are
indications that new estimates of the drama, particularly comedy, as well as of
the spectacular and artistic elements of festival performances are causing historians to reconsider the theatre of sixteenth-century Italy, this time in its own
terms. It is becoming clear that theatre historians, besides analyzing and tracing
the theoretical and technical contributions of the Italians, are going to have to
examine in more detail those courtly and festival productions that most typify
the learned theatre of the Italian Renaissance. And further, they are going to
have to relate their findings to those concerning the ever-popular and probably
overstudied *commedia dell' arte*; for it is far from certain that the *commedia
erudite* and the *commedia dell' arte* ought to be considered in isolation from one
another. It seems far more likely that a balanced estimate of the Italian Renaissance theatre will depend upon the cultivation of a perspective that can accommodate both forms simultaneously.

While the emphasis in Italian Renaissance studies is usually on the period 1500–1600, the one hundred years on either side also provide important indicators for understanding the origins and the consequences of the theatrical activity of the sixteenth century. This represents, nonetheless, a very long period of time, and it is convenient (although arbitrary) to think of the period as divisible into three parts: (1) the period prior to 1508, dominated by the humanist concern for the revival of classical learning and art; (2) the period between 1508, the year of Ariosto's *La Cassaria*, the first drama written and performed in the vernacular, and 1637, the date of the opening in Venice of the Teatro San Cassiano, the first opera house—a period dominated by courtly patronage, spectacle, and dramatic experiment; and (3) the period after 1637, during which the theatre became increasingly popular and professional, and the two theatrical forms most closely associated with Italy, the *commedia dell'arte* and the opera, were exported to the rest of Europe.

There is, moreover, a staggering amount of documentation and information available to the theatre historian, although it has not always been easy to impose a meaningful and coherent pattern on it. Our picture of the Italian theatre of the Renaissance is fragmented by the varying interests of the investigators— theatre historians, literary scholars and critics, art historians, musicologists, historians of popular culture. At times the work of the humanists, the *commedia dell'arte*, the opera, dramatic theory, stage practice, and scene design, and so on, each seems to occupy its own separate world.

DRAMATIC THEORY

Among the most influential and best known products of the Italian Renaissance are the theoretical treatises which, together with dramaturgical experiments in form and genre, continue to be studied, not only for the light they may shed on contemporary drama and dramatic criticism, but also because they played so large a part in determining the development of European theatre and drama in the seventeeth and eighteenth centuries. Indeed, there appears to have been no end to critical commentary and speculation in sixteenth-century Italy. (The most thorough discussion of the subject is by Bernand Weinberg in *A History of Literary Criticism in the Italian Renaissance;* and a good selection in English translation is available in *Literary Criticism: Plato to Dryden*, edited by Allan H. Gilbert.)

The humanist and scholarly veneration for classical civilization expressed itself in several ways. Dramatic forms and genres were based on Greek and Roman models. Latin, as the more accessible of the ancient languages, was used in place of the vernacular for literary and dramatic composition. And classical literary criticism provided the theoretical framework for neoclassicism. Relatively early in the sixteenth century, however, the choice between Greek and Roman dramatic models was made in favour of Rome; and even earlier, the proponents of Latin had been forced to give way to the growing use of Italian as a literary language. But dramatic theory developed into a full-fledged neo-classicism by embracing and reconciling both Greek and Roman critical traditions.

Early in the sixteenth century, Horace dominated critical thought: The most important of the early documents, Marco Girolamo Vida's *De Arte Poetica* (1527) and Bernardino Daniello's *La Poetica* (1536), are both Horatian in spirit. But because Horace had neglected to include a discussion of the orator or poet, the *Ars Poetica* was considered to be an incomplete rhetoric. At least it was so considered by the late classical commentators such as Donatus whose commentaries were attached to the versions of Horace that were available to sixteenth-century critics. And consequently there was a tendency to flesh out the Roman critic from other sources, especially Aristotle. There had been a translation of Aristotle's Greek text into Latin by Giorgio Valla as early as 1498, and the Greek text itself was published in 1508. Another edition in Greek, accompanied by a revised Latin translation by Allessandro de' Pazzi, appeared in 1536. In 1548 Francesco Robortelli published the first critical edition of the *Poetics*, and included not only another Latin translation, but an extended commentary as well. When, the following year, Bernardo Segni provided an Italian translation of Aristotle's treatise, the final step had been taken in initiating the *Poetics* into Renaissance critical thought.

The effect of Aristotle was immediately felt. The appearance in 1545 of Giraldi's commentary on Horace, in which he derived his definitions and discussion from Aristotle, marked the beginning of a practice that led ultimately to a nearly complete fusion (and confusion) of the two classical writers. Aristotle's *Poetics* and Horace's *Ars Poetica* were systematically compared and combined until they were, in the popular mind at least, virtually indistinguishable. The process is reflected in the title of Antonio Riccoboni's *Praecepta Aristotelis cum praecepta Horatii collata* (1592). And the effect found one of its best known expressions in Sir Philip Sidney's *The Defense of Poesie* (written 1583, published 1595; printed in Gilbert, *Literary Criticism*): "Poesy therefore is an art of imitation, for so Aristotle termeth it in the word *mimesis*, that is to say, a representing, counterfeiting, or figuring forth—to speak metaphorically, a speaking picture [cf. Horace]; with this end, to teach and delight [cf. Horace]" (p. 414).

In spite of their reliance on classical criticism, several critics wrote with considerable distinction and made important contributions to the history of dramatic theory. Antonio Minturno concerned himself with Italian literature and considered it against the background of classical theory and practice. Julius Caesar Scaliger, a resident of France, was a prime source of information for Sidney, and together with Vida and Nicolas Boileau provides evidence for the major stages through which neoclassical theory evolved. But the most significant theorist so far as the drama is concerned was Lodovico Castelvetro (1505–71), who made the conditions of performance and the limitations imposed by space, time, and the audience the bases of the theories embodied in his commentary

on the *Poetics* (1570). Of these theories, the most influential—and notorious—
is that of the three dramatic unities, still often mistakenly attributed to Aristotle. The Greek critic had certainly argued for the unity of action, and had
mentioned the unity of time in passing, but had said nothing concerning the
unity of place. Aristotle, of course, was concerned with artistic or aesthetic unity.
Castelvetro was concerned with audience reaction and argued that the representation of dramatic action must accord with what the audience knows to be true:
A play "cannot represent any action except such as occurs in one place and
within the space of twelve hours." And the unity of action—of prime importance for Aristotle—became for Castelvetro simply the necessary consequences
of the limitations of time and place: There was room for no more than one plot.
The idea of the unities clearly appealed to the current notions of verisimilitude,
and its survival even into the twentieth century is an indication of the failure of
theatre aesthetics to develop non-realistic principles.

Critical theory is of more concern to the theatre historian when it either reflects or influences practice, and the connection is usually closest when the writer
of criticism is also a playwright. Giangiorgio Trissino, for example, whose par-
aphrase and analysis of the *Poetics* preceded Robortelli's but was not published
until 1563, was the author of the tragedy *Sofonisba*, modelled after the Greek
fashion. And Giambattista Giraldi Cinthio, the author of the Seneca-inspired
Orbecche (1541), provided not only prefaces to his plays, but also full-scale
critical documents in which he defended his own practice, and he asserted that
classical models and methods were not necessarily the only ones appropriate in
a new age. (See especially *Discorsi intorno al comparre de e romanzi, della
commedie, e della tragedie*, 1554. Selections are printed in Gilbert, *Literary
Criticism*, pp. 252–273.) Finally, with Giambattista Guarini, whose replies to
attacks on his pastoral tragicomedy *Il Pastor Fido* (1585) were collected in 1601
under the title *Compendio della poesia tragicomica, tratto dai due Verati* (Gilbert, pp. 505–533), we have articulated a theory of tragicomedy that sheds
considerable light on European dramaturgy in the early years of the seventeenth
century.

The question remains, of course, as to the value of this critical theory to the
theatre historian. It is possible to argue that the documents of the sixteenth century provide evidence principally for the history of critical thought, and their
remoteness from theatrical practice makes them, like the treatises of Aristotle
and Horace, of only marginal interest so far as the history of the theatre is concerned. This would be to take a particularly narrow view of theatre history,
however, and it also fails to recognize an important difference between classical criticism and Renaissance criticism. Both Aristotle and Horace discuss dramatic genre and form, and both offer advice to the playwright; but they also
wrote after a major body of drama had been produced in their respective languages, and there is no indication that either had any particular effect on Greek
or Roman dramatic form. Renaissance criticism was both more insistently pre-
scriptive and apologetic, and more likely to have exerted an influence on the

composition of plays. Indeed, a standard explanation for the generally inferior quality of Renaissance Italian dramatic literature—of the *commedia erudite*, at least—is that it remained dominated by scholarly reconstruction of ancient practice and by theoretical precept, cut off from the life of Italian society. Tragedy in particular is held to have suffered under the conditions imposed by academicians and theorists. Joseph Kennard's analysis remains a commonly accepted one. Italian tragedy

> was the conscious product of cultivated persons who aimed at nothing nobler than the imitation of the ancients and the observance of impossible rules. It was suffocated by classical imitation. . . . These tragedies were the literary manufacture of scholars, writing without spiritual or intellectual contact with the world of action of the audience of busy cities. [*The Italian Theatre*, I, 137]

Even if we wish to disagree with either the estimate or the explanation of the drama's quality, we must take the critical writings of the Italian Renaissance into account, along with its dramatic literature. Finally, of course, although critics rarely addressed themselves directly to contemporary theatre practice, the existence of the neoclassical theatre is itself testimony to their influence.

There is one group of theoretical writings, however, that clearly did contribute directly to the establishment of a theatrical form and that consequently remains of considerable interest to the theatre historian. It consists, of course, of those writings associated with the early beginnings of Italian opera, in some respects an inevitable outgrowth of sixteenth-century theorizing and experiment. The men who "invented" opera were convinced that it had been the dramatic blend of words and music that had characterized Greek theatre, and they therefore studied ancient writings and experimented with musical drama in an effort to reconcile the demands of melody with those of poetry. The most important source of information on classical music was Boethius' *De Institutione Musica*, composed in the sixth century but readily available to Renaissance scholars as part of a complete edition of Boethius' works published between 1491 and 1499. In addition, musical treatises attributed to the Greek mathematician Euclid were rendered in Latin translation in 1498; Plutarch's commentary on the subject appeared in 1532; and pertinent materials by the Greek philosopher Aristoxenes, the astronomer Ptolemy, and Aristotle were provided by Giovanni del Grave. On the basis of these ancient theoretical writings—no classical music had survived—Renaissance writers developed their own theories. Between 1572 and 1581, Greek music and musical theory were discussed in a series of letters between Vincenzo Galilei, father of the astronomer, and Girolamo Mei. Galilei subsequently published his observations in *Dialogo della musica antica, et della moderna* (1581–82); and Mei's letters have been collected by Claude V. Palisca in *Girolomo Mei: Letters on Ancient and Modern Music* (1960).

Galilei was a member of the so-called Florentine Camerata, a group of musicians and writers devoted to the study and reconstruction of what they considered to be Greek music-drama. Included among its members were the composer Jacopo Peri and the poet Ottavio Rinuccino, whose *dramma per musica*, *Dafne* (1597)—of which only four short fragments survive —is traditionally held to represent the first modern opera; and Giulio Caccini, whose *Le Nuove Musiche* (1601), devoted to musical theory, contains the earliest known examples of Florentine monody, invented to replace the polyphonic system for the purposes of dramatic performance. (The documents and writings of the Camerata are listed in August Wilhelm Ambros, *Geschichte der Musik*, 3d ed., 1909; and the most important of them are printed in Angelo Solerti, *Le origini del melodramma* (1903).

THEATRE ARCHITECTURE AND STAGE DESIGN

As Italian scholars attempted to revive classical dramatic forms and classical theory, so they also attempted to rediscover and reconstruct what they believed to have been classical theatre structure. Renaissance knowledge of Greek and Roman theatres was derived principally from Vitruvius, whose *De Re Architectura* had been discovered in manuscript at St. Gall by Poggio Bracciolini in 1414 and printed at Rome in 1486 by the humanists Giovanni Sulpicio of Veroli and Pomponius Laetus. Further editions followed in 1496 and 1497. The first illustrated edition of Vitruvius, by Fra Giocondo Jocundus, appeared in 1511 and assumed a rectangular theatre. The first translation into Italian was executed by Cesare Cesariano in 1521. And about 1535 was founded in Rome the Accademia della Virtu, devoted to the study of Vitruvius and to the study of surviving Roman architecture. It was under the direction of the Academy that Giacomo Barozzi da Vignola (1507–73) produced his standard work of the orders of architecture, *Regola delli cinque Ordini d'Architettura* (1562–63). Another Italian translation was made in 1556 by Daniello Barbaro, who was also responsible for a combined Latin text and Italian translation, together with illustrations and commentary, which appeared in 1567.

All in all, before the end of the seventeenth century more than thirty editions of Vitruvius had appeared in Europe, and the architect's work had been translated into not only Italian, but also French (1547), German (1547–48), and Spanish (1602). (Although an abridgement appeared in English in 1692, it was based on a French translation. There was no complete English translation until the eighteenth century.) Among the non-Italian commentaries on Vitruvius we should note those of Guillaume Philander, which were published in 1544 and again, together with an edition of *De Re Architectura*, in 1550, 1552, and 1586. Philander is important for his citing of other classical authorities—especially Pollux and Flavius Cassiodorus—in his interpretation of Vitruvius' discussion of the theatre.

If we may judge by the number of editions, commentaries, and explanations of his work, and by the numerous treatises based on *De Re Architectura*, it is

difficult to overestimate Vitruvius' importance in the Renaissance. Vitruvius is
not particularly valuable for extending our knowledge of the Greek or Roman
theatre, but his brief comments on and discussion of theatre dominated theatrical theory and practice in Renaissance Italy in much the same way that Aristotle and Horace dominated Renaissance poetics. And the Vitruvian industry
was not lessened by the fact that the Roman architect's references to stage architecture and scene design were not easily understood or even reconciled. In
particular, it proved difficult to reconcile hints about the use of painted perspective scenery and the brief descriptions of the tragic, comic, and satyric scenes
(V.vi.9) with the description of the *scaena* that was supposedly to enclose these
scenes, with its architectural facade and *periaktoi* to effect scene changes (V.vi.8).
Actually, Renaissance theorists and architects were never able to determine the
relationship between the *frons scaenae* and the perspective set, and instead chose
to develop one or the other.

   In the fifteenth century Leon Battista Alberti had based his comments on theatre architecture on Vitruvius' writings, but by far the most influential work to
be based on the Roman architect's treatise was that of Sebastiano Serlio (1475–
1554), a pupil of the painter, architect, and stage-designer Baldassare Peruzzi
(1481–1536). Peruzzi left his notes and drawings for a projected edition of Vitruvius to Serlio, whose *Archittetura*, published in six books between 1537 and
1575, was conceived as an elaboration on Vitruvius. Book II, on perspective,
published in 1545, provides a discussion of matters relating to the stage and
includes a cross-section and plan of a theatre as well as scene designs based on
Vitruvius' descriptions. This book in particular proved immensely popular and
within seventy-five years had appeared in all the major languages of Europe.
(The English edition, translated from Dutch by Robert Peake, was published in
1611.) Serlio's treatment of the theatre is brief, and it does not really break new
ground, evidently summarizing the usual practice of the time; but for these very
reasons it is a valuable source of information for the theatre historian. Moreover, Serlio's section on the stage exercised a considerable influence on later
discussions: The scene designs in particular found their way into several editions of Vitruvius himself (for example, the French edition of Jean Martin in
1547 and Philander's 1552 edition) as well as being used by Daniello Barbaro
in his *Pratica della Perspectiva* (1559). Serlio visualizes the famous "scenes"
in terms of three-dimensional perspective, achieved by means of painted scenery, two-dimensional wings, and a raked stage. The Vitruvian *frons scaenae*
disappears entirely. And in spite of Andrea Palladio's attempt to restore it in
the Teatro Olimpico, begun in 1580, the *frons scaenae* was in fact destined to
be rejected in favour of a single proscenium arch and a perspective and sometimes changing scene.

   In fact, the development of the perspective scene was one of the most prominent features of Renaissance artistic and architectural theory and practice; and
once the proscenium arch had been selected over the *frons scaenae*, the stage-
scene became in effect a three-dimensional picture and thus subject to the rules

of painting. Theatre historians have perforce, therefore, found evidence for Renaissance stage design in writings by and about some of the leading artists of the quattrocento and cinquecento. A great deal of information concerning the period before 1550 is provided by Giorgio Vasari, whose *Lives of the Painters, Sculptors and Architects* was published in 1550 and again in 1568 in an enlarged edition. It is possible to trace the influence of the early theorists, such as Filippo Brunelleschi (1377–1446), credited with the "discovery" of perspective, and Leon Baptista Alberti (1404–72), author of *Della Pittura* (1436), the first written description of perspective construction, through Donato di Angelo Bramante (1444–1514), probably the greatest Italian architect of the High Renaissance, to men like Baldassare Peruzzi (1481–1536), one of the earliest of the Italian artists to design stage settings. (According to Vasari, Peruzzi designed the scenery for Cardinal Bibbiena's *La Calandria* in 1514.) Later writings on the subject of perspective include Daniello Barbaro's *Pratica della Perspectiva* (1559), Giacomo Barozzi da Vignola's *Due Regole dell Prospettive Pratica* (1583), and L. Sirigatti's *Pratica di prospettivo* (1596). Guido Ubaldus, described by his pupil Nicolà Sabbattini as "the Archimedes of Italy," produced his influential *Perspectivae libri sex* in 1600.

The student of theatre history may feel that excursions into the history of painting and architecture have taken us into foreign territory indeed. But it must be remembered that before the mid-seventeeth century, scene design was considered to be the responsibility of artists and architects, and even after that time the principles underlying stage design were established by artists. The real question becomes one of determining precisely how those artistic principles were translated into stage designs, and how those designs were actually executed on the stage. Even in those instances where the designs for play productions have been preserved or even published—as they often were in the Baroque period—there can be considerable difficulty in interpreting them in terms of the three dimensions of the stage. Fortunately, we do have sources of information available to us; and we are doubly fortunate in that the extant treatises and handbooks appear to reflect stage practice rather than offering merely theoretical blueprints for it. The earliest of these, as we have seen, is Serlio's *Second Book of Architecture* (1545), but other documents are even more important from the point of view of actual theatre production.

The earliest of these is by Leone de'Sommi (or di Somi) (1527–1592), the man in charge of theatrical productions at the court of Mantua, reputed author of the first Hebrew play, *The Comedy of a Marriage*, and the only man of his time to devote himself almost exclusively to the study of the theatre. His *Quattro dialoghi in materia di rappresentazioni sceniche* (*Four Dialogues concerning Theatrical Performances*), the first treatise on production and direction in the history of the theatre, was written about 1556 and is preserved in the Biblioteca Palatina, Parma. (The Italian text has been edited by Ferruccio Marotti. Portions of the third book appear in English translation in Allardyce Nicoll's *Development of the Theatre*, Appendix B, and in A. M. Nagler's *Source Book in Theatrical History.*) De'Sommi discusses dramaturgy, acting, costuming, and stage practice. A similar attention to the details and effect of lighting is to be found in the *Discorso della poesia rappresentativa e del modo di presentare le favole schemiche* (1598) of Angelo Ingegneri (ca. 1550–ca. 1613), the man who directed the famous performance of *Oedipus the King* at the opening of the Teatro Olimpico in 1583. (Although various scholars make reference to Ingegneri, there is no modern edition of his work, nor is there an English translation available.)

We are more fortunate with respect to Nicolà Sabbattini (1574–1654) and Joseph Fürttenbach the Elder (1591–1667), whose writings on the theatre, together with those of Serlio, are translated and collected in *The Renaissance Stage*, edited by Bernard Hewitt (1958). Sabbattini's *Manual for Constructing Theatrical Scenes and Machines* (1637–38), described by its translator John H. McDowell as "a work-a-day view of a practical technician" (*Renaissance Stage*, p. 42), is for that very reason of immense value to the theatre historian. In Book I, Sabbattini discusses theatre construction, audience arrangement, scene-building and painting, and lighting; in Book II he turns his attention to the *intermezzi*, the entr'acte episodes that necessitated devices for moving scenery and spectacular effects: Here we find detailed instructions on precisely how to achieve specific stage effects. The old-fashioned nature of much of Sabbattini's work indicates the extent to which the ordinary theatre technician and designer may lag behind the innovations of his more able or imaginative contemporaries. The theatre historian must be ever wary of assuming that the most advanced ideas and techniques were the norm.

The German writer Fürttenbach left us three formal treatises on theatre practice: *Architectura Civilis* (1628), *Architectura Recreationis* (1640), and *Mannhaffter Kunstspiegel* (1663), a collection of sixteen treatises on a variety of subjects, including perspective scenery and civil architecture. Like Sabbattini, Fürttenbach provides extensive descriptions of cloud and wave machines, and of lighting instruments and procedures. Although he tends to describe an ideal rather than actual practice, his treatises are second only to Sabbattini's manual in providing information about back-stage practice in the early years of the seventeenth century. And Fürttenbach not only tells us about Italian practice but also illustrates how it was adapted outside Italy.

Finally, we have two important treatises by the theatre architect and stage technician Fabrizio Carini Motta, who was employed at the Gonzaga court in Mantua. His *Trattato spora la struttura de' teatri e scene* (1673) is highly theoretical but is one of the earliest books devoted entirely to theatre architecture; and an unpublished manuscript in the Biblioteca Estense in Modena, *Costruzione de' teatri e teatrale machine* (1688), contains information concerning the chariot system. (Motta's work is forthcoming in English translation by Orville K. Larson. See Larson's article in *Theatre Survey* XXI, 1980, pp. 79–91.)

These then are our main sources of information concerning Renaissance Italian scene design and theatre practice. The principles and practices developed between 1550 and 1650 dominated European theatre of the next 150 years. Scene designers and architects continued, of course, to refine their practice, particularly with regard to the use of the flat-wing stage, and at least four important designers contributed to the theoretical discussion between 1672 and 1705: Giulio Troili, *Parodossi per pratticare la prospettiva* (1672); Andrea Pozzo, *Prospettiva de'pittori e architetti* (1693–1700); Ferdinando Galli-Bibiena, *L'architettura civile* (1711) and *Direzione* (1732); and Baldassare Orsini, *Dell Geometria e prospettiva pratica* (1771–73) and *Le scene del nuovo Teatro del Verzaro di Perugia* (1785). (Relevant selections from these works have been collected and translated by Dunbar H. Ogden in *The Italian Baroque Stage*.) The details of the work of these men lie beyond the scope of this discussion. It is sufficient to remind ourselves that theatrical design over more than two centuries had its origin in the sixteenth century.

The plethora of theory and generalized description can provide the historian with what appears to be a traceable line of development in the Italian theatre of the Renaissance. But ultimately the general picture thus constructed is found to lack specific substance, and the historian begins to apply general information to the hypothetical reconstruction of particular performances. In order to do so, it becomes necessary to determine the relationship between theory and practice, between general description and specific execution. And this relationship is traceable, not only in published scene designs and engravings, in dramatic texts and libretti, but also in drawings, diaries, letters, public documents, and various written accounts and descriptions of performances—in other words, the very detail that, painstakingly reconstructed, traditionally provides the historian with the basis for historical interpretations. If theoretical treatise and performance detail illuminate one another, or serve as checks on one another, so much the better for the historian.

We must bear in mind that the bulk of the evidence to be discussed in the following pages concerns the *commedia erudite*—the drama of academy and court—and the various forms of entertainment that accompanied or, in the case of opera, eventually replaced it at courtly festivals and, after 1637 at least, on the public stage. These forms included *intermezzi*, musical interludes of varying spectacular complexity; court ballets; pageant-jousts; on occasion even horse-ballets and mock sea-battles. Most plays or operas other than those performed after 1637 in the public theatres of Venice were performed only once or at most only a limited number of times, and the fleeting grandeur of the festival performances of which they were a part was often memorialized, not only by the publication of the play's text or the opera's *libretto*, but also by official descriptions of the event, illustrated with engravings of the scene designs. In the case of seventeenth-century Venetian opera, the complicated plots made it necessary to provide the audience with an *argumento*, which explained the situation at the beginning of the opera, a *scenario* or summary of the events of the piece, or even the complete *libretto*. The streaks of wax on many texts are testimony to the fact that they were bought and read by candlelight before and during the performance. While not all evidence comes so conveniently packaged, the great amount that does has proved a bonanza for historians and collectors.

SCENE DESIGN

Scene design has become an important and attractive area of study for theatre historians. Indeed, for the late sixteenth and seventeenth centuries in particular, it might be said that the history of stage design in Italy is the history of the theatre in Italy. The major artists and designers have been made the subjects of individual studies, and surveys of stage design such as Donald Oenslager's *Stage Design* are finding their way onto library shelves. At least two excellent surveys of Italian theatre in the Renaissance are based on the justifiable assumption that the pictorial and spectacular nature of this theatre contained its essence, and they proceed to analyze it in these terms. A. M. Nagler discusses festival performances in Florence between 1539 and 1637 in *Theatre Festivals of the Medici* (1964); and Cesare Molinari surveys the scene designs for fifty-seven productions between 1608 and 1969 in *Le nozze degli dei: Un saggio sul grande spettacolo Italiano nel seicento* (1968). Nagler's 136 illustrations are more than matched by Molinari's 278. Even so, the analyses provided by Nagler and Molinari represent a relatively recent phenomenon. For scene designs bear a peculiarly tenuous relationship to art history on the one hand and theatre history on the other. Art historians prefer art intended to be experienced in the form and medium in which they find it; theatre historians prefer real sets and real costumes and real theatres. The one has considered the ephemeral world of scenic production outside his or her province; the other has paid lip service to scene design but has felt, with some justification, that the engravings that make up tbe bulk of the evidence for it have at best an artificial relationship to the theatrical performance and belong more properly in an art gallery than in a theatre collection. The result has been that scene design has become a study and an art in its own right, with its own separate courses of study and sense of discipline, and that the extant designs themselves are sometimes treated as the stuff of their own history.

A contributing factor to this development is the undoubted attraction of the collectibility of designs. Not only are there substantial collections in expected places such as the Victoria and Albert Museum in London and the Uffizi Gallery in Florence, but private individuals have been able to accumulate impressive and valuable collections. Donald Oenslager writes of the pleasure of collecting in *Stage Design*, a practice he began with a purchase in Munich in 1923; and Robert L. B. Tobin, whose collection of scene and costume design is one of the most distinguished in the United States, began his acquisitions in the 1950s as a student at the University of Texas. Where such collections exist, they foster their own study on their own terms. To consider scene designs in the context of all other available information concerning the history of performance is the theatre historian's job of work, nevertheless; and however grateful we must be to the collectors, and however attractive we may find the designs of Peruzzi or Torelli or Santurini, we must view the drawings and engravings with the same sceptical eye we turn on any other piece of information purporting to be historical evidence. In the case of Renaissance scene design, we must bear the following points in mind.

In the first place, sketches and drawings intended as guides for those charged with the actual construction of the sets are rare. Most of the scene designs that have come down to us from the sixteenth and seventeenth centuries are in the form of engravings: some preserved in contemporary collections, some attached to specific published *libretti*, and some included in *Festival Books*, produced to commemorate a particular festive performance or series of performances.

Second, since stage designers usually did not prepare engravings of their own work, the relationship between the engraving and the original drawing must be inferred from what we know of both the designer's and the engraver's practice. We cannot automatically assume that an engraving is a faithful rendition of the drawing. In at least one instance, we know that three artists were involved in the production of the published designs. A book of designs attributed to the Italian designer Francesco Santurini (1616–91) features engravings by Melchior and Matthias Kusell, based on drawings of Santurini's designs by Caspar Am Ort. It is not clear whether Am Ort's sketches were based on what he saw on stage or on Saturini's own drawings. (The book in question is now part of the Robert Tobin collection.)

Third, the identification and date of a drawing are rarely obvious; and even engravings are occasionally difficult to link with a specific designer or performance. We must therefore distinguish among the following categories: (*a*) those drawings and engravings that reflect specific and identifiable performances; (*b*) those that can be linked to a specific theatre or place of performance even if not to a particular performance; (*c*) those that may be used only as indications of general practice—the more precisely dated the better.

Finally, and most important, we must try to understand the relationship between the scene design as we have it and the stage set it purports to represent. Besides the obvious imaginative leap from two dimensions to three, we must recognize that a drawing is a guide for the building of a set, not the other way around, and that an engraving is an artistic rendering in a non-theatrical medium of a drawing. In neither case does the design as executed in canvas and wood and paint directly influence the outcome.

Artists and architects who contributed their talents to the emerging theatre of the Italian Renaissance include da Vinci, Raphael, Peruzzi, Vasari, Serlio, Palladio, Scamozzi, Buontalenti, and Parigi; and their later, more theatrically specialized successors include Torelli, Santurini, and the Bibiena family. These and the names of a host of lesser designers, engravers, and draftsmen are the names to be reckoned with in the consideration of this theatre, rather than the names of playwrights or actors. Rarely in theatrical history has Aristotle's de-

nigrated spectacle achieved such prominence in production, or moved so close
to the centre of the theatre historian's attention. (The most convenient and authoritative source of information concerning the designs and the locations of
drawings, manuscripts, and so on is the *Enciclopedia dello spettacolo*, published in 9 volumes and a *Supplement* between 1954 and 1966. A worthwhile
survey of fifty-six of the most significant designs is available in *Italian Renaissance Festival Designs*, the catalogue of an exhibition at the University of Wisconsin, prepared by Arthur R. Blumenthal. And for the Medici court productions, the catalogue, *Feste e apparati medicei da Cosimo I a Cosimo II* by
G. M. Bertelà and Annamaria Petrioli Tofani, may be consulted.)

The work of the earliest scene designers is, of course, especially interesting,
if only because examples of it are so rare. But they are significant as well in
that they exist as sketches and drawings rather than as finished engravings. The
following designers and drawings are most notable:

Leonardo da Vinci (1452–1519)

Da Vinci provided designs and sketches for several entries and performances
at Milan during his stay there between 1482 and 1499. (The originals are now
lodged in several institutions in Milan, Paris, New York, and London.) One of
the most significant is a design for a revolving stage (British Library, Codex
Arundel 263) for the performance at some time between 1490 and 1495 of Angelo Poliziano's *Orfeo*. (It is reproduced in the *Enciclopedia dello spettacolo*
and in Blumenthal.)

Baldassare Peruzzi (1481–1536)

Peruzzi, more than da Vinci, deserves to be called the first modern stage designer. His nine extant designs are preserved in the Uffizi Gallery (four designs), in the Municipal Library at Siena (four designs), and at the Theatre Museum of Drottningholm, Sweden. Besides perspectives for tragic and comic scenes
and for triumphal arches, Peruzzi's legacy includes a plan and elevation for a
scene for a performance of Plautus' *Bacchides* in 1531 (Uffizi, Arch. 268, 269);
and a perspective scene in the Uffizi (291A) has been identified with the setting
for a 1514 production of Cardinal Bibbiena's *La Calandria*.

Aristotile da Sangallo (1481–1551)

One of the earliest representations of steps leading up to the stage is to be
found in a sketch for a city scene attributed variously to Aristotile da Sangallo
or to his cousin Antonio da Sangallo the Elder (1453–1534). The drawing, which
has been dated ca. 1530, indicates grooves on the stage—perhaps intended for
the moving into place of scenic panels. It also boasts three perspectives within
a single scene: It is the only known theatrical setting before 1589 calling for
three street perspectives. The intended performance is not known. (The drawing is reproduced in Blumenthal and in Oenslager's *Stage Design*. The original
is in the Oenslager collection.)

Bartolomeo Neroni (ca. 1500–71)

What is perhaps the earliest representation of a proscenium arch appears in a scene design attributed to Bartolomeo Neroni, devised for the 1560 performance at Siena of Alessandro Piccolomini's *L'Ortensio*. The proscenium arch—behind which appears a street in perspective—is clearly present in the original drawing; a crayon and ink copy of the same setting in the Theatre Collection of the National Museum in Stockholm omits the proscenium. A third version of the same design was executed as a chiaroscuro woodcut. The woodcut is dated 1589 and is signed "Hier. Bols.ˢ Senensis" (Giralomo da Bolsena). It describes Neroni as the "inventor." Impressions are preserved in the Metropolitan Museum of New York, in the Victoria and Albert Museum in London, and in the National Museum in Stockholm. (Both the original drawing and the woodcut are illustrated in Blumenthal.)

Giorgio Vasari (1511–74)

The first major figure to leave us a sizeable collection of scene designs is Giorgio Vasari, famous author of the *Lives* and in 1563 founder of the Accademia del Disegno in Florence. About 150 of his scene and costume desiqns are preserved in the Biblioteca Nationale in Florence. There are in addition many copies of his designs, both at the National Library and in the Gabinetto Disegni e Stampe of the Uffizi. (A. M. Nagler reproduces twenty-two of Vasari's designs for the festivities celebrating the wedding of Francesco de' Medici and Joanna of Austria in 1566 in his *Theatre Festivals of the Medici*, figs. 3–25.)

By Vasari's time, of course, Serlio had published his work on architecture (1545), and his designs for tragic, comic, and satyric scenes were beginning to achieve a prominence that constant reproduction has still done nothing to diminish. Within a few years of Vasari's death, Palladio and Scamozzi would design the only permanent theatre of sixteenth-century Italy to survive to our own time. And at the court of the Medicis in Florence, Bernardo Buontalenti (1536–1608)—Bernardo of the fireworks—would establish his credentials as theatre architect and scene designer by building a theatre in the east wing of the Uffizi and by contributing designs for the opening festivities in 1586. Buontalenti and his immediate successors in Florence—Giulio Parigi (d. 1637) and his son Alfonso (d. 1656)—together with Alfonso Rivarola called Il Chenda (1591–1640) at Ferrara, and Francesco Guitti (ca. 1605–45) at various centres, are representatives of the last generation of artists-architects-scene designers. With the establishment of a public opera house in Venice in 1637 and the debut of Giacomo Torelli (1608–78) as the designer for *La Finta Pazza* at the new Teatro Novissimo in 1641, the age of the professional scene-designer had begun. The new generation included Ferdinando Tacca (1619–86), who succeeded Alfonso Parigi at the Medici court in 1656, Francesco Santurini (ca. 1626–ca. 1685), Filippo Juvarra (1678–1736), and, to confine ourselves to the seventeenth century, the brothers Bibiena—Ferdinand (1657–1743) and Francesco (1659–1739). The remainder of the century saw Italian scene design and designers spread throughout Europe: Torelli and Tomaso Francini (1571–1648) to France, Cosimo Lotti (d. 1650) to Spain, Ludovico Burnacini (1636–1707) and Andrea Pozzo (1642–1709) to the court of the Habsburgs, the Bibiena family almost everywhere.

The main pictorial evidence for the work of these men has come down to us in the form of engravings, usually prepared by artists other than the original designers, and published with descriptions of festival performances or attached to operatic *libretti*. Engravers were competent artists in their own right and any attempts to reconstruct performances on the basis of their work or to determine the exact nature of a theatrical design must be made with the realization that the conventions of the engraver's art impose their own stamp on the engravings. Perhaps the best known of these men was the Frenchman, Jacques Callot (1592–1635), who was responsible for the engraving of many designs by Buontalenti and Giulio Parigi. (Something of the range of Callot's work is illustrated by the 338 prints included in *Callot's Etchings*, edited by Howard Daniel. His treatment of theatrical subjects is discussed in Gerald Kahan's *Jacques Callot: Artist of the Theatre*.) Callot also provided his own designs on occasion, such as for the performance of Prospero Bonarelli's *Il Solimano* in 1619. The published festival book contained six engravings of Callot's own designs (Blumenthal, figs. 52–54; Kahan, figs. 63–68); some of the original drawings are in the Devonshire collection and in the Uffizi. Other important engravers were Agostino Carracci (1557–1602), Remigio Cantagellina (1582–1630), Stefano della Bella (1610–64), and François Collignon (1609–57).

The survey of designers and designs here presented is illustrative rather than exhaustive, but the designers are generally the most significant of the period, and the designs that are noted are the most informative and the most often discussed by theatre historians.

Bernardo Buontalenti (1536–1608)

There exist descriptions of Buontalenti's designs for half a dozen productions between 1571 and 1600, and a few engravings. There also exist, however, numerous original drawings and sketches—of both scenes and costumes—attributed to Buontalenti, now to be found in the Uffizi and the National Library in Florence, and in the Victoria and Albert Museum in London. The most famous festivities with which Buontalenti is associated were those surrounding the marriage at Florence in 1589 of Ferdinand de'Medici and Christine of Lorraine, paricularly the *intermezzi* accompanying the performance of Girolamo Bargagli's *La Pellegrina*. No engravings or drawings of the perspective scenery for the play proper remain, but the pictorial record for the six *intermezzi* is particularly rich: engravings of the six sets by Agostino Carracci and Epifanio d'Alfiano—but even better, the original designs for four of the scenes—are preserved in the Victoria and Albert Museum; and in the Biblioteca Nazionale in Florence are nearly a dozen costume designs. (See Nagler, *Theatre Festivals of the Medici*, figs. 42–63.) Other drawings in the Uffizi and in various private collections have also been attributed to Buontalenti and the 1589 *intermezzi* (Nagler, fig. 41; Blumenthal, figs. 35, 36, 38).

Giulio Parigi (1580–1637)

Giulio and his son Alfonso succeeded Buontalenti at the court of the Medici. Giulio's designs in particular have become very well known through the large number of engravings prepared by himself, his brother, Remigio Cantagallina, Jacques Callot, and Stefano della Bella, the many copies of which can be found in all the major libraries and collections in Italy and in many non-Italian locations as well. At least seventy-five of the elder Parigi's designs appeared with published play texts and festival books between 1608 and 1625; another sixteen can be attributed to Alfonso through 1652. (More than fifty illustrations of the Parigis' work are provided by Nagler, figs. 68–126.) Unlike the case of Buontalenti, however, few of the Parigis' original drawings survive. Three of Giulio's costume sketches for a 1616 festive tournament are extant, two in the Biblioteca Nazionale and one in the Pierpont Morgan Library in New York City (Nagler, figs. 91, 95; Blumenthal, fig. 49). Other drawings in the Cleveland Museum of Art, in the Uffizi, and in the Oenslager collection are more doubtfully attributable to Giulio (Blumenthal, figs. 55, 56). The Biblioteca Nazionale does, however, contain a costume sketch by Alfonso for Andrea Salvador's *Flora*, performed in 1628 (Nagler, fig. 113).

Francesco Guitti (1605–45)

Guitti's short career spanned the years 1626 to 1638, but in that time he designed scenes for at least seven festival productions in Farrara, Rome, and Parma. All of the more than forty designs attributed to him survive in engravings by François Collignon and G. B. Torre attached to the *libretti* or festival books commemorating five performances (dates given are those of publication): (*a*) *Le Contessa* by G. B. Estense Tassane (1632); (*b*) *Erminia sul Giordano* by Giulio Rospigliosi (1637); (*c*) *Festa, fatta, in Roma* by V. Mascardi (1635); (*d*) *La Discordia Superato* (1638); (*e*) *Andromeda* (1638).

Giacomo Torelli (1604–78)

Torelli, who was influenced by Guitti, spent almost seventeen years between 1645 and 1662 in Paris, where most of his major work was done. But before he left Venice he was responsible for the designs of four productions that opened the Teatro Novissimo between 1640 and 1644. The editions of two of the operas, *Bellerofonte* (1642) and *Venere Gelosa* (1643), are illustrated with ten and twelve engravings respectively. (The edition of *Bellerofonte* also credits Torelli with the invention of the chariot system of scene changing.) Of the twelve engravings included in the *apparati scenici* for *Venere Gelosa*, however, only nine are of scenes for that production, and it has been conjectured that the remaining three were intended for the 1644 production of *Deidamia*. (A selection of the engravings is included in Per Bjürstrom's *Giacomo Torelli*, pp. 239–241, and in S. T. Worsthorne's *Venetian Opera in the 17th Century*, Appendix V.) There exists, in addition, a manuscript in the Biblioteca Federiciana in Fana that contains plans of the sets for *Bellerofonte*.

Ferdinando Tacca (1619–86)

Tacca succeeded Alfonso Parigi as scenographer and architect at the Medici court in 1656, but he is best known for his work with the Accademia degli Immobili, composed of stage-struck Florentine noblemen. It was for this group that Tacca designed and built a theatre and created sets for its productions. The scene designs for the operas *Hipermestra* (1658) and *Ercole Amante* (1661), published with the *libretti*, are especially useful for determining the possibilities of the new theatre.

Francesco Santurini (ca. 1626–ca. 1685)

While much of Santurini's work was done in Munich, he did designs for the Venetian opera as well: Indeed, we possess drawings of the scenes for *Adone in Cipro* (1676) and *Germanico sul Reno* (1676), now in the Musée de l'Opéra in Paris. A collection of thirty-nine of Santurini's designs, once belonging to Jacob Burckhardt, now form part of Robert Tobin's private collection.

The Bibiena Family (1670–1787)

Only two of eight scene designers belonging to the Bibiena family actually worked before 1700, but it is almost impossible to separate the work of Ferdinando (1657–1743) and Francesco (1659–1739) from that of the other family members, who dominated eighteenth-century stage design. It has been estimated that 80 percent of all eighteenth-century stage designs are attributable to the Bibienas. Their work survives in more than 200 engravings and etchings published in their own books (for example, Ferdinando's *Archittetura civile*, 1711), in opera *libretti*, and in festival books. There are extant, in addition, at least seven volumes of sketches and drawings of settings for court festivities, religious ceremonies, fireworks, and monuments: a book containing 452 sketches in the theatre collection of the Austrian National Library; another album presented to the Accademia di San Luca in Rome; a third in the Theatre Museum in Munich; and four more volumes of sketches at Harvard and in a couple of private collections.

One further large collection of architectural and theatrical drawings presents something of a puzzle. Dated about 1665, the collection of 238 architectural and theatrical drawings was at one time erroneously thought to have been the work of Torelli. A *GM* monogram on several of the drawings, together with the same initials in an architectural escutcheon with the date 1666, has prompted speculation that the drawings might be the work of one Giuseppe Maria Mitelli (1609–60), but there is no other evidence to link Mitelli with the theatre, and the identity of the artist responsible for the collection remains a mystery. Although the first group of 141 drawings includes a number of sketches of theatrical scenes, most of them are of architectural subjects such as gardens, altars, interiors, and so on. The second group of ninety-seven drawings, however, consists totally of scene designs. Until it is possible to identify and place these drawings more precisely, however, they can be of limited value to the theatre historian. (For a discussion of the collection see Oenslager, *Stage Design*, pp. 49–50.)

Finally, we should note the existence in the National Library in Turin, Italy, of ten volumes describing and commemorating ballets produced at the Court of Savoy between 1640 and 1660. Such commemorative volumes or *descrizione* are common for festival productions (see below), but these are particularly valuable because of the numerous illustrations of scenes and costumes that are included. The work of the ducal secretary, Tomaso Borgogno, each manuscript volume contains thirty to fifty large pages bound in red leather imprinted with gold and adorned with watercolour paintings. While these magnificent books would make a trip to Turin worthwhile, less affluent scholars are also able to consult photographic reproductions in the Yale University Theatrical Collection. (Allardyce Nicoll includes a dozen or so of the illustrations in *Stuart Masques*, and a few are discussed briefly by Gino Tani in Jean Jacquot, ed., *Les Fêtes de la Renaissance*, I, 221–233.)

OTHER GRAPHIC AND PICTORIAL MATERIAL

We are here concerned with a miscellaneous array of material dating from the closing years of the fifteenth century to the opening decade of the eighteenth, bearing on theatre buildings and stages both imagined and realized. Included are woodcuts illustrating editions of Plautus and Terence, drawings of theatres and stage plans, engravings of specific stages, sketches for stage machinery and scene-changing devices, and in three instances actual theatres that have survived into the twentieth century.

Woodcuts

Plautus and Terence were published in many illustrated editions throughout the sixteenth century, just as they appeared in illustrated manuscripts in the Middle Ages. Thirty-eight illustrated editions of Terence appeared between 1486 and 1614, together with another eight in translation. The Renaissance woodcuts, like medieval illuminations, seem on occasion to offer insight into contemporary staging conditions. Moreover, manuscript illumination and printed woodcut likely were not unrelated phenomena. As Cesare Molinari warns, "Any interpretation of the woodcuts must also consider the tradition of miniatures with which they belong" (*Theatre through the Ages*, p. 119). In general, that tradition was probably derived from late Roman practice augmented and altered by medieval practice and misconception. A case in point is the so-called *Térence des ducs*, a beautifully illustrated manuscript now housed in Paris in the Bibliothèque de l'Arsenal (ms. fr. 664). The frontispiece depicts actors (*ioculatores*) in the costume of *jongleurs*, evidently miming the action before a booth-like structure (*scena*) from which a figure, book in hand, reads the text aloud (*calliopus*). The audience (*populus romans*), confined within the *theatrum*, surrounds the performers. The miniatures illustrating scenes from the plays, however, dispense with the Calliopus and feature characters in fourteenth-century dress. Nevertheless, the picture presented by the frontispiece is in accord with the description of a theatrical performance found in John Lydgate's *Troy Book* (1513) and thus presents us with at least one late medieval or early Renaissance idea of a Roman theatre.

The Terence woodcuts seem clearly to derive from this or a similar tradition. The Ulm edition of Terence, published at Strasbourg about 1496 and illustrated by Albrecht Dürer, for example, depicts the orchestra as the playing area. Significantly, the woodcuts illustrating episodes from the plays do not suggest a theatre or a performance and are therefore of no interest to the theatre historian. An often-reproduced woodcut from the Venice Terence of 1497, labelled *Coliseus sive Theatrum*, again does not distinguish a stage from the semi-circular orchestra, although there are simple "mansions" on each side from which the actors apparently enter the playing area. Illustrations of editions of Plautus, on the other hand, sometimes differ radically from those of Terence. For instance, a scene from a 1518 edition of Plautus (reproduced by Donald Mullin in *The Development of the Playhouse*, fig. 2) features in the background three arched openings, through which can be seen what seem to be painted illustrations of open country. There is no indication that contemporary humanists either thought the two playwrights were originally performed under different conditions or that they mounted them differently in revivals (as, for instance, at Ferrara in the 1490s). We must therefore conclude that the woodcuts represent a graphic rather than a theatrical tradition.

The point is worth making, for theatre historians often reproduce woodcuts from editions of Terence—especially from the edition published at Lyons in 1493 by Johannes Trechsel—but exactly what they are evidence of is not always clear. Do they represent contemporary practice, or attempts to reconstruct ancient practice, or do they in fact represent an iconographic tradition not derived from stage performance at all? Those who argue for a representation of contemporary staging practice point to Pomponius' Roman productions of the Latin comic writers as at least the indirect inspiration for the Lyons illustrations and for those of the Venice edition of 1497, which was based on it. In a most thorough discussion of the problem, T. E. Lawrenson and Helen Purkis in *Le Lieu théâtral à la Renaissance* (1964) offer as supporting evidence for the possibility of a theatrical connection the fact that the supervisor of the Trechsel edition of 1493 and of the woodcuts prepared for it, Jodius Bodius Ascensius (1462–1535), had assisted at the performances of Terence at Ferrara in 1486 and 1487 before going to Lyons to assist Trechsel and marry his daughter. (They find no evidence to support the contention that Bodius had also been a pupil of

Pomponius at Rome.) They note that a comparison of the 1493 woodcuts with what we otherwise know of the Roman and Ferraran productions supports the thesis that the illustrations represent actual theatrical performance, but in a deliberately antiquarian style, and that subsequent variations in sixteenth-century Terence woodcuts are attributable to graphic tradition. On the other hand, Lawrenson and Purkis admit that neither Lyons nor Venice, where the editions were printed, were centres of dramatic production, and that the Trechsel Terence itself may be carrying on a medieval or antiquarian pictorial tradition. Certainly the Trechsel edition begat a family that persisted until Serlian perspective began to influence illustrations after mid-century; and in all later instances the artists clearly considered their cuts as decorations rather than representations of stage practice. We may allow Lawrenson and Purkis their scholarly conclusion: If we are unable to deny the possibility that the illustrations of the Terence editions of 1493 and of 1497 have the value of a theatrical document, it seems clear that the editions that follow depart more or less progressively from this possibility. Whatever use may be made of later illustrated editions of Terence, only those of 1493 and 1497 can be held to be of immediate use to the theatre historian.

One final piece of corroborative evidence that Terence-style "houses" were indeed used in contemporary productions is to be found in the manuscript of Angelo Beolco's *La Betia* (Biblioteca Marciana, Venice, ms. 637O). A drawing therein clearly shows three houses in a line, and Molinari, for one, suggests that this too reflects the staging at Ferrara. (Molinari also reproduces the drawing in *Theatre through the Ages,* p. 121.)

Stages and Theatres: Pictorial Evidence

Several drawings of theatres, ranging from the late fifteenth century to the latter half of the seventeenth, have survived.

A ground plan and elevation of a Roman theatre—in the Biblioteca Laurenziana in Florence—by Francesco di Giorgio (1439–1501), author of a treatise on architecture composed during the final years of his life, should be compared with the later illustrations of Vitruvius, such as those of Cesarino in 1521, in order to trace the developing interpretation of the Roman architect. (The drawing is reproduced in Molinari, *Theatre Through the Ages*, p. 124.)

A ground plan and elevation of a theatre designed for the 1531 performance, in Italian, of Plautus' *Bacchides* are preserved in two sketches attributed variously to Baldassare Peruzzi, his son Sallustio, or Antonio da Sangallo the Younger. The sketches are in the Uffizi Gallery in Florence.

The only extant plan of a seventeenth-century Venetian opera-house was discovered in 1927 in an album of thirty-six designs entitled *Teatro di Tor di Nova del C. Carlo Fontana.* The drawing is signed "Tomaso Belli [or Bezzi] ingegnere dell C⁹ Sud††ᵉ Teatro di Sᵗᵉ Giovanni Grisostomo." The SS. Giovanni e Paolo was built in 1639, and it has been determined that the plan dates from some time after 1678. A unique document, it shows a box theatre with five balconies, each with twenty-nine boxes. The album is preserved in the Sir John Soane Museum in London; the plan is reproduced in S. T. Worsthorne's *Venetian Opera in the Seventeeth Century* (Plate 5).

When Giacomo Torelli returned to Italy in 1652, he went to the Teatro della Fortuna at Fano, details of which are preserved in two sets of drawings and an engraving. Five drawings featuring the plan and elevation are to be found in the Bibliothèque de l'Opéra in Paris; eleven drawings of details of the decorations of the auditorium, and of plans for the stage and auditorium, are in the Biblioteca Federiciana in Fana; and an engraving by Ferdinando Bibiena, who was involved in restoring the theatre in 1718–19, shows the stage curtain, which was designed as a replica of the auditorium (*Enciclopedia dello spettacolo*, V, Plate 4). (This pictorial evidence is supplemented by an inventory of scenery in the possession of the Teatro della Fortuna in 1690. A copy is in the Biblioteca Federiciana. It is printed in Bjürstrom, *Giacomo Torelli*, pp. 249–250.)

With the exception of the material relating to the Teatro Olimpico, the Teatro Farnese, and the Court Theatre at Sabbionetta, discussed below, we have precious little other pictorial evidence concerning Italian theatres and stages. The theatre built by Buontalenti in the Uffizi for the Medici is known only through an etching of the hall done by Jacques Callot after a design by Giulio Parigi for a performance in 1617 of *La Liberazione di Tirreno e d'Arnea*, and through what appears to be a stylized impression of the theatre in Joseph Fürttenbach's *Newes Itinerarium Italiae* (1627). (Both engravings are reproduced in Nagler's *Theatre Festivals of the Medici*, frontispiece and fig. 101.) Finally, a series of miniatures in the State Archives in Bologna includes illustrations of a theatre for tournament-opera designed by Francesco Rivarola (Il Chenda) in 1639, and for a temporary amphitheatre erected in that city in 1627 (see Molinari, *Theatre through the Ages*, pp. 142, 150).

Stage Technology

We noted previously that an important question facing the theatre historian is that of determining precisely how scenes and scene changes were executed on the stage. The manuals and treatises of de'Sommi, Fürttenbach, and especially Sabbattini are invaluable in this respect; and supplementing their writings are several sketches and woodcuts that illustrate the behind-the-scenes working of stage machinery. Several drawings by da Vinci, for instance, indicate the kind of apparatus necessary for a particular effect. Antonio da Sangallo the Younger has left us a drawing, now in the Uffizi Gallery, of the *scaenae* and the *periaktoi* as he thought Vitruvius intended them. And in Vignola's *Due regole della prospettiva pratica*, published in 1583 by Egnazio Danti, are two diagrammatic woodcuts illustrating the proper design of a perspective scene and a method of shifting scenes by means of *periaktoi*.

But of more importance are two collections of drawings from the seventeeth century. The first is a set of thirty-nine drawings preserved in the Biblioteca Palatina at Parma (ms. 3708), thought by some scholars to be "probably"

Venetian and by others to be representative of production at the Teatro Farnese in Parma. Of the fifteen drawings featuring stage machinery, one is of special interest: what has been taken to be a reproduction of a chariot system for changing scenes, the invention of which is usually attributed to Torelli. (Many of the drawings are reproduced by G. Lombardi in *Archivo storico per le Provence Parmesi*, n.s. 9, 1909, pp. 1–52.) The association of the drawings with the Teatro Farnese, assumed by Lombardi and accepted as late as 1964 by Nagler in *Theatre Festivals of the Medici* (figs. 133–136), has been challenged by Cesare Molinari who, in an article in *Critica d'Arte* (1965), identifies some of the settings in the collection as those intended for an opera produced at the Teatro Vendramino di San Salvatore in Venice in 1675. And the Venice connection is strengthened by a similarity noted by Orville K. Larsen in *Theatre Journal* XXXII (1980) between the Palatine drawings and information provided by Sir Philip Skippon in his account of Venetian opera in the 1660s. (Sir Philip's account is discussed below.)

The second collection is not so problematic. Now in the Bibliothèque de l'Opéra in Paris, it contains designs for *Germanico sul Reno*, performed at the Teatro San Salvatore in 1676. In the words of a scholar who has studied the drawings: "The particular interest of the designs lies in the comparison offered between the fully decorated set and the bare mechanism, the pulleys and levers by which the apotheosis is contrived or the cloud opened . . . ." (S. T. Worsthorne, *Venetian Opera in the Seventeenth Century*, p. 48).

Theatres

Three spectacle theatres from Renaissance Italy have survived into the twentieth century: the Teatro Olimpico at Vicenza (1580–84), the Teatro Sabbionetta (1590), and the Teatro Farnese in Parma (1618). The best preserved of the three—nearly perfectly preserved—is the Teatro Olimpico, commissioned by the Olympic Academy of Vicenza, which appointed Andrea Palladio (1508–80) to design and supervise the construction of a classical theatre within a pre-existing building. Palladio, one of the most important architects and theorists of the later sixteenth century, had provided illustrations for Daniello Barbaro's edition of Vitruvius in 1556 and had expounded his views in his enormously influential *Four Books of Architecture* of 1570. Unfortunately, Palladio did not live to complete the project, which was seen to its completion by Vincenzo Scamozzi (1552–1616). Besides the completed theatre, there exists significant pictorial documentation, which hints at the process by which the theatre's design evolved but which also leaves unanswered the question of Palladio's intention for the *frons scaenae*. Did he intend street perspectives as designed and executed by Scamozzi, or did he intend to use *periaktoi* behind the openings? The evidence, in any event, consists of the following: a large (415 × 895 mm) pen-and-ink drawing by Palladio of the elevation of the *frons scaenae*, featuring a single large central arch, and a second sketch (378 × 806 mm), done at approximately the same time by Palladio's assistant, Giambattista Albanese, which reveals street perspectives behind the five openings in the *frons scaenae*. Both drawings are now on permanent loan to the Royal Institute of British Architects in London, from the Duke of Devonshire. (Both are reproduced in Blumenthal, figs. 21, 22; a larger rendering of Palladio's drawing is provided by George C. Izenour, *Theatre Design*, fig. 2.25.) In addition, there exist five drawings of street perspectives by Scamozzi: One drawing (reproduced by Blumenthal, fig. 23) is in the Devonshire Collection; four others are in the Uffizi.

Scamozzi was solely responsible for the second theatre that concerns us here, the Court Theatre at Sabbionetta, which although damaged, has been restored to something of its original state. Holding about 250 people, this intimate theatre has, like the Teatro Olimpico, semi-circular seating, but unlike the earlier theatre, the archless stage was designed to feature angled wings painted in perspective. Again, Scamozzi's ground plan and elevation for the theatre have been preserved in the Biblioteca Trivutziana in Milan (reproduced in Izenour, fig. 2.26).

Finally, we turn to the Teatro Farnese, designed by Giovanni Battista Aleotti (1546–1636), completed in 1618, and opened in 1628. With the exception of the Teatro Olimpico, this is the most frequently illustrated theatre from the period. Although badly damaged during World War II, the Teatro Farnese has been rebuilt and remains an important monument in the history of theatre architecture. It was evidently intended as a combination festival and tournament theatre; that is, the audience occupied a horseshoe of raised seats, separated from an open orchestra floor suitable for combats and displays, while the stage, complete with proscenium arch, was at one end of the structure. The hall's overall dimensions are approximately 86 metres by 32 metres. About 40 metres of its length is taken up by the stage, whose proscenium opening is 12 metres wide. A plan of the Teatro Farnese, alleged to be Aleotti's original plan, has been preserved in Parma (Nagler, fig. 128; Izenour, fig. 2.27). A plan of the theatre illustrating a performance of an equestrian ballet during *Le Nozze di Nettuno* (1728) is also extant (Izenour, fig. 2.28). If any of the drawings of stage machinery in the Palatina collection do represent practice at the Teatro Farnese, we can add this evidence to the important consideration of what went on behind the proscenium arch. Aleotti is usually credited with the invention of the painted flat wing moved on and off stage in grooves, which replaced both the older angled Serlian wings and the *periaktoi*; and his reputation as stage machinist is in part derived from the drawings in the Palatina collection. If they actually illustrate the workings at Venetian opera-houses, we may need a fresh, although not necessarily different, estimate of Aleotti's contribution.

DRAMATIC LITERATURE AND DRAMATIC TEXTS

The low estimation in which the drama of the Italian Renaissance has traditionally been held—often if not usually by critics who have not bothered to read it—has had a negative effect on the scholar who might otherwise choose

Italian drama to study, and it has also caused attention to be directed less to the intrinsic nature and worth of the Italian theatre than to the effect of various Italian theories and practices on other theatres of Europe. For without a drama of literary merit, it is somehow almost universally assumed that the theatre is fundamentally little more than a collection of superficial and fleeting effects, worth little concern in its own right. The usual charge is that Italian drama of the sixteenth century was imitative and artificial, a product of scholars and pedants divorced from the real concerns and the throbbing life of contemporary Italy. The theme is a constant one from the eighteenth to the mid-twentieth centuries, although some of the earlier estimates approved rather than objected to the imitative character of the drama. The popular attitude was confirmed and fed by Burckhardt's strictures on spectacle and, for English students at least, by Symonds' authoritative judgement in *The Renaissance in Italy* that Italy lacked the conditions for great drama—a free and sympathetic public, a centre of social and intellectual life, a "perturbation of the race in some great effort": "But in Italy there was no public, no metropolis, no agitation of the people in successful combat with an antagonistic force" (II, 98). Italian dramas, he argued, are "still and lifeless, designed to illustrate critical principles rather than to stir and purify the passions. They have no relation to the spirit of the people or the times. . . ." (II, 108–9). Minus Symonds' explanation, the view that Italy produced few plays of literary or theatrical merit continues to be echoed in most histories of the theatre.

Yet, on the other hand, the *commedia erudite* has not wanted for defenders, who have argued not only for the originality of the drama but also that it presents a valid picture of sixteenth-century Italy. The thesis has been argued mainly by Italian writers and mainly with respect to comedy proper. In particular, Ireneo Sanesi in *La Commedia* (1911–35, rev. 1954) views Italian comedy as a truly national theatre and as aesthetically rewarding, in spite of its derivative character. In English, Marvin Herrick's *Italian Comedy in the Renaissance* (1960) owes a good deal to Sanesi. (This book, together with Herrick's companion volume on Italian tragedy, provides a convenient survey of Italian drama of the Renaissance.) And Joseph Kennard, while reiterating Symonds' evaluation of the tragedies—"the literary manufacture of scholars, writing without spiritual or intellectual contact with the world of action or the audience of the busy cities" (*The Italian Theatre*, I, 137)—agrees with Sanesi in his estimate of comedy: "The Italian comedy of the *cinquecento* is a truly national theatre, reflecting social conditions, moral tendencies, sentiments, customs, in a clear and faithful picture of the society of the Renaissance" (I, 108).

Given the general attitude towards drama and theatre in the Italian Renaissance nonetheless, it ought not to come as a surprise to us that few texts have been analyzed as evidence for their own performance. We look in vain for studies of Ariosto's stagecraft or of Trissino's use of stage emblems. There are, of course, other reasons besides indifference to the aesthetic qualities of the dramas that militate against such studies. Many of the plays were indeed never more than academic exercises, and, if performed at all, were rarely performed more than once; if printed, they were intended and regarded as pieces of literature. The lack of permanent theatres, and the fact that the *commedia erudite* was normally performed by amateurs, meant that there was no on-going interaction between dramaturgy and conditions of performance, and that consequently the latter cannot be derived with any certainty from the former. The earliest humanist drama in fact was strictly literary, comprising imitations of the Roman drama in Latin, and probably representing a continuation of the medieval tradition of unacted school plays. Even after plays began to be written in the vernacular, their performance was limited to the academy or, more likely, to the court; and their publication formed part of the record of a past court entertainment—a historical event—rather than a script for potential performance.

The bulk of the dramatic texts that are available to us are in printed editions of the sixteenth and seventeenth centuries, and in general the student of theatre history must be prepared to ferret out these texts, and the occasional manuscript, from libraries in Italy and abroad. (In North America, excellent collections are held by the University of Toronto and the University of Illinois.) Relatively few of the hundreds of known plays of the Italian Renaissance are available in modern editions, and even fewer have been translated into English. Marvin Herrick's two volumes provide summaries of the content of over 200 comedies and 100 tragedies of the period; and Douglas Radcliff-Umstead found it expedient to include plot synopses of forty-seven Latin and Italian plays in *The Birth of Modern Comedy in Renaissance Italy* (1969). Such measures are deemed necessary in order to acquaint students with at least the content, the "what" of possible theatrical performance, but they can do little to indicate the "how" of performance. Actually, it is difficult to say what even a systematic study of the early editions would tell us: As literary documents they contain few if any stage directions and, as we have already noted, their authors as well as their performers were theatrical amateurs. Nevertheless, while their stage history is often obscure, some of these plays exerted a very great influence on later and foreign drama through literary transmission and occasional translation. For example, *Gl'Ingannati* (*The Deceived*), which appeared in 1538, had by 1600 run through twenty Italian editions and had been translated into French and Spanish as well as into Latin. By whatever intermediary literary route, the play provided Shakespeare with material for *Twelfth Night*. Also, Ariosto's I *Suppositi* (1509) was acted in George Gascoigne's version at the Inns of Court in 1566. And Guarini's *Il Pastor fido* (1590) not only influenced John Fletcher's *The Faithful Shepherdess*, but in Sir Richard Fanshawe's 1647 English translation has retained a small niche in the English dramatic tradition. Thus, even as literature, Italian plays have contributed to the history of the theatre.

The increasing use of music in dramatic performance, culminating in the *dramma per musica* and the opera of the seventeenth century, adds another dimension to the analysis of texts as theatrical documents. In an ideal world, the words to be sung and the musical notation indicating how they were to be sung would have come down to us as a unit, in the way that words and punctuation are a unit. (In both instances, of course, we would ideally be equally able to assume that the words, the punctuation, and the musical notation reflected performance practice.) In fact, however, the conditions of both producing and preserving operas, which tended to separate words and score, and the subsequent scholarly and critical habit of treating music and drama as separate art forms, have conspired against the ideal.

The sad fact is that the music woven into the courtly performances of the sixteenth century is for the most part not available to us, although its use is recorded in letters and diaries and in the formal accounts published to commemorate performances. (We know of at least thirty theatrical productions before 1540 that made use of music.) Even after the turn of the century, musical scores were only indifferently preserved. For the heart of early opera was the work of the poet. The earliest opera for which the music has survived, for instance, is *Euridice*, written by Ottavio Rinuccini. But not only do we tend to gloss over his name in favour of the play's musical composer, Jacopo Peri, but we also forget that the words were set to music by Giulio Caccini as well. Both musical settings exist. Nor was this an isolated instance of the constant element in opera being the *libretto* rather than the music. What then does the text of such an opera consist of? Even in the case of an acknowledged master of the new genre, Claudio Monteverdi (1567–1643), most of his music intended for a dramatic or semi-dramatic performance has been lost. For his second opera, *Arianna* (1608), we possess the *libretto* but only the music for the heroine's famous lament. Not surprisingly, the extent to which the relationship of music to words has reversed itself since the early seventeenth century is reflected in the fact that most histories of the opera indicate that the only part of *Arianna* that still exists is the lament.

The attitude that vested the poet rather than the composer with authority in the writing of an opera persisted into the early years of the professional opera in Venice. *Libretti* were set to music by various composers, and the "text" of an opera consisted of some combination of *argumento, scenario,* and *libretto.* S. T. Worsthorne summarizes the situation:

And all that remained to testify to a performance was often the duodecimo, paper-bound book with the print wax-stained from the little candle, by the light of which the story was followed in the theatre. The music, either in parts or score, was never printed, irrespective of the success of the work . . . [but] was allowed to moulder in some lumber-room of the theatre. [*Venetian Opera in the Seventeenth Century*, p. 119]

In fact, we owe much of the knowledge we do have of the music of the operas of the period to one Marco Contarini, whose collection of 112 operatic scores (the *Codices Contarinian*) is preserved in the Marciana Library in Venice, the gift of one of his descendants. In general, then, the poet was the senior partner in seventeenth-century opera. It was not until 1677 that we find an instance of the composer's rather than the poet's name being attached to an opera. It was a situation not destined to change until the early years of the eighteenth century.

But poets were not the only cross composers had to bear; nor was the cavalier treatment of their music by publishers the only impediment to a proper consideration of musical texts. By the last quarter of the seventeenth century, tbe singers were making demands that were reflected in the printed *libretti*. In the *libretto* of *Il Genserico* (1669) we find the earliest indication that additional arias had been inserted during the performance and were therefore included by the printer in order to please the performers. These arias—the result of impromptu composition during rehearsals—seldom form part of manuscript scores. Moreover, Worsthorne points out that successive editions of a given *libretto* were sometimes altered so that lines originally written as dialogue became quatrains in order to facilitate setting them as arias by the next composer. He offers as an example Nicolà Minato's *Scipione Africano* (1664) which, originally set to music by Pier Francesco Cavalli, was changed to accommodate more arias, arranged by Bonaventura Viviani. Operas were thus constantly undergoing change; "for no producer," writes Worsthorne, "would dare include in a new production music that the audience might know" (p. 122).

Writing the history of performance on the basis of "texts" composed, written, and preserved under these conditions clearly presents formidable difficulties. Indeed, the generally chaotic state of opera composition, transmission, and performance reached such levels of incohesion in Germany that it has rendered the history of pre-nineteenth-century opera almost inaccessible. Opera had been exported to Salzburg as early as 1618, and before the end of the century it was being performed in Innsbruck, Munich, Prague, and especially Vienna. But to the problems in Italy and Venice were added others: Composers were active in different places; *libretti* were constantly being adapted and translated; the same work appears under different titles, or different works under the same title; music was lifted from other works, including other operas, for insertion into new operas; and lost and fragmentary scores and *libretti* are common.

The reason that there have been few attempts at sorting the evidence of scores, *libretti*, and *scenari* and at synthesizing this evidence with information about staging and scene design—Worsthorne's book is a notable exception—is the tendency to treat drama, music, and theatrical performance as belonging in different categories. This has been particularly detrimental with respect to the opera, which receives far more attention as a species of musical composition than it does as a kind of dramatic performance. More than twenty-five years ago, Joseph Kerman complained that "dramatic unawareness underlies almost all current writing about opera," and he expressed his conviction that opera ought to be treated as "a drama, not a harmony exercise" (*Opera as Drama*, p. 16). There is some indication that Kerman's wish may be coming true, that the dramatic qualities of operatic performance are beginning to be appreciated. At some universities the production of opera has become a joint responsibility of departments of theatre and music. But if the history of the Italian theatre of the sixteenth and seventeenth centuries is to be understood and written, it will be necessary for theatre historians to view the *dramma per musica* of the turn of the century through the lens of the sixteenth-century theatre and with an appreciation of the role of music in theatre. And we must learn to recognize musical notation as an integral part of some dramatic texts.

WRITTEN EVIDENCE

Official Descriptions

Besides the texts of plays, the *libretti*, and the *argumenti* or *scenari* of opera, there were often published official descriptions of festival performances. The occasion—a wedding, a baptism, a royal reception—was not only commemorated but was made public in this way, and the festival patron glorified. Most of the festivals discussed by Nagler in *Theatre Festivals of the Medici* were the subjects of published descriptions. (Angelo Solerti's *Musica, ballo e drammatica*, 1905, provides an important collection of details from such descriptions, together with other archival material, for the period 1600–37 at the Medici court.) The performance that opened the Uffizi theatre in 1586, Giovanni Bardi's *L'Amico fido*, is recorded in such a *descrizione*, by Bastiano de Rossi, as is the *barriera* (barriers) engaged in at the same theatre in 1613. In the latter instance the official description is probably the work of the designer of the tournament, Giovanni Villifranchi. Both accounts are rich in detail, and both pause in their descriptions of the performances to offer brief descriptions of the theatre and the audience. (See Nagler, pp. 58–69, 119–125.) A description of a tournament in Padua in 1637 indicates that the theatre erected for the event was, according to Per Bjürstrom, "the first example in Venetia in which the parterre theatre, with the stage as the focal point, is combined with the tournament theatre's arrangement of boxes" (*Giacomo Torelli*, p. 38). And some idea of Torelli's last efforts, for the inauguration of the Teatro della Fortuna in 1677, is preserved for us in *Descrizione de Gli Apparati, et intramezzi nel dramma Il Trionfo della Continenza*. These examples suffice to illustrate the range of information these descriptions provide. However much they might tend to inflate the glory and the significance of a particular performance, they cannot help but provide a perspective on performance otherwise almost universally denied us in the study of theatre history.

Letters

The private correspondence of the great and near great provides another source of information concerning theatrical performance. The letters are often very revealing in their frankness. Perhaps the best known letter writer from the very early years of the sixteenth century is Isabella d'Este (1474–1539), daughter of Ercole I, Duke of Ferrara and related by family or marriage to most of the ruling houses of northern Italy. Isabella's letters are many and are concerned with many matters, including, on occasion, matters of concern to the theatre historian. In a letter to her husband, Francesco Gonzaga, Marquis of Mantua, Isabella wrote of a new comedy by Ercole Strozzi, with dances in the middle, performed on May 10, 1493 at a wedding entertainment in Ferrara. But of most interest is a series of descriptive letters concerning the festivities surrounding the 1501 marriage of Isabella's brother Alfonso to Lucrezia Borgia. Six comedies were performed on a wooden stage about the height of a man; scenery was used; and Isabella was bored. (See Julia Cartwright Ady, *Isabella d'Este*, I, 199.)

In the same year was written a much-quoted letter from Sigismondo Cantelmo to Duke Ercole d'Este, describing a carnival performance at Mantua. (The letter appears in Ady, I, 183–185, and in the same translation in Lily B. Campbell, *Scenes and Machines on the English Stage during the Renaissance*, pp. 45–46n.) Cantelmo's description is not always clear. He writes, for example: "The back of the stage was hung with cloth of gold and foliage, as required for the recitations, and the sides were adorned by six paintings of the Triumphs of Caesar by the famous Mantegna [Andrea Mantegna, 1431–1506]." The paintings referred to were once thought to have been stage scenes, but there is a better possibility that they were intended as wall decorations for the auditorium. We ought also to compare this description with a phrase used by Sulpizio da Veroli in his epistle of dedication to the 1486 edition of Vitruvius. He uses the words "Picturatae scenae faciem" to refer to Pomponius' stage. But as Molinari notes, the reference could be to painted scenery or to pictures hanging on a backdrop (*Theatre through the Ages*, p. 119).

Other early performances have been made famous by being described in letters. A 1508 production at Ferrara of Ariosto's *Cassaria* is described in a letter to Isabella d'Este from Bernardino Prosperi, in which he expresses his admiration for the scenery designed by Pellegrino and evidently used for all the dramatic performances of the Carnival:

It has been a view in perspective of a town with houses, churches, belfries and gardens, such that one could never tire of looking at it, because of the different things that are there, all most cleverly designed and executed. I suppose that this will not be destroyed, but that they will preserve it to use on other occasions" [quoted in Edmund G. Gardner, *The King of Court Poets*, pp. 323–24].

A few years later, Baldassare Castiglione, the famous author of *The Courtier*, described the stage setting for the first performance, at Urbino, of Cardinal Bibbiena's *La Calandria* (1513) in a letter to Lodovico Canossa (quoted in Campbell, pp. 49–50, and in Nagler, *Source Book in Theatrical History*, p. 71). Again, there is considerable admiration expressed for "the art of painting and well-conceived perspective" that characterized the scene, designed by Girolamo Genga.

And it is a letter dated March 8, 1519, from Alfonso Paoluci to the Duke of Ferrara that provides us with information concerning the scene designed by Raphael for Ariosto's *I Suppositi*. (Paoluci's detailed account can be found in G. Campori, *Notizie inedite di Raffaello da Urbino*, pp. 126–129.)

These were, of course, not the only letter writers of the period, and as the sixteenth century wore on, other sources of information became available to us and we are less dependent on such occasional and sporadic tidbits of information. An exception is a letter by Jacopo Cicognini, detailing the 1611 presentation at a carnival at the Medici court of a *mascherata*, a combination of ballroom dancing and operatic scenes. This is our principal primary source, and it forms the basis of Nagler's reconstruction of the event in *Theatre Festivals of the Medici* (pp. 116–118).

Contemporary History and Biography

By far the most important work in this category is Vasari's *Lives*, which we have noted on previous occasions. Details of stage machinery (especially in his life of Cecca), Peruzzi's set for Bibbiena's *La Calandria*, the setting and temporary stage designed by Aristotile de Sangallo (1482–1551) for the marriage of Duke Cosimo I and Eleonore of Toledo (1539), the festival preparations for the nuptials in 1565 of Francesco de' Medici and Joanna of Austria (worked on by Vasari himself)—all this and more is described in this indispensable book. But other, less well known authors also make their contributions. Francesco Sansovino (1521–86) published two works, one on Italian cities (1576) and one on Venice (1581), both filled with information on a variety of topics, including the theatre, although the accuracy of the information is sometimes in doubt. In the seventeenth century, Giovanni Pietro Bellari throws light on the opinion of the time concerning theatre and opera in *Vite de' Pittori* (1628), as does Christoforo Ivanovich in *Minerva sulla Tavolina* (1681). But none of them approaches Vasari's stature as a source of crucial information.

Diaries and Journals

Various people feel compelled to record their impressions of daily life: Officials keep journals of the public activities with which they are associated; travellers are prone to record what they saw while on tour. Some of these sources are published; others are not. Some of them are useful to the theatre historian in a general way; others offer specific information on specific performances or theatres. One of the most astonishing collections of facts concerning Venetian life in the early sixteenth century is the sixty large volumes of Marino Sanudo the Younger's *Diarii*, in which the author reported on matters literary and artistic, customs, commerce, public works, and festivals from 1495 until his death in 1536. (The diary was published 1879–1903.) But most diaries are less formidable. The painter Federico Zaccaro (ca. 1540–1609), for example, has left us *Il passagio per Italia* (1608) in which several theatrical performances are described. (See Nagler, *Theatre Festivals of the Medici*. Zaccaro's description of backstage machinery at Mantua in 1608 is printed in Nicoll, *Stuart Masques*, p. 126.)

Florence and the Medici court are particularly well documented in this manner. Agostino Lapini's *Diario fiorentino* (ed. Giuseppe Odoardo Corazzini, 1900) is useful for the last half of the sixteenth century, providing a chronicle of the events, for instance, surrounding the opening of the Uffizi theatre in 1586. The early years of the seventeenth century are documented in Francesco Settimani's *Diario* in the state archives in Florence (printed in *Notizie e documenti intorno la vita di Francesco Settimani fiorentino*, 1875), in the anonymous *Storia d'Etichetta evvero Diario d: Corte*, and in the diary of Cesare Tinghi, Chamberlain to Ferdinando I and Cosimo II. Two volumes of this last work, comprising a total of 1,323 leaves with both sides used, covering the period July 22, 1600, to November 9, 1623, were well known when, about the turn of the present century, Angelo Solerti discovered in the Florence State Archives a "Diario del Gherardini," which proved on examination to be a third volume of Tinghi, for the period November 11, 1623, to March 1626. (The most significant extracts from Settimani and Tinghi, together with other archival material, are printed in Solerti's *Musica, ballo e drammatica*.)

Foreign travellers to Italy also recorded their impressions. The manuscript journal of Barthold von Gadenstadt (1560–1631), who travelled in Italy 1587–89, is preserved in the Herzog August Bibliothek in Wolfenbuttel. *Coryat's Crudities* (1611) by Thomas Coryat records theatrical performances in Venice. Later accounts include a description by Richard Lascelles in *Italian Voyage* (1670) of a Roman performance of 1630 designed by Giovanni Lorenzo Bernini (1598–1680), and an account of Venetian opera by Alexandre de Saint-Didier in *La Ville et la République de Venice* (1680). (Selections from Coryat and Saint-Didier are printed in Nagler, *Source Book in Theatrical History*, pp. 259–61, 261–67.) Of particular interest is Joseph Fürttenbach's *Newes Itinerarium Italiae* (1627), in which the German architect and stage designer records his journey to Italy about 1610. Fürttenbach was especially interested in architecture, festivals, processions, and performances; and he was impressed with Parigi and the marvels of the Medici palace. John Evelyn witnessed performances of four operas at the Teatro Novissimo and the Teatro SS. Giovanni e Paolo in 1645, including a performance of *Ercole in Lidia*, designed by Torelli. Evelyn's *Diary* records the visits. We also have the important record of a less well-known English traveller, Sir Philip Skippon, who has left us an account of Venetian opera which he saw as a young man in the 1660s, first published in *A Collection of Voyages and Travels* (1732). Included are diagrams of stage machinery. (Orville K. Larson reproduces the drawings and discusses Skippon's account in *Theatre Journal*, 32, 1980, pp. 448–457.) Finally, we have the notes on Venetian stage craft, including an early box set, made by the Swedish artist Nicodemus Tessin when he visited the Teatro San Salvatore and the Teatro SS.

Giovanni Crisostomo in 1687. (See an article by Orville Larson in *Theatre Survey* XXI, 1980, pp. 79–91.)

FESTIVAL PRODUCTIONS

Italian festival productions were spectacular, and so long as scholarly interest in the theatre was conditioned by classical models and a literary bias, they were neglected and despised in equal measure. In fact, it is no real exaggeration to say that the serious study of the Italian festival theatre did not begin until well after the end of World War II. A general introduction to the subject was provided by Pietro Gori in two books on Florentine productions: *Le Feste fiorentine attraverso i secoli* (1926) and *Firenze magnifica* (1930). But Gori provided no detailed study of the performances and no scholarly apparatus to sustain his generalizations. Federico Ghisi's *Feste musicale della Firenze Medicea* (1939) is a musicological study. Since the war, however, at least partly through the efforts and initiatives of the Centre National de la Recherche Scientifique and the publications it sponsors, a new interest has developed. Cesare Molinari followed his *Spettacoli fiorentini del quattrocento* (1961) with *Le nozze degli dei* (1968). And for English-speaking students, Nagler's *Theatre Festivals of the Medici* remains a most valuable source of information, as does Howard Mayer Brown's *Sixteenth-Century Instrumentation* (1973), which provides reconstructions of the instrumentation for eight *intermedii*.

Of most significance, earlier negative estimates of these festival productions have undergone a complete transformation. Thus in 1973 Roy Strong, a leading apologist for the arts of the Renaissance, offered the following observation:

To a great extent the court fête and its context represented one of the most profound philosophical positions taken up by Renaissance writers and artists, who genuinely believed in the importance of the role of art and letters in the service of the State. All over Europe poets, architects, painters, sculptors and musicians united to create these ephemeral spectacles. . . . No other art form demonstrates so fully the passionate belief held during the Renaissance of the union of the arts. The court fête could express philosophy, politics and morals through a unique fusion of music, painting, poetry and the dance, all terrestrial manifestations of that overall cosmic harmony which they believed governed the universe and which the art of festival tried so passionately to recreate on earth. Few things, therefore, can give us such a vivid insight into the workings of the Renaissance mind. [*Splendor at Court*, pp. 16–17]

We noted earlier that in general the study of the Italian Renaissance theatre has isolated elements for examination and offered us a fragmented picture of the whole. Strong substitutes for this analytic view a new synthetic view, which postulates the festival as a theatrical mode that functioned as something more than the sum of the various arts it comprised.

The most appropriate way to pursue such a synthesis is to concentrate on specific festivals, and to reconstruct them in as much detail as possible. The main centres of the court fête were Ferrara, Mantua, Naples, and perhaps above all Florence, which, under the Medici family, became the Athens of sixteenth-century Italy.

Possibly the best known performance from sixteenth-century Italy is the one that served to inaugurate the Teatro Olimpico in 1585. The theatre is, of course, still extant, and the significance of the occasion prompted considerable unofficial commentary among the *intellettuale*. The event was considered historically significant even in 1585, and while later generations might dispute the significance or the reasons for believing the performance significant, the cumulative effect of the surviving evidence has been to ensure the opening of the Teatro Olimpico a permanent place in the history of the theatre. In addition, the survival of the theatre itself has ensured its continuing role in that history to the present day. (See Gino Nogara, *Cronache degli spettacoli nel Teatro Olimpico di Vicenza dal 1585 al 1970.*)

The play chosen for production was Sophocles' *Oedipus the King*, in an Italian translation by Orsatto Giustiniano (1538–1603). The text—*Edipo Tiranno di Sofocle Tragedia. In lingua volgare redatta dal Clariss. signor Orsatto Guistiniano, Patritio Veneto*—was published the same year. The performance was under the direction of Angelo Ingegneri (ca. 1550–ca. 1613), whose plans and accounts are among the records and papers of the *Accademia Olimpico*, preserved in manuscript in the Biblioteca Bertioliana in Vicenza, and in a collection of letters and accounts concerning the performance in the Biblioteca Ambrosiana in Milan. Included in the Milan collection as well are a letter from Scamozzi, co-designer of the theatre, to Leonardo Valmarana; a letter from Alessandro Tessame to Ingegneri; letters concerning the production by Giacomo Dolfin, Antonio Riccoboni, and Filippo Pigafetta; and observations and remarks by Sperone Speroni and Giovanni Vincenzo Pinelli. (All of this material is printed in Alberto Gallo, *La prima rappresentazione al Teatro Olimpico con i progetti e le relatione dei contemporanei*, 1973.)

Of these accounts, one of the most detailed and certainly the best known to English speaking students is the letter from Filippo Pigafetta to an unknown correspondent. (Nagler prints an English translation in *Source Book in Theatrical History*, pp. 81–86.) Pigafetta was exceedingly impressed by the physical theatre: "Even the smallest detail seems to have been executed by Mercury and adorned by the Graces themselves." And he was equally pleased with the choice of play: "Thus in the most famous theatre of the world, the world's most excellent tragedy was given" (p. 84). He also reveals, besides the names of the translator and director, that the choral music was composed by Andrea Gabrieli, organist of St. Mark's, and the costumes designed by Giovan Battista Maganza. (The choruses from *Edipo Tiranno*, with Gabrieli's music, were published separately in 1588. The costume designs by Maganza, preserved in various collections, are reproduced by Nogara and by Gallo, and also by Léo Schrade in *La Représentation d'Edipo Tiranno au Teatro Olimpico*, 1961.) This first performance at the Teatro Olimpico is recognized as a singular event in both the history of architecture and the history of scenography.

REFERENCES

Ady, Julia Cartwright. *Isabella d'Este*. 2 Vols. London, 1915.

Ambros, August Wilhelm. *Geschicte der Musik*. 3d ed. 4 Vols. Leipzig, 1909.

Bertelà, Giovanna Maria, and Annamaria Petrioli Tofani. *Feste e apparati Medici da Cosimo I a Cosimo II*. Florence, 1969.

Bjürstrom, Per. *Giacomo Torelli and Baroque Stage Design*. Rev. ed. Stockholm, 1962.

Blumenthal, Arthur R., ed. *Italian Renaissance Festival Designs*. Madison, Wisconsin, 1973.

Brockett, Oscar G. *History of the Theatre*. 3d ed. Boston, 1977.

Brown, Howard Mayer. *Sixteenth-Century Instrumentation: The Music for the Florentine Intermedii*. American Institute of Musicology, 1973.

Brubaker, David. *Court and Commedia: The Italian Renaissance Stage*. New York, 1975.

Burckhardt, Jacob. *The Civilization of the Renaissance in Italy*. Tr. S.G.C. Middlemore. New York, 1954 [1860; 1867].

Campbell, Lily B. *Scenes and Machines on the English Stage during the Renaissance: A Classical Revival*. New York, 1960. [1923]

Campori, G. *Lettere artistiche inedite*. Modena, 1866.

———. *Notizie inedite di Raffaello da Urbino*. Modena, 1863.

Corrigan, Beatrice. "Italian Renaissance Comedy and Its Critics: A Survey of Recent Studies." *Renaissance Drama*. n.s. V (1972), 191–211.

———. "Opportunities for Research in Italian Renaissance Drama, 1967." *Research Opportunities in Renaissance Drama* XI (1968), 9–20.

———. "Problems in Staging Italian Renaissance Dramas." *Research Opportunities in Renaissance Drama* XII (1969), 7–11.

Cruciani, Fabrizio. *Il Teatro del Campidoglio e le Feste Romane del 1513, con la ricostruzione architettonica del teatro di Arnaldo Bruschi*. Milan, 1968.

D'Ancona, Alessandro. *Origini del teatro italiano*. 2 Vols. Turin, 1891.

Daniel, Howard, ed. *Callot's Etchings: 338 Prints*. New York, 1974.

Enciclopedia dello spettacolo. Founded Silvio D'Amico. 9 Vols. Rome, 1954–62. *Supplement 1955–1965*. Rome, 1966.

Evelyn, John. *Diary*. Ed. E.S. de Beer. 6 Vols. Oxford, 1955.

Gallo, Alberto. *La prima reppresentazione al Teatro Olimpico con i Progetti e le relazioni dei contemporanei*. Milan, 1973.

Gardner, Edmund G. *The King of Court Poets: A Study of the Work, Life and Times of Lodovico Ariosto*. London, 1906.

Ghisi, Federico. *Feste musicale della Firenze Medicea (1480–1589)*. Florence, 1939.

Gilbert, Allan H., ed. *Literary Criticism: Plato to Dryden*. Detroit, 1962. [1940]

Gori, Pietro. *Le Feste fiorentine attraverso i secoli*. 2 Vols. Florence, 1926.

———. *Firenza magnifica*. Florence, 1930.

Herrick, Marvin T. *Italian Comedy in the Renaissance*. Urbana, 1960.

———. *Italian Tragedy in the Renaissance*. Urbana, 1965.

———. "Opportunities for Research in Italian Comedy of the Renaissance." *Research Opportunities in Renaissance Drama* IX (1966), 13–16.

Hewitt, Bernard, ed. *The Renaissance Stage: Documents of Serlio, Sabbattini, Fürtten-*

bach. Tr. Allardyce Nicoll, John H. McDowell, George R. Kernodle. Coral Gables, Florida, 1958.

Izenour, George C. *Theatre Design.* New York, 1977.

Jacquot, Jean, ed. *Les Fêtes de la Renaissance.* 3 Vols. Paris, 1956–75.

———. *Le Lieu théâtrical à la Renaissance.* Paris, 1964.

———. *Musique et Poesie au XVIe siècle.* 2d ed. Paris, 1973.

Kahan, Gerald. *Jacques Callot: Artist of the Theatre.* Athens, Georgia, 1976.

Kennard, Joseph Spencer. *The Italian Theatre from Its Beginning to the Close of the Seventeenth Century.* 2 Vols. New York, 1964. [1932]

Kerman, Joseph. *Opera as Drama.* New York, 1956.

Kernodle, George R. *From Art to Theatre: Form and Convention in the Renaissance.* Chicago, 1944.

Lapini, Agostino. *Diario fiorentino.* Ed. Giuseppe Odoardo Corazzini. Florence, 1900.

Larson, Orville K. "Giacomo Torelli, Sir Philip Skippon, and Stage Machinery for the Venetian Opera." *Theatre Journal* XXXII (1980), 448–457.

———. "New Evidence on the Origins of the Box Set." *Theatre Survey* XXI (1980), 79–91.

Laver, James. "Stage Designs for the Florentine Intermezzi of 1589." *Burlington Magazine* LX (1932), 294–300.

Lawrenson, T. E., and Helen Purkis. "Les Editions illustrées de Terence dans l'histoire du théâtre. Spectacles dans un fauteuil." In *Le Lieu théâtral à la Renaissance.* Ed. Jean Jacquot. Paris, 1964.

Lombardi, Glauco. "Ill Teatro Farnesiano di Parma." *Archivo Storico perle Province Parmesi publicato dalla R. Deputazione di Storia Patria* n.s. 9 (1909), 1–52.

Minor, Andrew C., and Bonner Mitchell, eds. *A Renaissance Entertainment: Festivities for the Marriage of Cosimo I, Duke of Florence in 1539.* Columbia, Missouri, 1968.

Mitchell, Bonner. *Italian Civic Pageantry in the High Renaissance: A Descriptive Bibliography of Triumphal Entries and Selected Other Festivals for State Occasions.* Florence, 1979.

Molinari, Cesare. "Disegni a Parma per uno spettacolo Veneziano." *Critica d'arte* XI n.s. no. 70 (1965), 47–64.

———. *Le nozze degli dei: Un saggio sul grande spettacolo Italiano nel seicento.* Rome, 1968.

———. *Spettacoli fiorentini del quattrocento.* Venice, 1961.

———. *Theatre throught the Ages.* Tr. Colin Hamer. London, 1975.

Mullin, Donald C. *The Development of the Playhouse: A Survey of Theatre Architecture from the Renaissance to the Present.* Berkeley and Los Angeles, 1970.

Nagler, A. M. ed. *A Source Book in Theatrical History.* New York, 1959.

———. *Theatre Festivals of the Medici 1539–1637.* New Haven and London, 1964.

Nicoll, Allardyce. *The Development of the Theatre.* 5th ed. London, 1966.

———. *Stuart Masques on the Renaissance Stage.* New York, 1968. [1938]

Nogara, Gino. *Cronache degli spettacoli nel Teatro Olimpico di Vicenza dal 1585 al 1970.* Vicenza, 1972.

Oenslager, Donald. *Stage Design: Four Centuries of Scenic Invention.* New York, 1975.

Ogden, Dunbar H., tr. *The Italian Baroque Stage: Documents by Giulio Troili, Andrea Pozzo, Ferdinando Gallie-Bibiena, Baldasari Orsini.* Berkeley, 1978.

Palisca, Claude V., ed. *Girolomo Mei: Letters on Ancient and Modern Music*. Rome, 1960.

Petrioli, Annamaria. *Mostra di disegni vasariani. Carri trionfali e costumi per la genealogia degli dei (1565)*. Florence, 1966.

Radcliff-Umstead, Douglas. *The Birth of Modern Comedy in Renaissance Italy*. Chicago. 1969.

Sanesi, Ireneo. *La Commedia*. Rev. ed. 2 Vols. Milan, 1954.

Sanudo, Marino. *I Diarii di Marino Sanuto*. 58 Vols. Venice, 1879–1903.

Schrade, Léo. *La Représentation d'Edipo Tiranno au Teatro Olimpico (Vicence, 1585), avec la musique des choers d'Andrea Gabrieli*. Paris, 1961.

Settimani, Francesco. *Notizie e documenti intorno la vita di Franceso Settimani fiorentino*. Florence, 1875.

Skippon, Philip. *An Account of a Journey Made through Part of the Low Countries, Germany, Italy and France*. In *A Collection of Voyages and Travels*. London, 1732, vol. VI.

Solerti, Angelo. *Musica, ballo e drammatica alla corte Medicea dal 1600 al 1637*. Florence, 1905.

————. *La origine del melodramma: Testimonianze dei contemporanei*. Turin, 1903.

Sommi, Leone d'. *Quattro dialoghi in materia di rappresentazioni sceniche*. Ed. Ferruccio Marotti. Milan, 1968.

Strong, Roy. *Splendor at Court*. Boston, 1973.

Stuart, Donald C. *The Development of Dramatic Art*. New York, 1960. [1928]

Symonds, John Addington. *The Renaissance in Italy: Italian Literature*. 2 Vols. New York, 1964. [1881]

Vasari, Giorgio. *The Lives of the Painters, Sculptors and Architects*. Tr. A. B. Hinds. 4 Vols. London and Toronto, 1927. [1550; 1568]

Vitruvius. *The Ten Books on Architecture*. Tr. Morris Hickey Morgan. New York, 1960. [1914]

Walker, D. P., ed. *Les Fêtes de Florence (1589)*. Vol. I: *Musique des Intermèdes de la «Pellegrina»*. Paris, 1963.

Weinberg, Bernard. *A History of Literary Criticism in the Italian Renaissance*. 2 Vols. Chicago, 1963.

Worsthorne, Simon Towneley. *Venetian Opera in the Seventeenth Century*. Oxford, 1954.

2

THE COMMEDIA DELL'ARTE

Easily the best known and possibly the most studied of Italy's contributions to the world's theatre is the *commedia dell'arte*. It flourished for 200 years (ca. 1550–ca. 1750) and left an indelible mark on European theatre. It was, moreover, from at least the earliest years of the seventeenth century the subject of treatises and discussions by its various apologists and practitioners; and the twentieth century has seen a continued and renewed interest in the form. The student can turn to a number of substantial studies: Maurice Sand, *Masques et Bouffons* (1862), which later appeared in English as *The History of the Harlequinade* (1915); Winifred Smith, *The Commedia dell'Arte* (1912); Pierre Louis Duchartre, *La Comédie italienne* (1925), translated 1929; Cyril W. Beaumont, *The History of Harlequin* (1926); Kathleen M. Lea, *Italian Popular Comedy* (1934); Allardyce Nicoll, *The World of Harlequin* (1963); Giacomo Oreglia, *The Commedia dell'Arte* (in Italian 1961, in Swedish 1964, in English 1968). That the *commedia dell'arte* has occasioned more analysis and commentary than its more literary cousin, the *commedia erudite*, may be due to the fact that, as an improvised form, it cannot speak for itself as conventional dramatic texts seem to do in a culture habitually oriented to the written word. And this was as true in the seventeenth century as it is now.

The focus of attention in considering the *commedia dell'arte* is, in fact, the actor, and the definition of the form must be in large measure a definition of a style of acting. "It is at once the attraction and the limitation of a history of the commedia dell'arte," writes Kathleen Lea, "that it must be written from the green-room. The privilege of familiarity is thrust upon us at a price. Once behind the scenes, there we remain . . . tantalized by laughter in the auditorium and glimpses from the wings" (*Italian Popular Comedy*, I, 5). We should note, nonetheless, that this perspective is precisely what we miss in the study of the learned drama. The question remains of the extent to which the acting style of the *commedia dell'arte* masks accords with that of the *commedia erudite*. Conversely, of course, we should also like to determine to what extent the scenic and musical attributes of the latter found their way into the production of the popular comedy. While we are here following convention by treating the two theatres separately, we ought to keep these questions in mind.

Clear evidence concerning the *commedia dell'arte* does not appear before the middle of the sixteenth century, and yet before 1600 the form had spread throughout much of Europe. Early records—municipal, parliamentary, ducal, legal—are scanty, but archival searches have yielded references to several troupes of professional actors: the company of the *Gelosi* (1568–1604), under Flaminio Scala and later Francesco Andreini; that of Alberto Naselli or Zan Genassa (1571–84); the *Confidenti* (1574–1639), under Vittoria Piissini and later Flaminio Scala; the *Uniti* or united companies (1578–1640), under Bernardino Lombardi; the *Desiosi* (1581–99); the *Accesi* (1590–1628), under Pier Maria Cecchini; the *Fideli* (1601–52), under Giovan Battista Andreini, son of Francesco. Two pieces of documentary evidence are of particular importance.

(*a*) A theatrical contract, dated February 25, 1545, and signed by eight actors before the notary Vincenzo Fortuna, established an acting company under the leadership of "Ser Maphio known as Zanini" and set out the conditions of their association. This is the earliest Italian theatrical contract to have survived and indicates a high degree of organization and expertise on the part of the players. (The Italian text can be found in Ester Cocco, *Giornale storico della letteratura italiana* (LXV [1915]; an English translation is provided in Oreglia, *The Commedia dell'Arte*, pp. 140–143.)

(*b*) In 1568, a description of a performance of "a comedy *all' improvviso* in the Italian style" before the Duke of Bavaria at the castle of Trausnitz was published. The *Discorsi*, by the court musician Lodovico Massimo Troiano, is the earliest account of a *commedia dell'arte*. (The pertinent portions are provided in English translation in Oreglia, pp. 4–10.)

Such evidence from the sixteenth century as we have suggests that the *commedia dell'arte* was a reasonably well-developed form by mid-century. Its earlier history, however, has been—probably will remain—the subject of highly speculative theory. Among the most prominent theories are the following: (*a*) that the form developed from the Atellan farce as it continued to be performed through the Dark Ages by Roman *mimi*; (*b*) that it was brought to Italy by Byzantine mime actors after the fall of Constantinople in 1453; (*c*) that it developed from improvisations of the plays of Plautus and Terence;, (*d*) that it grew out of the Italian farce of the early sixteenth century; (*e*) that it represents some combination of the first four theories. Whatever its origins, the *commedia dell'arte* is known to us principally through evidence that dates from the seventeenth century and even later: through *scenari*, the plot outlines that served the troupes as dramatic texts; through various forms of written evidence, ranging from informal letters to published dissertations; and through a large volume of pictorial evidence.

SCENARI AND DRAMATIC TEXTS

There are extant more than 1,000 *scenari* or plot outlines with brief directions for properties, characters, entrances, and exits, which served as the bases for performances of the *commedia dell'arte*. They are preserved in at least ten manuscript collections and one printed edition, all dating between 1611 and 1735. The relatively late dates of some of the collections are, of course, simply *ad quem*, the most recent possible date for the *scenari* in the collections. There is little doubt that many of the *scenari* had been acted for many years before they found their way into a particular collection. Scholars have tried to establish the acting dates of *scenari* by tracing their variants through other miscellanies and published plays. While this is an uncertain procedure at best, researchers can sometimes provide approximate dates of *scenari* on the basis of theme and style.

The major manuscript collections, discussed by Kathleen Lea in the first volume of *Italian Popular Comedy*, are the following: (*a*) the collection of Basilio Locatelli, dated between 1618 and 1622, in the Biblioteca Casanatense, Rome, containing over one hundred texts (printed in A. Valeri, *Gli scenari inediti di Basilio Locatelli*, 1894); (*b*) the collection of Ciro Monarca, dating from the mid-seventeenth century and containing forty-eight *scenari*, also in the Casanatense; (*c*) two small collections of twelve *scenari* each in the Vatican Library (Barb. lat. 10244, 3895), dating from the late seventeenth century; (*d*) fifty-one *scenari* held in the Civic Museum in Venice; (*e*) the Modena Collection of the Este Library and the Modena State Archives (twelve *scenari*); (*f*) the collection of twenty-two texts of Father Placido Adriani in the Biblioteca Communale of Perugia; (*g*) a collection of twenty-three *scenari* in the Biblioteca Nazionale, Florence (published by Adolfo Bartoli, *Scenari inediti della commedia dell'arte*, 1880); (*h*) copies made in 1700 of two collections in the Biblioteca Nazionale in Naples, containing a total of 183 *scenari*; (*i*) the so-called Corsini Collection of one hundred texts, at one time housed in the Biblioteca Corsiniana in Rome, but now in the Accademia dei Lincei; and (*j*) a collection of Harlequin *scenari* by Domenico Biancolelli (1640–88) in a French translation by T. Gueullette, in the Bibliothèque de l'Opéra in Paris with a copy in the Bibliothèque Nationale. Curiously, the earliest of the collections that have come down to us is found in a printed edition. Flaminio Scala's *Il teatro delle favole rapresentative*, containing fifty of the author-actor's *scenari*, appeared in 1611. (An English translation was published in 1967 by Henry F. Salerno.)

From the *scenari* we learn about property lists, typical actions, the movements of characters, the outline of the action; but they are at best sketchy and confused sources of information. On the other hand, there is at least one instance of a famous player-manager who has left us a corpus of full-fledged dramatic texts. Giovan Battista Andreini (ca. 1578–1654), leader of the *Fideli*, was the author of eighteen plays, several of which he published in Paris in 1625 in *Lo Specchio, composizione sacre e poetica*; he produced others over the next fifteen years. These little-studied and little-valued compositions—termed "very obscure" by Duchartre—have nonetheless a significance that is not always appreciated. Derived from the medieval *sacre rappresentazione* and the later *intermezzi*, Andreini's plays may provide a hint as to what the *scenari* of the *commedia* were like once they were fleshed out by improvisation. Moreover, the texts of the plays are liberally provided with stage-directions and with prefaces that give us details about the use of scene changes and apparatus, music, dance, costume, and stage action. The occasional frontispiece, such as for *La Florinda*, which represents a Scottish forest in which a towered castle, a circular temple, a rustic hut, four hunters, a horse, and a dog are featured, appears to be modelled after the published engravings accompanying the *commedia erudite*. Finally, in *Le Due commedie in commedia*, Andreini used the play-within-a-play technique and thereby indicates some of the conventions of presentation: the advertisement by bill and procession, the use of the prologue, the use of a curtain. The *Fideli* performed regularly at the ducal courts of Mantua and Ferrara, and at the royal house of France as well. Under these circumstances, it seems reasonable to posit a reciprocating relationship between the *commedia dell' arte* and the *commedia erudite*. It seems unlikely that Andreini was active in two totally divorced theatrical worlds.

WRITTEN EVIDENCE

The written evidence for the *commedia dell'arte* tends to affirm the extent to which the popular theatre was performance centered. Much of it—letters, commonplace books, treatises, and apologies of various kinds—was the work of the actors themselves. The most pertinent documents and extracts from documents have been collected and printed (in Italian) in the following volumes: Alessandro d'Ancona, *Origini del teatro italiano* (1891); Luigi Rasi, *I comici italiani* (1897–1905); Enzo Petraccone, *La commedia dell'arte* (1927); Vito Pandolfi, *La commedia dell'arte* (1957–60).

A large number of letters concerning the *commedia dell'arte* have survived; they are particularly illuminating concerning the off-stage lives of the actors, the organization and interplay of the various acting companies, and the movements of the companies throughout Italy and Europe. They shed very little light, however, on the actors' craft. We learn, for instance, why the Gelosi were exiled from Mantua in May 1579. Pleased by a performance, the Duke called for the author. When three actors proceeded to claim the credit, his pleasure turned to anger, and the three unfortunates were jailed and the company banished. The details are contained in a letter now in the Modena archives. Letters from October 1591 contain an account of a feud between actors and refer to a plot to slash and disfigure an actress' face. And a series of letters and records from 1580 illustrate that even a prince might not usurp his ducal father's prerogatives. Prince Vincenzo of Mantua issued a license to the *Uniti* company without his father's permission. The Duke's ensuing displeasure was felt by both actors and son. (These and other incidents are discussed, and the letters quoted, in English translation, in Winifred Smith's *Italian Actors of the Renaissance*.) Of a more formal and literary nature are the *Lettere* of Isabella Andreini (1562–1604), wife of Francesco and the most celebrated actress of the *commedia dell'arte* of all time. The *Lettere*, printed six times between 1607 and 1647, comprise a series of discussions of emotions, particularly love, and may have been used by the actress in her stage roles.

Of more direct pertinence to the actual performance of the *commedia dell'arte* are the commonplace books kept by the actors as convenient sources of jokes, songs, anecdotes, and stock scenes—in short, *lazzi*—which they used to flesh out their performances of the *scenari*. These are variously alluded to as *zibaldoni*, *repertori*, *generici*, *doni*, *dote*, or *squarci*. Their survival means that we have at least the stuff if not the style of performance. (Rasi quotes extensively from the *zibaldoni* in *I comici italiani*.)

The *zibaldoni* also had their literary counterparts. Francesco Andreini's *Bravura del Capitano Spavento* (1607), a series of fantastic discourses by the Braggart Captain, is only the most famous of several publications devoted to such material: Antonio Pardi, *Le stupende forze, e bravure del Capitano Spezza Capo* (1607); G. C. Croce, *Vanto ridicoloso del Trematerra* (1619); *Rodomuntadas castellanas* (1607); Lorenzo Franciosini, *Rodomontadas espanolas* (1627). Such collections furnished players with specimens and examples for the compiling of their own gag-books. Later in the century, a famous Harlequin, Evaristo Gherardi, provided an important collection of scenes in *Le Théâtre italien* (1694), which offers descriptions of and comments on the acting of the scenes as well.

Nor were actors loath to go into print in defense of their calling. Pier Cecchini, besides quarreling with many of the most important actors of the time, also provided a defense of the *commedia dell'arte* and its players in *Brevi discorsi intorno alle comedie, comedianti e spettatori* (1614) and *Frutti della moderne comedia et aviso a chi le recita* (1628). (A manuscript by Cecchini, entitled *Discorso sopre l'arte comica*, dated 1607, is printed in Pandolfi, *La commedia dell'arte*.) A defense of actors was also undertaken by Niccolo Barbieri in *La Supplica* (1634). And we have one instance at least in which generalized accounts in support of the actors and their craft were focussed on a specific life. Angelo Costantini, a distinguished interpreter of the mask Mezzettino in his own right, in *La Vie de Scaramouche* (1695) provides us with the biography of Tiberro Fiorelli (1602–94), the most famous interpreter of the role of Scaramuccia and possibly the greatest European actor of the seventeenth century.

Finally, we must note the writings of Luigi Riccoboni. Riccoboni (1675–1753)—interpreter of the lover Lelio—was the director of the troupe invited by the Duke of Orleans in 1716 to re-establish regular performances of the *commedia dell'arte* in Paris. Riccoboni's efforts to accommodate Italian improvisation to the demands of a French-speaking Parisian audience finally resulted in a new tradition, which utilized improvisation in the performance of French plays. But while the old spirit of improvisation was there, the new tradition represented in fact the beginning of the end for the *commedia dell'arte*. The new emphasis was on literary comedy and tragedy and away from improvisation, and it was to culminate later in the eighteenth century in the reforms of Carlo Goldoni, who pursuaded his actors to abandon their masks and to speak only the words written for them by the playwright. Riccoboni's *Histoire du théâtre italien* (1728, 1730) represents his attempt to legitimize the *commedia dell'arte* both by postulating its antecedents in Latin comedy and by urging its reform on the basis of a written text. The author's essentially serious, even scholarly, purposes are reflected as well in his later writings on the theatre. *De la réformation du théâtre* (1743, 2d ed. 1747) speaks for itself. And *Réflexions historiques et critiques sur les différents théâtres de l'Europe* (1738), translated as *A General History of the Stage* (1741, 1754) is a serious attempt at a comparative survey of the theatres of Italy, Spain, France, England, Holland, Flanders, and Germany. So far as the *commedia dell'arte* is concerned, Riccoboni's attitude never changed. He yields to no one in his respect for the skills of Italian actors, crediting them with the ability "to touch the Great and Pathetic" in regular drama, and citing his own company's success with *Merope* and *Andromache*. But of the traditional *commedia improviso* he writes:

But if true *Comedy* shall be lost among the *Italians*, they will always retain a kind of *Comedy*, tho' not deserving that Appellation, and more properly to be called *Farce*; I mean the ancient mercenary *Comedy* which was played *extempore*, and succeeded to the *Latin* Comedy, which at first indeed was low and immodest, but afterwards was improved into greater Decency and Correctness. Should the Ruin of Learning become general in *Italy*, and should her *Species* of *Dramatic* Poets ever be extinct, the ignorance of the People would give them a Relish for this kind of *Comedy* or *Farce*. It is therefore to be presumed, that it will continue but too long should it be once introduced, but its Reputation can never be solid, because it must always depend upon the Abilities of the Actors. [*General History*, p. 65]

Riccoboni's published opinions are generally confirmed by a manuscript entitled *Il teatro italiano*, found in the Bibliothèque Nationale, containing a "Discorso" on the *commedia all'improvviso*, and six *scenari*. (See *Discorso della commedia all'improvviso e scenari inediti*, edited by Irene Mamczarz.)

Riccoboni is a valuable resource, but he appeared late in the history of the *commedia*. Of more importance for an understanding of the popular theatre in the sixteenth century is Tammaso Garzoni's *La prazza universale di tutte le professioni del mondo enobli et ignobli* (1586), where we find descriptions—not always flattering—of touring troupes, masks, and actors. For the seventeenth century we are most indebted to Andrea Perrucci's *Dell'Arte rappresentativa, premeditate ed all'improvviso* (1699), a detailed handbook on all aspects of the art by a bishop of the Church who had clearly missed his calling.

Perrucci is especially valuable for an appreciation and understanding of the actor's technique. He describes rehearsal practices, analyzes the behaviour and actions of the particular masks on stage, provides representative specimens of speeches and dialogues, and advises would-be actors to master the intricacies of formal rhetoric. We learn, for example, something of the stage behaviour intended to indicate a night scene. The actors, he writes, are prone "to grope about, to bump into each other, to make grimaces, to climb up ladders and to indulge in a variety of silent actions" (quoted by Nicoll, *The World of Harlequin*, p. 137). Given the conventional nature of the *commedia dell'arte*, it is likely that the techniques described and prescribed by Perrucci obtained pretty well throughout the seventeenth century.

PICTORIAL EVIDENCE

It is when we turn to the iconography of the *commedia dell'arte* that we realize that our perspective is not totally that of the green room. The actor is what is most commonly depicted, true; but it is the actor in the costume and posture of the conventional mask that is presented, and however modified by artistic considerations, the representations seem undeniable evidence of the impressions made by the actors-masks in performance. The hundreds of drawings, engravings, and paintings of the *commedia dell'arte* produced between the end of the sixteenth century and the end of the eighteenth century provide valuable information concerning changes undergone by particular masks as they were interpreted by different actors in different countries over a 200-year period. Much of this pictorial material has been reproduced. The following volumes are especially useful in this respect: Duchartre, *The Italian Comedy;* Nicoll, *Masks, Mimes, and Miracles;* Fausto Nicoloni, *Vita di Arlecchino;* Pandolfi, *La commedia dell'arte;* the 1964 Benjamin Blom reprint of Winifred Smith, *The Commedia dell'Arte*. The most important pictorial sources are as follows, noted in approximately chronological order.

Le Bal costume sous Charles IX

In *The History of the Harlequinade* Maurice Sand refers to a painting which depicts several members of the court of Charles IX as masks of the *commedia dell'arte*, including the king himself as Brighella and the Duke of Guise as Scaramouche. Luigi Rasi, in *I comici italiani*, similarly refers to the painting. However, when Pierre Duchartre attempted to examine the painting, he could find no trace of it. What he did find, in the Museum of Bayeaux, was a painting titled (misleadingly) *Le Bal costume sous Charles IX*. Duchartre believes this to have been the painting Sand and Rasi had in mind, although he doubts that they had examined it, for although members of the court do appear in the picture and are identified in a legend at the foot of the painting, none of them is in the role that Sand assigned him and there is no Scaramouche visible at all. The picture, painted on wood (not canvas as indicated by Nicoll in *Masks, Mimes, and Miracles*), depicts a troupe of Italian players—probably that of Alberto Ganassa—together with the court personages before what appears to be a perspective scene. It is attributed to Frans Porbus the Elder (1545–81) and has been dated on the basis of the figures and the legend between 1570 and 1574, thus making it the oldest iconographic document for the *commedia dell' arte* extant. (See Duchartre, *The Italian Comedy*, pp. 82–86.) Allardyce Nicoll includes a reproduction of another painting attributed to Porbus (fig. 224), noting that it was, in 1931 at least, in the possession of Mme Wenner Gren, Stockholm. Beyond suggesting that this painting may be the earliest pictorial representation of the *commedia dell' arte*, Nicoll offers no further comment.

The Trausnitz Frescoes

We have noted the description of Lodovico Massimo Troiano of a *commedia dell' arte* performance at the castle of Trausnitz in 1568. The Duke of Bavaria later (1576) had executed two series of frescoes evidently commemorating the performance. One was done on the walls of his bedchamber; the other on the spiral staircase or *narrentreppe*. Watercolour drawings of the *narrentreppe* paintings were done in 1841 and are now in the National Museum of Munich. Kathleen Lea, who discusses the frescoes and includes some reproductions in small, offers the following comment based on an eyewitness examination of the paintings:

The artist does not appear to have attempted to represent consecutive scenes from any one comedy. Zanni occurs twenty-four times, Pantalone fifteen, the maid seven, the lovers six, his lady five, and the "Ruffiana" twice. It is the peculiar value of these frescoes that no fancy for the buffoon as a decorative grotesque has distorted the delineation of dress and attitude. They appear as life-like as they are life-size. [*Italian Popular Comedy*, I, 16]

Recueil Fossard

Early in this century, in the uncatalogued reserves of the National Museum of Stockholm, Agne Beijer discovered a collection of sixteenth-century engravings compiled by one M. Fossard for Louis XIV of France. *Recueil de plusieurs fragments des premières comédies italiennes qui ont été représentées en France sous le regne de Henri III, Recueil dit de Fossard conservé au Musée National de Stockholm* was published in 1928. The entire collection is reproduced as a supplement to the 1966 Dover reprint edition of Pierre Duchartre's *The Italian Comedy*. These remarkable pictures depict the various masks going about their stage business—dancing, discoursing, playinq practical jokes (usually risqué), engaging in amorous horseplay (always risqué). The bawdy nature of the represented scenes is emphasized by the oversized phallus sported by Pantalone. In the Trausnitz frescoes this mask appears as an old man; in the Recueil Fossard he is very clearly virile—a portrait made typical in later renderings. It has been suggested as well that the eighteen prints may represent scenes from the same comedy. (See Cesare Molinari, *Theatre through the Ages*, p. 160.)

Les Compositions de rhetorique de M. Don Arlequin

In the Bibliothéque Nationale in Paris there is a pamphlet so titled, dedicated to King Henry IV of France. The document has been dated ca. 1601 and is attributed to Tristano Martinelli, thus making him the first-known Arlecchino. The pamphlet consists of seventy pages, fifty-six of which contain only a two-line rhyme—evidently intended as the rhetorical compositions. The remaining pages contain the Dedication, some miscellaneous verse, and six illustrations, three of which present Arlecchino in exactly the same way as he appears in the Recueil Fossard. (See Duchartre, *The Italian Comedy*, pp.340–348.)

Corsini Watercolours

The Corsini collection of *scenari* is distinguished by its 101 illustrations: each title-page is illuminated with a scene or a group of characters from its scenario. The drawings have little to commend them as works of art in their own right, but for this very reason may well represent important evidence for the theatre historian. (Eleven are reproduced in Nicoll, *The World of Harlequin*, figs, 12–15, 31, 60, 77, 81, 86, 87, 92; but unfortunately there is no published collection of the entire series.) The drawings are crude and naive, but they do indicate dress and properties, and as Kathleen Lea observes, "Once we come to understand their notation these drawings can tell us more about the stage of the commedia dell' arte than the decorative grotesques of Callot" (*Italian Popular Comedy*, I, 139).

The McGill Feather Book

In the Wood Library of Ornithology at McGill University in Montreal is one of the most bizarre iconographical records of the *commedia dell'arte* known. It consists of a book containing 156 pictures, 112 of which are of birds (hence the location of the book), but all of which are executed in feathers. The birds in the collection are often depicted with their own skins and beaks and claws as well. For the theatre historian, however, the interest lies in a series of fourteen pictures of characters from the *commedia dell'arte*. In all, nineteen different figures appear in the fourteen pictures. The first leaf of the series (leaf 100 of the book) depicts a man standing under a tree—both composed of feathers. A sign on the tree identifies the figure as "Leander," and in the upper right corner of the leaf is the inscription, "LICHOMEZI"—Li Comici. Oddly, although the book has been known since 1923 when it was purchased from a London bookseller, and although it was the subject of several articles written between 1927 and 1961, it has played little part in the study of the *commedia dell'arte*. Nicoll reproduced some of the pictures in *The World of Harlequin* but did not describe the book; and Pandolfi reproduced three of the pictures in *La commedia dell'arte* but failed to mention the book's location. It was left to

Beatrice Corrigan to provide a reasonably complete discussion of the book in a place where theatre historians were likely to come across it (*Renaissance Drama*, n.s. II, 1969). The feather book was executed in 1618 by Dionisio Minaggio in Milan—this much is clear from the inscription on the first leaf. But Corrigan argues that the pictures do not merely represent typical masks, but are portraits of actual actors, all of whom performed in Milan between 1615 and 1618. Thus, she maintains, the book is "one of the most important iconographical documents of the early seventeenth century" (p. 181). If she is correct, we have on leaf 111 the only portrait of Lelio (Giovan Battista Andreini) and Florinda (Virginia Andreini) together as they appeared on the stage. Other actors identified by Corrigan include Federico and Benedetto Ricci, Niccolo Barbieri, and Silvio and Giovan Battista Fiorillo. Of even more interest to the theatre historian is her suggestion that, having been drawn from the actual wearers, the costumes shown have a special claim to authenticity.

Callot's Engravings

The aesthetic value of Jacques Callot's etchings of the *commedia dell'arte* is certainly higher than that of the Corsini watercolours, and they have consequently been reproduced and copied to such an extent that not only has it become difficult to imagine the masks without being influenced by Callot's renderings, but copies and imitations sometimes pass for originals. Nevertheless, the excellence of the work must not be allowed to distort our judgement of the value of the etchings as evidence for the performance of the *commedia dell'arte*. Unlike Callot's engravings of tournaments and entries, which record actual events and have therefore true historical value, those depicting the masks rarely reflect specific actors or performances. They have been described by George Kernodle as "a kind of fantasy capturing the essence of movement and appearance" (quoted by Gerald Kahan, *Jacques Callot*, p. 9). This is especially true of Callot's major work based on the *commedia dell'arte*, the *Balli di Sfessania* (1622), which features costumes, postures, and names otherwise unknown. "It is almost as though," writes Kahan, "Callot has created an abstract visualization of the theatrical ideal" (p. 9). While the twenty-four figures of the *Balli di Sfessania* represent Callot's masterpiece on the *commedia dell'arte*, he was also responsible for other series of relevant etchings: *Les Trois Pantalons* (1618); *Les Deux Pantalons* (1616); and *I Capricci* (1617, 1621), in which several masks are featured. (All of Callot's etchings of the *commedia dell'arte* are reproduced and discussed by Kahan, pp. 7–25.) In order to determine the nature and significance of these etchings, however, it is wise to consider them in the context of Callot's work in general. We should note especially his treatment of figures in the *Gobbi* or *Dwarfs*, the *Beggars*, and the *Fantasies*. (See Howard Daniel, *Callot's Etchings*.)

Later Artistic Renderings

Artists major and minor, known and unknown, have found artistic inspiration in the *commedia dell'arte*. Claude Gillot (1673–1732) was fond of portraying actors, supervised scenery and costumes at the opera, and published *Le Théâtre italien*, a volume of engravings based on plays. (See Duchartre, pp. 35, 38, 39, 79, 81, 85, 186, 200, 252.) Gillot's pupil, Jean-Antoine Watteau (1684– 1721), also painted scenes from the Italian comedy (Duchartre, pp. 36, 37, 89, 189, 275; *L'opera completa di Watteau*, ed. Giovanni Macchia). A Dutch collection of *scenari* from the eighteenth century is illustrated with engravings by G. J. Xavery (Duchartre, *passim*). Other artists who have contributed to the iconography of the *Commedia dell'arte* include the scene designer Ludovico Burnacini (1636–1707), Giovanni Domenico Ferretti (1692–1769), and Johan Probst (1673–1748). Examples of their work are to be found in a collection of illustrations assembled by David Allen and Benjamin Blom and appended to the 1964 reprint edition of Winifred Smith's *Commedia dell'arte*. Also included are reproductions of thirty-two anonymous Dutch engravings from the early eighteenth century, depicting actors—many unmasked—playing contemporary musical instruments (pp. 308–315).

The *commedia dell'arte* has always been a popular subject for artists, and to a large extent popular conceptions of the art have been determined by artistic impressions of it. Until such time as a proper and systematic survey and history of the renderings are done, however, theatre historians must be wary of confusing stage tradition with iconographic tradition.

REFERENCES

Bartoli, Adolfo. *Scenari inediti della commedia dell' arte*. Florence, 1880.

Beaumont, Cyril W. *The History of Harlequin*. London, 1926.

Cocco, Ester. "Una compagnia nella prima metà del secolo XVI." *Giornale storico della letteratura italiana* LXV (1915), 55 ff.

Corrigan, Beatrice. "Commedia dell'Arte Portraits in the McGill Feather Book." *Renaissance Drama* n.s. II (1969), 167–188.

D'Ancona, Alessandro. *Origini del teatro italiano*. 2 Vols. Turin, 1891.

Daniel, Howard. *The Commedia dell'Arte and Jacques Callot*. Sydney, 1965.

Daniel, Howard, ed. *Callot's Etchings: 338 Prints*. New York, 1974.

Duchartre, Pierre Louis. *The Italian Comedy: The Improvisation, Scenarios, Lives, Attributes, Portraits, and Masks of the Illustrious Characters of the Commedia dell'Arte*. Tr. Randolph T. Weaver. New York, 1966.[1929]

Felver, Charles S. "The *Commedia Dell'Arte* and English Drama in the Sixteenth and Early Seventeenth Centuries." *Research Opportunities in Renaissance Drama* VI (1963), 24–34.

Kahan, Gerald. *Jacques Callot: Artist of the Theatre*. Athens, Georgia, 1976.

Lea, Kathleen M. *Italian Popular Comedy: A Study in the Commedia Dell'Arte, 1560– 1620, with Special Reference to the English Stage*. 2 Vols. New York, 1962.[1934]

Macchia, Giovanni, ed. *L'opera completa di Watteau*. Milan, 1968.

Mamczarz, Irene, ed. *Discorso della commedia all' improvviso e scenari inediti*. Milan, 1973.

Molinari, Cesare. *Theatre through the Ages*. Tr. Colin Hamer. London, 1975.

Nicolini, Fausto. *Vita di Arlecchino*. Milan, 1958.

Nicoll, Allardyce. *Masks, Mimes, and Miracles*. London and New York, 1931.

————. *The World of Harlequin: A Critical Study of the Commedia dell'Arte*. Cambridge, 1963.

Oreglia, Giacomo. *The Commedia dell'Arte*. Tr. Lovett F. Edwards. Intr. Evert Sprinchorn. New York, 1968.

Pandolfi, Vito. *La commedia dell'arte*. 5 Vols. Florence, 1957–60.

Perrucci, Andrea. *Dell'arte rappresentativa, premeditata e all' improvviso*. Naples, 1699.

Petraccone, Enzo. *La commedia dell' arte*. Naples, 1927.

Rasi, Luigi. *I comici italiani*. 3 Vols. Florence, 1897–1905.

Riccoboni, Luigi *A General History of the Stage*. 2d ed. London, 1754.

————. *Histoire de théâtre italien depuis la décadence de la comédie latine*. Paris, 1728, 1730.

————. *De la reformation du théâtre*. Paris, 1747.

Salerno, Henry F., tr. *Scenarios of the "Commedia dell'Arte": Flaminio Scala's "Il Teatro delle favole rappresentative."* New York and London, 1967.

Sand, Maurice. *The History of the Harlequinade*. 2 Vols. New York, 1915.

Schöne, Gunter. "Die Commedia dell'arte—Bilder auf Burg Trausnitz in Bayern." *Maske und Kothurn* V (1959), 74–77, 179–181.

Smith, Winifred. *The Commedia dell'Arte*. New York, 1964. [1912]

————. *Italian Actors of the Renaissance*. New York, 1968.[1930]

Valeri, A. *Gli scenari inediti di Basilio Locatelli*. Rome, 1894.

3

THE THEATRE OF THE SPANISH GOLDEN AGE

SCHOLARSHIP

For English-speaking students and especially for those familiar with the Elizabethan theatre, the theatre of sixteenth- and seventeenth-century Spain seems
both foreign and oddly familiar. Spain's rigid Catholicism helped to prolong
the life of the medieval religious dramas—the *autos sacramentales*—for nearly
200 years after the demise of their English counterparts. And the secular drama
itself, patterned after the three-act form devised and perfected by Lope de Vega,
with its seemingly endless variations on the themes of honour and justice,
sometimes appears to present an oversimplified and puzzling idealization of
characters and issues. On the other hand, the similarities between the two theatres are obvious. Following the publication in 1967 of N. D. Shergold's *History of the Spanish Stage from Medieval Times until the End of the Seventeenth
Century*—the standard work in English on the subject—one scholar was moved
to remark:

So striking are the parallels in their evolutionary development that a specialist in English
. . . may well experience a sense of reminiscence in reading Shergold's early chapters:
a feeling that the reader has encountered the subject before in a different key. . . . The
evolution of the stage itself and hence the nature of theatrical tradition is much alike in
the two countries. . . . [John Loftis, in *Research Opportunities in Renaissance Drama*
XII, 1969, p. 25].

The parallel, of course, is not perfect, but provided that it is not allowed to lull
us into a false sense of familiarity, it can serve as a basis for arriving at an
understanding of the history of the Spanish theatre.
    That history can be divided chronologically into three periods: that prior to

the opening of permanent theatres in Madrid, the Corral de la Cruz in 1579 and the Corral del Príncipe in 1583; that between the opening of the theatres and the introduction of Italianate staging at court in the 1620s; and the remainder of the seventeenth century. While there was theatrical activity at various centres throughout Spain, particularly at Seville and Valencia, it was Madrid that emerged as the major centre of theatrical activity, providing, in the *corrales*, in the court, and in the Corpus Christi celebrations, opportunities that drew the major dramatists to the Spanish capital. Regulations concerning the theatre emanated from Madrid, and the "Protector" of both hospitals and *corrales* was a member of the Council of Castile. And finally, it is wise to bear in mind the tripartite division of the Spanish theatre: the religious theatre, the court theatre, and the commercial theatre.

Attempts to write the history of the Spanish stage have differed mainly insofar as they have made use of material in the various public and royal archives of Spain. Published dramatic texts have, of course, been available to all investigators, but archival material is by its nature not only more difficult to consult, but even difficult to learn about. The historiography of the Spanish stage is punctuated by the periodic publication of documents laboriously retrieved from Spanish archives, and the subsequent use of the documents in reconstructing theatrical conditions and in reinterpreting stage history.

The earliest attempt at a history of the Spanish theatre was Casiano Pellicer's *Tratado histórico sobre el origen y progresos de la comedia y del histrionismo en España* (1804) which, as Shergold points out, seems to have been based on an address by the author's father, Juan Antonio Pellicer, delivered to the Royal Academy of History in 1792. (The manuscript containing the address is still in the Academy's library: ms. Est. 27 gr. 5a. E. no. 147.) Both father and son wished to demonstrate the "legitimacy" of the Spanish drama by emphasizing its classical regularity, and they therefore pretty much ignore anything before Juan del Encina (1469–1529), often considered the father of Spanish drama. Casiano Pellicer, however, proved himself a worthy progenitor of Spanish theatre historians by consulting original documents in the accountant's office and archives of the Reales Hospitales General y Pasión (now housed in the Archives de la Diputación Provincial, Madrid). Of more importance for modern researchers is the fact that some of the material available to Pellicer—the account book of the Teatro del Príncipe for example—is no longer extant, and we are therefore dependent upon his work for our knowledge of it.

Spanish scholars of the late nineteenth and early twentieth centuries continued to make use of archival materials, although the results would indicate that there is a right way and there is a wrong way to do it. The right way is illustrated in the work of J. S;nchez Arjona and Cristóbal Pérez Pastor. The former consulted documents from the municipal archives for his *El teatro en Sevilla en los siglos XVI y XVII* (1887) and published original materials in *Noticias referentes a los anales del teatro en Sevilla desde Lope de Rueda hasta fines del siglo XVII* (1898). Pérez Pastor made an entire career of searching archives and publishing the documents he found concerning the theatre and drama. The most important for theatre history are the two volumes of *Neuvos datos acerca del histrionismo español en los siglos XVI y XVII*, the first series published in Madrid in 1901, the second in Bordeaux in 1914. The wrong way to deal with archival material is illustrated by D. Ricardo Sepúlveda, whose *El Corral de la Pacheca* appeared in 1888. Unlike Pérez Pastor, Sepúlveda did not work with the original documents and did not himself engage in archival searches. Instead, he simply printed in chronological order extracts from documents sent to him by archivists. Such a procedure was almost bound to produce an unbridgeable gap between interpretation and data, and it comes as no surprise that Sepúlveda confused two theatres and was actually writing about the Corral del Príncipe, which opened in 1583, rather than the Corral de la Pacheca, which disappeared the same year. (This confusion is not the only mischief perpetrated by Sepúlveda: We will return to his work later in this chapter.)

The earliest work in English devoted to an overall view of the Spanish Golden Age theatre is *The Spanish Stage in the Time of Lope de Vega*, by H. A. Rennert, published in 1909. Rennert made use of Pellicer's study, and he also took account of Graf von Schack's multi-volume *Geschichte der Dramatischen Literatur und Kunst in Spanien* (1845–46). More importantly, he made extensive use not only of the compilations and documentary references of Sánchez Arjona and Pérez Pastor, but also of Emilio Cotarelo y Mori's *Bibliografía de las controversias sobre la licitud del teatro en España*, which had appeared in 1904. Rennert quotes extensively from published documents but made no attempt himself at archival research. Nevertheless, the relationship between such research and the writing of Spanish theatre history was established, and fresh interpretations of that history would depend in large measure on what new materials could be found. (Cotarelo y Mori, whose early researches were used by Rennert, continued the tradition of consulting municipal archives and published his results in half a dozen volumes between 1911 and 1934.)

The writing of history is, of course, more than the collecting and publishing of data. It involves as well the evaluation and analysis of evidence. And in the case of theatre history, it must involve the analysis as a document of production of the single most constant piece of evidence for theatrical performance—the play text. There was surprisingly little detailed study of dramatic texts as evidence for conditions of performance before the 1935 publication of R. B. Williams' *The Staging of Plays in the Spanish Peninsula prior to 1555* and William Hutchinson Shoemaker's *The Multiple Stage in Spain during the Fifteenth and Sixteenth Centuries*. While both books have been criticized for being thesis bound—Williams for insisting too strongly on precise scenes and locations, Shoemaker for finding the influence of the medieval French *décor simultané* everywhere—they are significant for their introduction of self-conscious method in the treatment of evidence. Shoemaker in particular is under-rated in this respect. He acknowledges the various compilations of theatrical materials, but rightly observes: "But in none of these works have the scanty miscellaneous facts been adequately analyzed or properly correlated and interpreted. In fact, no study has brought to light the plans and methods by which fifteenth and sixteenth century plays were performed'' (p. 1). He goes on to discuss difficulties encountered by scholars attempting to interpret evidence for the Spanish stage.

Shoemaker decries unwarranted generalizations based on a handful of contemporary accounts. He is particularly concerned about extending the remarks of Cervantes, Agustín de Rojas, and Juan Rufo concerning the theatre of Lope de Rueda to other stages and other times: "Their remarks constitute, at best, a one-sided and partial picture of the Spanish stage in the second half of the sixteenth century" (p. 2).

He notes that in many instances it is impossible to connect a particular dramatic text with a particular kind of stage, that the performance of most extant plays cannot be determined as to place and circumstance. Shoemaker avoids potential problems here by assuming that methods of presentation could have been readily adapted to a variety of locales. This may be true, but what then exactly can play texts tell us about the available stage resources? We seem to be left with resources common to any stage or playing area. What Shoemaker did not do, but what is hinted by his discussion, is to categorize dramatic texts according to what we *do* know about them (or might be able to find out)—their publishing history, their variants, their manuscript versions, in a very few instances their performance history. Nevertheless, his perception that our inability to connect texts with specific times and places of performance is indeed a difficulty has too often been ignored by theatre historians.

Finally, Shoemaker laments the paucity of iconographical evidence for staging before the seventeenth century. There are no miniatures in the manuscripts of Spanish and Catalan plays, and woodcuts from sixteenth-century title-pages are unreliable as indications of stage practice, since there is rarely any indication that the illustrator had performance in mind. Shoemaker goes on, nevertheless, to point out that there may have been an iconographic tradition common to the various arts, that some objects are regularly presented in the same way. "If it is discovered," he writes, "that such an object became a part of the scenery for a play, the stage settings may very well have resembled the conventional form of the object that the spectators were accustomed to seeing in the arts and probably in real life" (p. 4). Like Williams, however, Shoemaker finds his principal evidence for staging methods in the stage directions and lines of the dramatic text.

Shoemaker's comment that no study had really explained the methods of fifteenth- and sixteenth century dramatic production was echoed thirty years later by L. L. Barrett, who noted in an article in *Research Opportunities in Renaissance Drama* (1966) that in spite of the labours of Pérez Pastor, Rennert, and others "none of them has given a full picture of any performance, complete with all the facts. It may well be that no one ever can, for lack of solid documentary evidence. . . ." (IX, 9). The lack of "solid documentary evidence" was at least partially remedied shortly thereafter by the publication of Shergold's *History of the Spanish Stage* (1967). Shergold's book is based on original archival research as well as on a close examination of dramatic texts and is concerned, in the author's words, "with buildings, stages, scenery, machines, actors" (p. 549). Moreover, fresh archival material continues to be published in a series of volumes edited jointly by Shergold and J. E. Varey, who between them have made the sources for Spanish theatre history a two-man operation. (See the section on archival documents below.) Barrett's point, nevertheless, remains valid; for documentary evidence alone—however voluminous—is not going to present us with the full picture of a performance he wants. It may be necessary, as he notes, "to interpret subjectively certain probable though unverified facts" (p. 9). Once again, empirical, data-based—data *confined*—history yields to the historical and speculative imagination.

It would be a mistake, however, to underestimate the contributions of Pellicer, Pérez Pastor, Cotarelo y Mori, and especially "los profesores ingleses" to the study of the Spanish stage. The authors of recent, interpretive studies readily acknowledge their debts to the archival reseachers. Othón Arróniz, for instance, bases his *Teatros y escenarios del Siglo de Oro* (1977) on published archival materials, analyzing the material circumstances that surround the representation of the plays. And the possible interpretations of the Spanish theatre based on the documentary evidence are taken a step closer to Barrett's "full picture" in the work of José María Díez Barque, who in *Sociología de la comedia española del siglo XVII* (1976) attempts to relate the social function of the drama to the contemporary system of values, and to determine its effect on the political and social life of the individual. This kind of investigation obviously necessitates a detailed examination of the Spanish audience, its expectations, and its reaction to what it saw in the theatre. Díez Barque picks up on the point in *Sociedad y teatro en la España de Lope de Vega* (1978), where he analyzes the total social, economic, and professional organization of the seventeenth-century Spanish theatre, including the sociocultural structure of the audience, in order to obtain partial conclusions concerning the complex relationships between the world of the stage representation and the real world of the spectators. It is inconceivable to contemplate such studies without the availability of archival material.

ARCHIVAL DOCUMENTS

The centrality of archival research for the writing of Spanish theatre history is reflected both in the extensive use of documents and in the increasing volume of their publication. The municipal archives of many Spanish towns have yielded information concerning theatrical activities, but the repositories of most interest are located in Madrid. The richest collections are the following:

a. *Archivo de la Diputación Provincial, Madrid.* Here are found the documents connected with the hospitals and the *cofradías* that financed them, and until 1615 controlled the *corrales*. (Pellicer discusses documents from this archive which are now lost.)

b.   *Archivo Municipal, Madrid*. While the municipal archives contain some material from the sixteenth and early seventeenth centuries, the bulk of it dates from the 1630s and later, after the municipality acquired ownership of the *corrales*. Shergold notes that two sets of files are of particular importance: (1) one concerned with theatrical leases and their sale every four years from 1641 to 1719; and (2) one consisting of builders' estimates and accounts for repairs to the theatres for roughly the same period. In addition, the municipal archives contain the Corpus Christi files dealing with the annual performances associated with that festival, as well as the "Libros de Acuerdos," the minute books of the City Council.

c.   *Archivo Histórico de Protocolos, Madrid*. This is the legal records office and contains contracts relating to actors and the theatre. Shergold points out that the pertinent material is difficult to cull from the Archivo de Protocolos and that we therefore must continue to rely on the findings of Pérez Pastor, who published a good deal of this material in his two volumes of *Nuevos datos acerca del histrionismo español en los siglos XVI y XVII*.

d.   *Biblioteca Nacional*. Three manuscripts are of particular importance: (1) *Genealogía, origen, y noticias de los comediantes de España* (ms. 12.917–12.918); (2) *Anales o historia de Madrid, desde el nacimiento de Cristo hasta el año 1658* by Antonio León Pinelo (ms. 1764); and (3) *Papeles del Buen Retiro* (ms. H. 125.2280).

e.   *Archivo del Palacio Nacional, Madrid*. Again, Shergold has been able to zero in on two sets of documents: (1) the accounts of the Royal Chamber 1623–37, useful for helping to establish the chronology of the drama; and (2) a large bundle of papers dating mainly from the period 1665–1700, featuring the complete expense accounts for several court plays, including *Hado y divisa de Leonardo y Marfisa* (1680), Calderon's last court play.

The publication of this material, as we have seen, has been going on since the turn of the century. To the volumes by Sánchez Arjona, Pérez Pastor, and Cotarelo y Mori already cited we can add *Documentos para la biografía de D. Pedro Calderón de la Barca* (1905) and *Noticias y documentos relativos a la historia y literatura españolas* (1910–26) by Pérez Pastor; and *Ensayo sobre la vida y obras de D. Pedro Calderón de la Barca: Parte Primera* (1924) by Cotarelo y Mori. (There is no second part.) But the most systematic publication of archival material has been undertaken in recent years by the English scholars N. D. Shergold and J. E. Varey. In 1961, the pair produced *Los Autos Sacramentales en Madrid en la epoca de Calderón 1637–1681: Estudio y documentos*, a chronologically arranged collection of documents from the Corpus Christi files of the Archivo Municipal. Included are documents concerning the formation of acting companies and the various payments and actors involved; legal contracts concerning the building of pageant wagons and scaffolds, the placing of awnings, the blocking off of side streets, and the building of *tarascas* or dragons; information concerning the organization, route, and timing of the procession; financial and administrative accounts; and Calderón's *memorias de apariencias*, notes on the intended staging and effects of his *autos*. Also included are six drawings of *tarascas*—Corpus Christi dragons—and two ground plans for the staging of *autos*. (See below.)

An even more ambitious project of Varey and Shergold consists of eight volumes—published and projected—of archival source materials, entitled *Fuentes para la historia del teatro en España*, undertaken under the auspices of Tamesis Books of London. Six volumes are devoted to the seventeenth century. Volume I, *Representaciones palaciegas 1603–1699*, is to consist of a series of documents relating to the court theatre, from the Archivo del Palacio Nacional. Volume II is intended to be an edition of *Genealogía, origen y noticias de los comediantes de España*. Volumes III-VI—*Teatro y comedias en Madrid . . . Estudio y documentos*—contain materials relating to the commercial theatre in Madrid between 1600 and 1699, drawn from the municipal archives. The amount and variety of information thus made available is impressive. We learn the dates of plays; we have information concerning dramatists and actors; we have access to documents concerned with staging, scenery, and costumes; we discover the details of theatre administration. We can trace the relationship between the hospitals and the city of Madrid so far as the *corrales* are concerned; we find documents relating to the system of leasing the theatres; we have contracts specifying repairs to the theatres; we have details concerning entrance fees, the renting of rooms, the policing of the *corrales*, and the prohibition of plays. For the second half of the century there are three main groups of documents dealing with the commercial theatre: (*a*) the leases (*arriendos*) which were normally renewed every four years; (*b*) the petitions submitted for compensation when a performance at a *corral* was cancelled in order for the actors to appear at court (*certificados de baja*); and (*c*) correspondence concerning repairs to the *corrales*.

The data derived from these documents tend on the whole to be useful in a cumulative and statistical way. That is, details take on meaning and significance only in the context of countless other details, and together they provide support for generalizations concerning historical trends and common practices. This is true of most leases, documents of repair, municipal records, account books, and decrees. Rarely are we able to reconstruct a specific performance from the information we have; and rarely does any single archival document or group of documents provide us with enough pertinent information for it to be singled out for special attention. There are, of course, exceptions; and some documents elicit greater interest because they are categorically important, offering—either collectively or in themselves—a proportionally greater amount of information than others; or because they refer to events of particular interest; or because they are unique or rare and therefore our only source of information on a topic.

The *certificados de baja*, for example, submitted by the lessees of the *corrales* when requesting compensation for performances cancelled because of royal command performances, are especially common after mid-century and can prove valuable in several ways. Since the title of the cancelled play and the title of the play performed at court are often mentioned, the *baja* documents help in dating the plays. More importantly, in the process of making a case for compensation, they also provide incidental pieces of information on particular performances, on rehearsals, on acting companies, and so on.

Another group of documents of particular importance—also preserved in the municipal archives of Madrid—are Calderón's *memorias de appariencias* for the years 1659–81. Calderón was the sole provider of *autos* during these years, and the *memorias* are fairly detailed and explicit descriptions of the staging that the playright envisaged for the performance of his *autos*.

These "memorias" [writes Shergold], give much fuller descriptions of the effect required than do the often perfunctory stage-directions. The "memorias" also sometimes give a brief glimpse of an earlier draft of the auto, though there was a tendency, for reasons of cost, to discourage major changes once the "memoria" was in the hands of the contractor. [*History of the Spanish Stage*, p. 478[.

Calderón was not in fact the only playwright to provide such *memorias de apariencias*. They also exist (Archivo Municipal, 2–199–3) for the two *autos* of 1687, written by Francisco Antonio de Bances López-Candamo. (These were published in 1916 by F. Cuervo-Arango y González Carvajal.)

Court performances were often followed by published written descriptions or *relaciones*, but occasionally archival materials include details that offer a closer and sometimes behind-the-scenes view of theatrical activity at court. For instance, in connection with Calderón's *El mayor encanto amor*, performed in 1635 before the court on a stage floating on a lake, we have a long memorandum by the stage designer, the Italian Cosimo Lotti, in which the idea for the performance was initially set out in some detail. (The memorandum is printed in Pellicer, *Tratado histórico*, II, 146–166.) Calderón, who was evidently expected to provide dialogue for the spectacle, replied to Lotti in a letter which is now located in the Library of the Hispanic Society of America. (It is printed by L. Rouanet in *Revue Hispanique* VI, 1899, pp. 196–200.) The playwright objected that Lotti's scheme was unworkable but expressed his willingness to consider some of Lotti's devices, a few of which were in fact incorporated into the ultimate performance. The published version of the play (1637) includes stage-directions, however, that differ in certain respects from those described in both the memorandum and the letter. (See Shergold's discussion, pp. 280–284.)

A few years later, on February 4, 1640, a new theatre, designed by Lotti, was opened at the Palace of Buen Retiro. The opening of the *Coliseo*, as it was called, is described in a newsletter preserved in the Biblioteca Nacional (ms. 8177). The newsletter describes the theatre as a *corral de comedias* as well as a *coliseo*, and indicates that the performance was open to the public. This evidence, together with the published text of the play performed for the occasion,

Rojas Zorrilla's *La gran comedia de los bandos de Verona*, suggests that the *Coliseo* incorporated features of the *corral*. (A drawing of the ground plan of the *Coliseo*, if authentic, also supports the idea that the structure of the commercial theatre influenced the court stage. See below.)

Information concerning the theatre can sometimes come from unexpected sources, themselves the result of unexpected—even bizarre—events. In February 1662 elaborate preparations were made for a performance at the Palace of Buen Retiro of Calderón's *El Faetonte* or *El hijo del Sol, Faeton*. Just before the performance, however, a plot to burn the scenery and the theatre was discovered. Subsequently, the retiring governor of Buen Retiro, the Marqués de Heliche, confessed to the crime and was tried and imprisoned. The whole episode is recorded in documents from the Biblioteca Nacional: the indictment (ms. 6751), the trial (ms. 2280), a newsletter concerning the event (ms. 2396). For the theatre historian, the importance of the episode lies in the information contained in the documents concerning the stage that had been erected for the performance of Calderón's play. (See Shergold, pp. 326–327.)

Documents that appear to establish the beginnings of an institution or a practice tend to receive a good deal of attention, sometimes more than they deserve. A case in point involves the evidence for the rise of professional actors. An often-cited reference to actors, found in the *Nueva Recopilación*, an eighteenth-century compilation of laws, is dated 1534, and refers to "players—men and women" (*commediantes, hombres y mugeres*). Unfortunately, current opinion has it that the reference is probably false and had its origin in a seventeenth-century sumptuary law. (See Shergold, p. 151n.) Nevertheless, the date seems not far off. In his *Ingeniosa comparación entre lo antiguo y lo presente* (1539), the humanist Cristóbal de Villalon refers to six players employed by the Cathedral of Toledo; and a document in the Archivo Histórico Nacional, dated 1543, refers to a group of actors under Hernando de Córdoba of Seville receiving eight ducats for performing a *farsa* before the Duchess of Osuna. Here the contemporary documents of 1539 and 1543 are clearly more trustworthy than a source prepared 200 years after the fact.

On the other hand, a document can on occasion attain the status of a primary source even though it dates from a period later than what it purports to discuss. The document in the Biblioteca Nacional entitled *Geneología, origen, y noticias de los comediantes de España* was compiled some time between 1700 and 1721. It consists of two volumes of biographical information on actors and actresses of the seventeenth century. Little is known of its origin or the circumstances of its compilation. A comparison of the manuscript with the records of the Cofradía de la Novena, the actors' guild, indicates that the *Geneología* is based at least in part on these records. (The archives of the Cofradía de la Novena are housed in the Theatre Museum in Madrid.) But it seems also clear that some information came to the compiler by word of mouth or was collected from other sources. Shergold suggests as one possible source Luis Quiñones de Benavente's *Ioco-seria, burlas veras o reprehension moral, y festiua de los de-*

sordenes publico (1645), a collection of one-act farces that make allusions to actors. The upshot is that, while the *Geneología* may not be totally reliable in every detail, the information it contains on the biographies and families of players, the types of role they undertook, and the acting troupes they belonged to cannot be ignored. (See Shergold, pp. 531–533.)

PICTORIAL AND GRAPHIC EVIDENCE

There is pictorial and graphic evidence for all three kinds of theatre found in Spain during the Golden Age, but none of it can be dated before 1626 and some of it dates from as late as the middle of the eighteenth century. There is one notorious instance of a drawing done in 1888 being assigned to the early seventeenth century. (Most of the pertinent graphic material is included in Shergold, *History of the Spanish Stage*, and in Shergold and Varey, *Los autos Sacramentales*.)

Court Theatre

There are extant four drawings of ground plans of court theatres, dating from the seventeenth and eighteenth centuries. The earliest is of the ground plan of the Palace of Alcazar in Madrid, by Juan Gómez de Mora. It is dated July 15, 1626. On it is marked the *salon de comedias*. Another plan of the palace, dating from the eighteenth century, also indicates the theatre, but shows it much reduced in size. (Both drawings are reproduced in F. Iñiguez Almech, *Casas reales y jardines de Felipe II*, pp. 229, 242.)

Another pair of drawings, ostensibly of the theatre in the Palace of Buen Retiro, are reproduced and discussed in Shergold's *History of the Spanish Stage*. The first (fig. 3; discussed p. 329) must actually be deciphered from two sources, only one of which is of an early date. Shergold notes that among the Barbieri papers in the Biblioteca Nacional there is what appears to be a rough version (ms. 14.004) of a drawing published (redrawn) by Cotarelo y Mori in 1924 in his *Ensayo sobre la vida y obras de D. Pedro Calderón de la Barca* (p. 202). The drawing bears the notation "2–458–24," but Shergold was unable to find the original drawing in that box in the Municipal Archives of Madrid. He suggests, nonetheless, that both drawings have the same source, that the Barbieri sketch and the Cotarelo y Mori copy (which dates from the nineteenth century) are derived from the same plan. The date of this original plan is taken to be 1655, the date which appears on the Cotarelo y Mori copy. The second drawing was discovered by Sr. Miguel Molina Campuzano and first published by Shergold (figs. 29, 30). It shows a ground plan of the Buen Retiro palace made about 1712 or 1713 by an assistant to the French architect Robert de Cotte. Since this plan has the same general appearance as that published by Coterelo y Mori, Shergold holds that it attests to the authenticity of the 1655 drawing. And, he argues, it is important in other respects:

The details it gives of the layout of the stage and also the means of access to it; the fact that it shows the relation of the Coliseo to the rest of the Retiro Palace; and the proof that it provides that, apart from the apparent extension at the rear . . . the theatre underwent no extensive remodelling in the second half of the seventeenth century [p. 330]

Although Italianate scene and set design became a part of courtly theatrical production after 1615, when the Italian Cosimo Lotti was imported by Philip IV, and although Lotti's work and influence are attested to from various sources, we have no actual designs for Spanish productions that are attributable to him. In fact, compared especially with the plethora of drawings and engravings emanating from seventeenth-century Italy, our pictorial evidence for Spanish scene designs is pitifully small. There exist only two complete sets of designs for any production before 1700.

The first is a set of drawings by Francesco Herrera el Mozo in the Austrian National Library, Vienna (Codex 13217), consisting of the frontispiece and four stage sets made for *Celos hacen estrellas* by Juan Vélez de Guevara. The most probable date is 1672, and the most probable place of production the Palace of Alcazar. Another design by Herrera, featuring a frontispiece with a lowered painted curtain, now preserved in the Uffizi in Florence, was also likely made for the same performance. The four scenes depict the house of Mars, a garden, ruined farm buildings, and a rustic scene surmounted by a star and gods in the sky above. The drawings are evidently of stage sets after construction rather than designs for the building of sets, and were intended to illustrate the manuscript of the play.

The second is a set of twenty-four pen-and-ink drawings of scenes designed by Baccio del Bianco, Lotti's successor at the Spanish court, for Calderón's *La fieri, el rayo y la piedra*. (They are preserved in the Biblioteca Nacional, ms. 14.614. Shergold reproduces six of the drawings, figs. 8–13; Cesare Molinari, *Theatre through the Ages*, pp. 204–205, provides twenty of them, with annotations.) The drawings illustrate a manuscript of the play prepared in connection with a performance in Valencia in 1690 and may therefore not be the original designs from which the scene-painters worked. The play originally had been performed in 1652, published in 1664, and reprinted with new stage-directions in 1687. Since Baccio del Bianco died in 1657, we may safely assume that he was responsible for the designs of the 1652 production, but the three different versions of the text, with three different sets of stage-directions, suggest not only that producers adapted the play for different performances, but that it is also possible that the drawings were doctored to reflect the 1690 text more closely than the original performance of 1652. (The three versions of the text and their scenic requirements are discussed by Shergold, pp. 306–310.)

Other than a theatre design attributed to the painter Francisco Ricci (Shergold, fig. 6), only two further engravings from the seventeenth century throw any light on theatrical practice. Both engravings, now in the Bibliothèque Nationale in Paris, were executed by the Flemish engraver Harrewyn, and both represent scenes from court performances (Shergold, figs. 7a, 7b). They are significant in that, although mainly concerned with the scene on stage, they also depict a portion of the audience, including the King and Queen, who are seated under a canopy.

Autos Sacramentales

Ground plans for the stages and carts used in the annual performance of religious plays at the Feast of Corpus Christi have been preserved in the municipal archives of Madrid. (See Shergold, figs. 20–26.) The plans for 1635–36, 1644, and 1665 are especially useful. The one for 1635–36 (fig. 21) illustrates the special measures taken when, after the 1634 festival, the King ordered the Council of Castile to invite other Councils to view the *autos* with it. The platform for spectators was so extended that it surrounded three sides of the stage, and the carts had consequently to be moved to the back of the stage rather than, as other documents indicate, being placed at the sides of the platform. This new arrangement, however, evidently continued, for it is so indicated in the plan and elevation for the performance of 1644 (fig. 22). The detailed features and explicit dimensions shown in this drawing have contributed to its use as a blueprint by Richard Southern for a reconstruction of the stage. (Southern's sketch is published in *Le Lieu théâtral à la Renaissance*, edited by Jean Jacquot, and is reproduced in Oscar Brockett's *History of the Theatre*, 3d edition.) A drawing of a plan for the 1665 performance shows four carts instead of two (a change that had taken place in 1647) and shows too that, once again, in order to accommodate a larger audience, the side carts were removed to the rear of the stage. A second drawing, undated but probably from 1666 (fig. 25), confirms the configuration of the first and emends the dimensions. The fact that drawings appear to have been made only when special arrangements were necessary accords with other evidence that the usual arrangement of carts was to have one on each side and two at the back of the acting platform. A drawing from 1692, showing a cross-section of the stage for the performance of *autos* at the palace (fig. 26), needs to be considered along with the written documents dealing with the production, but provides important clues as to the size and dimensions of the carts. (See Shergold, pp. 487–489.)

Other pictorial evidence concerning the Corpus Christi performances includes a drawing of a cart made in connection with a contract from 1646 (fig. 23), and a number of designs for *tarascas* or Corpus Christi dragons. These peculiar constructions, perhaps derived from the comically fierce dragon featured in earlier, medieval Corpus Christi processions, had by the middle of the seventeenth century acquired some constant characteristics, and the meaning of *tarasca* had been modified. By this time, the dragon usually had moving wings, a woman invariably stood or sat on its back, and the word referred not to the dragon, but to the woman. Examples can be found in Shergold's *History of the Spanish Stage* (figs. 27, 28, 32) and in Shergold and Varey's *Los autos sacra-*

mentales (figs. 2–4, 6–8). One of the designs printed by Shergold (fig. 28) is by José Caudi, a Valencian architect and designer of triumphal cars during the reign of Charles II (1665–1700), whose work on *auto* carts and *tarascas* is otherwise known only through written documents.

Corrales

Maps of Madrid and drawings associated with the renovation of the Corral del Príncipe constitute part of the graphic evidence for the Spanish *corral*, its location, and its structure. Two seventeenth-century maps of the city are reproduced and discussed in M. Molina Campuzano, *Planos de Madrid de los Siglos XVII y XVIII* (1960). And two drawings illustrating changes in the Corral del Príncipe are reproduced by Shergold: The first (fig. 14) shows plans for an extra room in 1587; the second (fig. 15) depicts a proposed permanent roof to replace the canvas awning in 1713.

Of more importance are two sets of drawings of the two Madrid *corrales*, in which the ground-plans are clearly laid out. The first set, in the Archivo Municipal (B–134–24, 3–135–8), dates from 1735. They were first published by Varey and Shergold in 1951 and are reproduced in *Shergold's History of the Spanish Stage* (figs. 16, 17). Both drawings show the stages, and both include scales that allow the calculation of exact measurements. The stage of the Corral del Príncipe was approximately 28 feet wide by 23 feet deep, not including a semi-circular projection of about 5 feet at the front of the stage. (The measurements are in Castilian feet, which equal about 28 cm. Therefore the stage measured approximately 7.8 metres by 6.4 metres.) The drawing of the Corral de la Cruz is more difficult to interpret, but Shergold estimates the size of the stage as 29 feet (plus a 5-foot projection) by 26 feet, or about 8 metres by slightly over 7 metres. The late date of the drawings might on the face of it tend to invalidate them as evidence for the *corrales* of the seventeenth century, but there is no evidence of restructuring of the ground plan of either *corral*, and it is therefore assumed that the 1735 drawings reflect the situation in the late seventeenth century in any event, and likely that of a much earlier period as well.

The second pair of drawings of Madrid's two *corrales* is preserved among the Armona papers of the Biblioteca Nacional (Shergold, figs. 18, 19). Both sketches were redrawn and the copies are to be found in a 1785 manuscript housed in the library of the Academy of History. The redrawings are enscribed 1730, and this may indeed be the date of the original drawings, but Shergold notes that "the inscription 'theatro *antiguo* . . .' which appears on both of them may mean that they were made later, from memory, perhaps specially for inclusion in the 1785 manuscripts" (*History of the Spanish Stage*, pp. 409–410n.). Unlike the 1735 drawings, these are not drawn to scale and the size of some features is consequently distorted. Nevertheless, they provide clear detail of features mentioned in written documents and confirmed by a long description in Luigi Riccoboni's *General History of the Stage* (pp. 88–91).

The redrawing of the Corral del Príncipe in the library of the Academy of

History features as well in the sad saga of the so-called Comba sketch. In Ricardo Sepúlveda's *El Corral de la Pacheca*, published in Madrid in 1888, there is found an illustration, signed by J. Comba, titled "Picura del Theatro Antiguo del Príncipe *Ano de 1660*." For reasons difficult to comprehend, this picture became part of the baggage of theatre history and was reproduced and cited as a seventeenth-century drawing. If this were in fact true, the sketch would be a prize indeed. Unfortunately, it was made specifically to illustrate Sepúlveda's book and in Shergold's words, "shows more imagination than accuracy" (*History of the Spanish Stage*, p. xx). Shergold first demonstrated the truth about the Comba sketch in an article in *Le Lieu théâtral à la Renaissance* in 1964, and repeated his findings in 1967. Comba's drawing, which purports to be of the Corral del Principe in 1660, is based partly on material found in Sepúlveda's text—including quotations from Pellicer—and partly on the drawings of the theatre in the Academy of History. Comba tried to be accurate, and he tried to communicate the flavour of the period, but his picture is the product of a nineteenth-century imagination, not an exact factual rendering. Nevertheless, error dies hard, and the drawing continues to illustrate books on theatre history. In fact, of half a dozen popular and readily accessible introductory texts in the field, all of them published or revised after 1967, only one notes that the sketch was done in 1888 for Sepúlveda's book and that it is inaccurate in many details. (The question remains: In these circumstances, why print the picture at all?) Another gives no indication of the date or the reliability of the illustration, and a third indicates—ambiguously—that it was prepared from information available in 1660. In two instances, Juan Comba is identified as a seventeenth-century artist. Comba, it appears, is a ghost who refuses to be exorcised.

DRAMATIC TEXTS

Humanist drama—sometimes in Latin, occasionally in Italian—was written and performed in Spain during the early years of the sixteenth century. But the real beginnings of secular drama in Spain are linked to Juan del Encina, whose *Carnival Plays* of 1494 represent one of the earliest instances of secular drama for which a performance can be established. Encina visited Italy around the turn of the century and the new learning is reflected in the eclogues that he subsequently wrote. The Italian influence continued in the work of Bartolome de Torres Naharro, who published his collected plays in 1517 under the title of *Propalladia*. In Portugal, the court poet to King Manuel I, Gil Vicente, was also experimenting in drama, writing in both Portuguese and Spanish. Rarely, however, are these early plays linked to a specific performance, and rarely do the rubrics give any indication of the conditions under which they might have been performed. Evidence for staging is limited to the texts, and since we cannot be sure that we are not dealing with literary exercises, the reconstruction of staging practice on the basis of these texts is a chary business.

With the publication shortly after his death, however, of the plays of Lope de Rueda (ca. 1505–1565), we find ourselves dealing with the printed texts of plays that were indeed performed by professional players. And after the opening in 1579 of the Corral de la Cruz and in 1583 of the Corral del Príncipe, we can often associate play texts with specific places of performance. The published dramatic texts of the great Spanish playwrights, then, have been a major source of information concerning the staging practices at the *corrales*, and it is only prudent to examine the volume and nature of that evidence.

The total number of plays involved is staggering. It has been estimated that more plays were written and performed in Spain during the one hundred years following the building of the Corral de la Cruz than were produced in the rest of Europe combined. The total sometimes suggested (30,000) may be an exaggeration, but even allowing for the same incremental factor that appears to have inflated the output of Lope de Vega, we must put the total number of plays at close to 15,000. Although there is no ready record of the number of extant plays, if we postulate a survival rate roughly the same as that for Elizabethan plays, we must guess that at least 5,000 plays are available for analysis. Obviously, few scholars have world enough and time to engage in such an activity, and the reasonable alternative has been to concentrate on the plays of the most influential and famous dramatists: Cervantes, Lope de Vega, Vélez de Guevara, Tirso de Molina, Alarcón, Calderón, and Rojas Zorrilla. But even these few playwrights were responsible for a body of drama equal to half the estimated output of the Elizabethans. Cervantes and Alarcón had relatively modest outputs, about sixteen and twenty-four plays, respectively; but Rojas has eighty plays attributed to him, and of Calderón's 111 *comedias*, one hundred are extant, together with seventy *autos*. Tirso de Molina wrote more than 300 plays, as did Vélez de Guevara. The prodigious Lope de Vega, however, dominated the Spanish stage for fifty years and in the process established a record for sheer quantity of plays that is unlikely ever to be broken. In *The New Art of Writing Plays* (1609) Lope noted that he had written 483 *comedias*; in his *Eglogo a Claudio* (1628) he claimed to have written "mil y quinientos" (1,500) plays; and shortly after his death, in *Fama póstume*, his friends credited him with 1,800. Modern scholarship has determined that a more accurate figure would be 800 *comedias*, about 400 hundred of which are extant. Even the diminished figures are awe-inspiring. Given Lope de Vega's, Tirso de Molina's, and Calderón's dominance over the Spanish stage there is every reason to hope that an examination of their plays would reveal a good deal about contemporary theatrical conditions.

The published text of a performed play is clearly a valuable document for a theatre historian, but such texts are seldom production documents—that is, texts used as scripts for a performance or texts based on a specific performance—and in order to evaluate their worth as evidence for production, we must have some idea of the process by which plays were produced and printed. The usual procedure was this. The playwright (*poeta*) sold his play, presumably in an autograph manuscript, to the manager of the acting company (*autor*), who prepared the script for production by cutting and altering as he thought necessary. Actors' copies were prepared from this acting text. Since in the early years, especially, plays were considered of no literary interest, once they were no longer performed, their texts were discarded. The result is that very few autographs or producers' copies have survived, and a great bulk of dramatic literature has been lost to us. The plays that have come down to us did so principally in a printed form. As the seventeenth century wore on, there was an increasing demand for reading texts of the plays, and booksellers responded by printing plays either singly (as *sueltas*) or in small collections of about a dozen. Sometimes *sueltas* were later bound together to make a collected volume. It is postulated as well that some texts were prepared for publication on the basis of a memorial reconstruction on the part of a person hired to attend a performance of a play.

The possibilities for the introduction of changes in the text between the playwright's original manuscript and the printed texts are obviously very great: The producer, the actor, the bookseller, the man attempting to memorize lines—all could and no doubt did contribute something to the text as we have it. About this there can be no disagreement. But the almost universal lament that the texts of all Golden Age plays must therefore be regarded as corrupt carries an implication that ought not to go unchallenged. The question of the playwright's intentions and his authority over the text of a play is one we have touched on before. If we assume that the "real" play exists only in the dramatist's original intentions, or in the autograph manuscript which presumably embodies those intentions, then clearly we are dealing with "corrupt" texts. On the other hand, if we wish to argue that the real play is more accurately represented in its performance text, we cease to mourn the loss of the author's autograph, rejoice in the existence of producers' and actors' copies, and even take a benign view of our memorizer. Since it seems on the whole more likely that printers' copy was derived from producers' copies than from any other source, it is similarly likely that, so far as theatre historians are concerned, the possibility of corruption is confined principally to the activities of the printer.

In some instances playwrights undertook the preparation of their own plays for publication. This was true of Lope de Vega and Tirso de Molina, for example. This certainly makes textual editors more comfortable, but theatre historians must weigh the obvious authority of such theatre-wise dramatists against the possibility that the published version of a given text is directed at readers rather than at an audience in the theatre, or that it reflects an ideal as opposed to an actual performance.

Spanish dramatic texts are useful in determining the general theatrical conditions under which the plays were intended to be performed. The large number of texts available for analysis allows for constant cross-checking and for a relatively clear idea of the minimum theatrical resources available for their performance. Since stage-directions in printed texts may or may not reflect actual stage practice, they must be consulted with caution, and most of our information must be derived from the dialogue. This is the basic method used by Shoemaker and Williams in the 1930s. Where they may have erred was in assuming the existence of certain stage resources and staging methods and then interpreting the evidence of the texts with those resources and methods in mind. A better method would be to attempt to find correlations between available non-textual information about theatrical resources and the evidence of the play texts; that is, what the external evidence suggests might have been available for a production must be balanced against what the text demands for performance, and what the text seems to require must be balanced against the limitations of production established by external evidence.

This is Shergold's procedure. By examining the extant texts of Cervantes, Juan de la Cueva, and Lope de Vega, he determines that Lope de Vega had in mind basically the same stage as did the earlier dramatists, although Lope's more abundant stage-directions specify details (for example, a curtain at the rear of the stage) not indicated in Cueva's few rubrics. A number of plays call for a character to descend from a "hill" in full view of the audience, but there is no indication of the way in which this was done. Shergold suggests either a permanent or a temporary staircase from the upper gallery onto the main stage, but this remains a possibility only. Certain costumes and properties were clearly called for and obviously available: tables, benches, an occasional dais. Shergold similarly relies on Lope's plays to establish theatrical conditions between 1604 and 1635:

There are the same references to the two doors that gave access to the stage, and two groups of characters frequently use them to make simultaneous and symmetrical entrances and exits. Many stage-directions mention windows, a balcony, a wall, and a tower, and curtains continue to be drawn back to reveal dead bodies, pieces of painted scenery, altars, interiors, and a wide variety of other scenes and effects. [*History of the Spanish Stage*, p. 219]

Shergold also examines plays by Lope's contemporaries and successors and suggests that it is possible to reconstruct the *corral* stage of the last half of the seventeenth century in a similar manner to that done for the earlier period. A similar method was employed by L. L. Barrett, who took a list of single and multiple curtain effects drawn from over 1,000 plays and examined the stage-directions for them in the published editions in order to determine that "a recessed area of some size did exist on the public stage in sevententh-century Spain" (*Research Opportunities in Renaissance Drama* X, 1967, 25–31).

We might recall as well that it was Barrett who noted in 1966 that, even with our knowledge of general stage conditions and resources, we still do not have a complete picture of Spanish plays in performance. In that 1966 article he went on to suggest another way of approaching dramatic texts, which might help to fill in that picture. The method he suggests brings us back to Spanish archives and the manuscripts of Spanish plays and it also brings us to the possibility of experiment to help establish possibilities and eliminate impossibilities. Barrett

examined play manuscripts in the Biblioteca Nacional. He found few producers' copies, but he did find more than one manuscript each for a number of
plays and, further, that these copies differed from each other. He found, for
example, that Montalbán's *Como padre y como rey* exists in four manuscripts:
(a) an actors' copy, with annotations for staging; (b) another different performance copy, with different staging annotations; (c) a copy seemingly intended
for reading, or perhaps printing; and (d) "a curious mixture, apparently of two
plays: the first act is doubtful in origin . . . while the other two acts show
signs of having been used for acting" (*Research Opportunities in Renaissance
Drama*, IX, 11–12). Similarly, the manuscripts of Vélez de Guevara's *A lo que
obliga el ser rey* indicate staging arrangements evidently as intended by the
playwright, and as altered by the producer; and two of the three manuscripts of
Claramonte's *El major rey de los reyes* also differ in their staging requirements,
while the third provides a detailed description of the staging, intended for a
reader. Barrett suggests that a systematic analysis of such differences might
provide valuable insight into the performance of these particular plays. What
he did specifically, however, was to "block" forty of the texts he found and
to read and time his "performance" of them in an effort to come to terms with
the plays as performed. The procedure, Barrett admits, ignores the literary and
the historical in favour of the dramatic, and it is not likely to produce publish-
able results, but it is, he believes, a useful exercise for the undergraduate teacher.
He is doubtless too modest: A researcher who consistently engages in such an
exercise—who even on occasion manages to mount a full-scale production of
one of the plays—is obviously in a better position to interpret the staging requirements of a text than someone who has never tested conceptions against
actual practice. And manuscripts, when available, provide far better texts on
which to practice than edited and printed readers' texts.

WRITTEN EVIDENCE

References to the theatre of varying value to the theatre historian appear in
critical treatises, in books of history and antiquarianism, in memoirs, in correspondence, in travellers' accounts, and even in fiction. Rarely is such information central to an understanding of the Spanish theatre, and it must usually
be interpreted with some care, but it provides perspectives on the stage that are
the product of a wide range of attitudes. Moralists worry about the evil effects
of stage performance; letter writers and diarists comment upon personal relationships; foreign travellers compare Spain's theatre with their own; literary
theorists debate the merits of classical versus modern dramaturgy; playwrights
defend their own practice and attack that of their rivals; and invective sometimes adds its own flavour.

Early References

Early references to the theatre are inconclusive, but their scarcity highlights
the information they provide. Cristóbal de Villalón (ca. 1505–1558), in his *In-*

geniosa comparación entre lo antiguo y lo presente (1539), refers in passing to six skilled players employed by the Cathedral of Toledo. Fray Francisco de Alcocer, in *Tratado del Juego* (1559), mentions indecencies and improprieties associated with acting, but what is more intriguing, he also discusses the use of various devices, including the actors' masks. If masks were still being used as late as 1559, the use was surely on the wane, for this is the last reference we have to them.

Actually, the three most frequently cited sources for information concerning Spanish professional theatre before the opening of permanent theatres are all relatively late. Juan Rufo y Gutiérrez (1547?–1625) was the author of a collection of witticisms and maxims, *Las seyscientas apotegmas* (1596), in which he found occasion to describe the theatre of Lope de Rueda, who had died thirty years before. Rufo notes the discomforts of the innyard, the paucity of costumes and properties, and Lope de Rueda's exceedingly limited repertory. This picture of a crude and primitive theatre is echoed in *El viaje entretenido (The Entertaining Journey)* a novel by Agustín de Rojas Villandrando, published in 1603. The primitive quality of the early theatre is also Cervantes' theme when in the Prologue to *Ocho comedias y ocho entremeses nuevos* (1615) he recalls the impression made upon him in his youth by Lope de Rueda. Cervantes contrasts this theatre—which clearly he remembers with affection and admiration—with the sophisticated stage of 1615, and it is he who provides us with perhaps the most widely known description of the theatre of Lope de Rueda:

There were no figures which arose or seemed to arise from the centre of the earth through the hollow of the stage, which at that time consisted of four benches arranged on a square, with four or five boards upon them, raised about four spans from the ground. . . . The furnishings of the stage were an old woolen blanket drawn by two cords from one side to the other, which formed what is called a dressing-room, behind which were the musicians, singing some old ballad without the accompaniment of a guitar. [quoted by Rennert, *The Spanish Stage in the Time of Lope de Vega*, pp. 17–18]

These three accounts must, of course, be balanced against what Lope de Rueda's plays tell us about the conditions of their own performance, and what archival documents tell us about the playwright's activities. There is little doubt that all three descriptions are cast in the mold of "how far we have come from the bad old days" and must be read accordingly. Even Cervantes' pleasurable recollection is couched in the same terms. We must, moreover, be somewhat wary of treating Rojas' work of fiction as a treatise intended to convey factual information about a world outside itself. It is a comic novel, not an objective document. Nevertheless, Rojas was an actor for a time, and there is no reason for his deliberately falsifying the picture of an actor's life that he paints. It becomes rather a matter of interpreting what he says with a degree of literary sophistication. One point that we must certainly bear in mind is the particular genre of the novel and the particular conventions of that genre. *El viaje entretenido* was not the only picaresque novel of the period, and, as Shergold points out, "it became almost a conventional *topos* of this kind of literature that the 'picaro' should fall in with a troupe of players, and become, for the time being, one of their number" (*History of the Spanish Stage*, p. 513). (A convenient collection of this fiction is *La novela picaresca española*, edited by Angel Valbuena Prat.) Added to the picaresque novel's general tendency to caricature, then, is a more specific collection of type-figures from the theatrical world: the foolish dramatist, the impoverished troupe-manager, the immoral actress. Such conventions must be allowed for. When they are, descriptions such as those of Rojas may take their place as *bona fide* evidence for theatrical history.

Descriptions of Theatres

Our single most important description of a *corral* as it appeared in the last decade of the sixteenth century is provided by the critic Alonso López Pinciano (1547?–1622) in his *Philosophia antigua poetica* (1596). The author gives us an account of a visit to the Corral de la Cruz to see a performance of an adaptation of a play by Euripides. It is not clear whether the visit was actual or imaginary, but in either event, the details discussed and the criticisms made suggest a knowledge based on experience. Pinciano mentions the tuning of instruments, a curtain, the appearance of the actors, costumes, and décor; he describes the quarreling over benches and seats, the fruit-seller and his occasionally misdirected aim.

The seventeenth-century theatre is more extensively documented, as we would expect. There are several descriptions of the interiors of *corrales*, although none of them is in great enough detail to allow an accurate reconstruction. One of the earliest occurs in a manuscript attributed to one Morisco. The author notes chairs and benches in the *patio*, women of the common people in a gallery, distinguished persons in another gallery. (The passage is quoted by Rennert, pp. 323–324.) A much more detailed description of the visit of a gallant to the theatre is provided by the dramatist Juan de Zabaleta in *Día de fiesta par la tarde* (1666). Here we get a glimpse of the green-room, the actors and actresses, the *cazuela* or "stew pan" where women sat, a fruit-seller, and various members of the audience—all in a way which stresses the very human and social quality of an afternoon at a *corral*. (The description is printed by Rennert, pp. 334–338.) Finally, we should take account of a play that has a theatrical performance for its subject. The first act of *La Baltasura* (ca. 1630?) represents the interior of the Corral de la Olivera in Valencia and features dialogue by spectators in the theatre. (See Rennert, p. 278n.)

The place of the theatre in the social and political life of Madrid can, of course, be inferred from a multitude of documents in the archives. For one specific period in the latter half of the seventeenth century, however, we have evidence of particular value. Jerónimo de Barrionuevo (1587–1671), from August 1, 1654, to July 24, 1658, wrote regularly to the Dean of Saragossa commenting on contemporary life and customs in Madrid. Barrionuevo's *Avisos*—constituting a kind of journalistic gossip column—offer a discussion of political and foreign news, details of crimes and scandals, and notices of new plays, fiestas, and fashions.

Foreign Visitors

Some of our main sources of information concerning the theatre in seventeenth-century Spain—as they were in Italy—are the reports and diaries of visitors from abroad. (A bibliography of this material has been compiled by A. Farinelli, *Viajes par España y Portugal desde la Edad Media hasta el siglo XX*.) Not all such accounts are extensive and some still languish in manuscript in official archives. Shergold mentions an account of the visit of Prince Cosimo of Tuscany in 1668–69 (Biblioteca Medicea-Laurenziana ms. Med. Pol. 123) and another by the Englishman Thomas Williams in 1680 (Cambridge University Library ms. Dd. vi. 80). And others mention theatrical affairs only briefly and in passing, for example: Maréchal de Bassompierre in his *Journal de ma vie*, or the correspondence of the British Minister at Madrid 1690–99, Alexander Stanhope, who provides some information concerning the court theatre of the time. An anonymous English work, *A New Account of Spain*, published in London in 1703, offers an unfavourable impression of a *corral* at Cadiz in the last decade of the seventeenth century. (See an article by G. E. Wade in *Bulletin of the "Comediantes"* X, 1958.) And *Lettres écrites de Madrid en 1666 et 1667*, attributed to one "Muret," contains a description of the theatre at Buen Retiro and the adjoining "sale des balets."

More extensive and interesting observations are offered by the Comtesse d'Aulnoy in her *Relation du voyage d'Espagne* (1693), excerpts from which are quoted by Rennert (pp. 330–333). Madame d'Aulnoy recounts visits in 1679 to a *corral* in San Sebastian, to a performance of the opera *Alcina* at the Buen Retiro theatre, and to the performance of an *auto* in Madrid. The lady was not always favourably impressed. She found fault with the physical stage, with the audience, with the *gracioso* or clown at the *corral*; with the "wretched machinery" at the Buen Retiro; with the quality of the *auto*. On the other hand, she approved the dancing of the actresses at the *corral*, and admired the architecture and decoration of the Buen Retiro. Also of considerable interest is the narrative of Francis van Aerssen, also known as Antoine de Brunel, who visited Spain in 1654–55 and published his *Voyage d'Espagne* in 1665. (An English translation, *A Journey into Spain*, appeared in 1670, with no indication that it was a translation.) Once again, we find the *corrales* compared unfavourably with what the author has known elsewhere. But of most importance is Aerssen's (or Brunel's) long description of the celebrations in Madrid of the Feast of Corpus Christi (quoted by Rennert, pp. 325–328). Of special note is the fact that Aerssen observes that the carts stood round the stage—an indication, according to Shergold, that the number of carts had been increased from two to four for each play. A work generally bound with the *Voyage d'Espagne*—*Relation de l'Etat et Gouvernement d'Espagne* (1666) by François

Bertaut—also provides a description of Madrid's theatres (Rennert, pp. 328–329).

Critical Theory

Compared with the Italian preoccupation with dramatic and critical theory, Spanish critical writing appears very meagre indeed. It begins much later, toward the close of the sixteenth century, and it follows in general the conventional controversy: classical rules and rigidity versus the newer, less constrained conception of drama reflected in most of the professional theatre. But also involved was the old concern over the possible immorality of the stage; and rendering the debate lively were personal animosity and invective. (A list of documents is provided by Cotarelo y Mori, *Bibliografía de las controversias sobre la licitud del teatro en España*. See also Margaret Wilson, *Spanish Drama of the Golden Age*, pp. 24–38.)

The last decade of the sixteenth century saw the first full-blown Spanish rhetoric and poetic based on Italian precedent. Juan Diaz Rengifo's *Arte poética española*, a standard treatise on rhetoric, was published in 1592. In 1596 appeared Lopez Pinciano's *Philosophia antigua poética*, a systematic exposition of Aristotle in the manner of the Italians. He conflates and confuses Aristotle and Horace, discusses drama as an imitative art, insists on the rigid distinction between tragedy and comedy, advocates a five-act structure, and defends the three unities. (His suggestion that theatrical performances ought not to last longer than three hours may have been based on his experience at the Corral de la Cruz as well as on theoretical grounds.) The *Philosophia antigua poética* obviously had little effect on what was played on Spanish stages, but this was not because it found no sympathetic readers, even among those who had ambitions as playwrights. The great Cervantes himself entered the lists on the side of classical decorum in *Don Quixote* (1605) and, in a passage generally thought to have been directed mainly at Lope de Vega, and certainly reminiscent of the similar strictures of Sir Philip Sidney, laments the passing of the regular drama (such as his own *Numantia*) and the absurdity of the new style, which violated canons of probability and sense. "And yet," writes Cervantes, "there are people who think all this perfection, and call everything else mere pedantry" (in Clark, *European Theories of the Drama*, p. 62).

One of those who did think "everything else mere pedantry" was Lope de Vega. At least partially in answer to Cervantes, he wrote his *Arte nuevo de hacer comedias en este tiempo* (*The New Art of Writing Plays in this Age*) (1609). (Both Cervantes' and Lope's remarks are included in Barrett H. Clark's *European Theories of the Drama*.) Lope, of course, was an exceedingly successful playwright and happily twits the classicists with the fact while he simultaneously argues his own theory of the necessary subordination of art to nature. As a theoretical document, *The New Art* is not important; as a justification for its author's dramatic practice, it has historical significance. By 1609, at any rate, the battle of the ancients and moderns was really over. The historian and literary critic Francisco de Cascales (1564–1642) reiterated an extreme conservative view in *Tablas poeticas* (1617), but a year earlier Ricardo de Turia had argued in *Apologética de las comedias españoles* that classical precepts were not applicable to modern circumstances. (The playwright Juan de la Cueva had championed the new drama as early as 1606 in *Egemplar poética* but the treatise was not published until 1774.)

What kept the controversy going for a few years longer was clearly personal animosity on the part of several writers towards Lope de Vega, and an equivalent determination on the part of the playwright's friends to defend him. Cristóbal Suárez de Figueroa (1571?–1644) launched a personal attack on Lope in 1617 in *El pasajero* (*The Traveller*). An even more virulent attack by Pedro de Torres Rámila is known only through the replies it prompted from Lope and his friends, who evidently destroyed every copy they could find of *Spongia*, as it was called. The most significant refutations of Torres Rámila were the *Expostulatio spongiae* (1618) by several writers, and Tirso de Molina's *Cigarrales de Toledo* (1621), although Lope himself contributed a couple of verse satires and a long allegorical poem (*La filomena*) in his own defense.

The moral objections to stage plays, which found their most prominent expression in the historian Juan de Mariand's *Tratado contra los juegos públicos* (*Treatise against Public Plays*) (1609), were reasserted in the 1620s after the defeat of the classicists, and Francisco de la Barreda felt compelled to defend the modern theatre on moral as well as aesthetic grounds in his *Invectiva y Apologia* (1622). With the possible exception of Diego de Vich's *Breve discurso de las comedias y de su representacion* (1650) there is little else in Spanish dramatic theory or criticism until the eighteenth century.

DESCRIPTIONS OF COURT PERFORMANCES

Events that took place at royal or ducal courts or that involved royal or noble personages were, of course, far more likely to be described and chronicled than were performances at the *corrales* or even those of the Corpus Christi *autos*. Special festivities, which might include the performance of a play, were laid on for the usual reasons: to celebrate a wedding or a birth, to honour a guest, to mark a royal birthday. Neither their number nor their extravagance is nearly so great in Spain as it was in Italy, but on occasion the solemn Spaniards approached their more effervescent Italian cousins in the mounting of spectacle. Such festivities were often described in published *relaciones*, the Spanish equivalent of the Italian *descrizioni*. (See J. Alenda y Mira, *Relaciones de solemnidades y fiestas públicas de Espanña*.) Moreover, plays performed during these celebrations were often published with far more lavish stage-directions and descriptions than usual.

A special form of entertainment, unique to courtly festivities, was the masque, similar to that exploited in England by Ben Jonson and Inigo Jones but destined in Spain to remain a less elaborate precursor of the more elaborate

court play *à l'Italienne*. Prime sources of information concerning these early
masques and masque-like entertainments at the Spanish court are *Relaciones de
las casas sucedidas en la corte de España, desde 1599 hasta 1614* by the historian Luis Cabrera de Córdoba; *Fastiginia o fastos geniales* by T. Pinheiro da
Veiga; and a 1605 report on the experiences in Spain of the English ambassador
by Robert Treswell. (Treswell's description is printed in John Sommers' *Fourth
Collection of Scarce and Valuable Tracts*.) It is principally to these documents,
for instance, that we owe our considerable information concerning a masque
performed at the festivities in 1605 in Valladolid celebrating the birth of Prince
Philip (later Philip IV), although there exists, in addition, an anonymous *Relacion* (printed with N. Alonso Cortes' edition of Pinheiro da Veiga's *Fastin-
ginia*).

Masques were essentially aristocratic and, more importantly, amateur entertainments. But Spanish aristocratic households did not shrink from the performance of regular drama as well. Such amateur performances at the residence
of the Duke of Lerma are recorded by Cabrera de Córdoba, and we possess
relaciones of specific performances there in 1614 and 1617. Lope de Vega's *El
primio de la hermosura*, acted in 1614 by court ladies and members of the royal
family, is described in a manuscript *relacion* first published by F. Ramírez de
Arellano and J. Sancho Rayón in 1873. (It is reprinted, together with the text
of the play, in Lope's *Obras*, XIII.) We learn that the performance took place
in an open-air theatre on a river bank, and the set was influenced by the medieval *décor simultané*. At one end were a mountain, a cave, and a temple; at
the other, another mountain on which was Circe's cave. In between were a palace, another temple, and a castle—all elaborately painted. The entire set is described in considerable detail, as are the costumes and the action of the play,
which concluded with a masque danced by the ladies of the court. (See Shergold, pp. 252–255.)

Similar detail is provided in the two *relaciones* by Pedro de Herrera and Fernandez de Caso, describing the performance in 1617 of Luis Vélez de Guevar-
a's *El caballero del sol*. The mechanical changing of scenes replaced the *décor
simultané* of the earlier performance, and Fernandez de Caso refers to "everything revolving," the set as well as the costumes changing. This may be a reference to a revolving set. Once again, the river setting was utilized, this time
with a platform on one side of the river for the play and another on the other
side of the river for the spectators. A ship sailed up the river, from which the
protagonist disembarked to begin the play. It is clear from the *relaciones* that
El caballero del sol was only one of a wide variety of events that went on for
several days and that included the procession of triumphal cars, fireworks, another play, ballets, and music. (See Shergold, pp. 255–258.) The proper analysis and evaluation of the part, then, depends upon a careful consideration of
the whole.

Amateur court performances continued into the reign of Philip IV (1622–
40). Three plays were performed at Aranjuez in 1622. The text of the first,

Conde de Villamediana's *La gloris de Niquea*—interpolated with descriptions of the scenery used—is extant, and the performance is described in both prose and verse by Antonio Hurtado de Mendoza in *Fiesta que se hizo en Araniuez a los años del Rey nuestro señor D. Felipe IIII* (1623). Mendoza refers to the play as an "invencion" and thereby stresses the prominence of spectacle over text. The stage, its facade, the scenery, the performance—all are described in detail, and the text generally corresponds with the description. We have only the text of the second play, by Mendoza himself (which he included in the *Fiesta* of 1623), but again elaborate scenic devices are clearly called for. The third play, Lope de Vega's *El vellocino de oro*, is also the subject of a verse account by Mendoza in *Fiesta*, an account that records that the play failed to reach its conclusion because the scenery caught fire. (For a discussion of all three performances, see Shergold, pp. 268–274).

Descriptions of performances designed by Cosimo Lotti are especially interesting. Although the Italian designer's career in Spain from 1626 to his death in 1643 is traceable in account-books, occasional references in official reports, newsletters, and other archival documents, none of his Spanish designs has survived, and written descriptions of his work are scarce and disconcertingly brief. Lope's descriptions of Lotti's scenery for *La selva sin amor* (1629) is included with the published text of the play (*Obras*, V). Diego Jiménez de Enciso's *Júpiter vengado* (1632) is chronicled by Hurtado de Mendoza in *Convocacion de las Cortes de Castilla* (1632), but little detail is included. For Calderón's *El mayor encanto amor* (1635) we have Lotti's own memorandum concerning the staging and Calderón's reply to it. (See above.) Two huge and elaborate triumphal cars, designed by Lotti for the Carnival of 1637, are described in a *relacion* by A. Sánchez de Espejo. A Jesuit newsletter describes a stage designed and built by Lotti in the Retiro for a "poetic competition" in 1638, This is not very much to go on. In fact, the most detailed description of a performance designed by the Italian is an anonymous, undated account, with an unmentionably long title, of a play acted in 1640 in the Jesuit college in Madrid to celebrate the centenary of the Order. (There is a copy in the Biblioteca Nacional.) The play, *Obrar es durar* by the Jesuit P. Valentín Céspedes, was staged in the court manner, with tranformations and three scenes in detailed perspective—a castle scene, a hill scene, and a garden of flowers. The stage featured a proscenium arch formed by two interlocking trees. A cloud hung over the stage for the use of Fame, and the whole stage was illuminated with artificial light. It was, in short, a performance fit for a king, and it was performed before Philip IV on October 5. A second performance followed three days later.

Two further descriptions are complemented by other sources of information. In 1648 Gabriel Bocángel y Unzueta composed the second of two masques in celebration of the birthday of Mariana of Austria, niece of Philip IV. (The first masque had been performed the previous year.) *El nuevo Olimpico* called a "royal performance and a festive masque," survives in a text generously provided with rubrics and including an account of the production by Bocángel himself. There are in addition two letters by the author referring to the performance in the Biblioteca Nacional (ms. 8391) and another, undated *Relacion* by Juan Francisco Dávila. In 1652 occurred the first performance of Calderón's *La fiera, el rayo, y la piedra*. Besides the three versions of the text and the set of designs by Baccio del Bianco noted earlier, the performance is described in an anonymous printed newsletter (Biblioteca Nacional ms. 2384) and in León Pinelo's *Anales o historia de Madrid* (Biblioteca Nacional M.S. 1764).

The last court performance of the seventeenth century for which we have a description is that of Calderón's *Ado y diuisa de Leonido y de Marsia*, acted at Carnival on March 3, 4, 5, 1680, in celebration of the King's wedding. The text of the play and a "Descripcion de la comedia" between the first two acts in a different hand are preserved in manuscript in the Biblioteca Nacional (ms. 9373). (See Calderón, *Obras*, XIV.) Other manuscript copies of the play are to be found in the Biblioteca Nacional (ms. 16.743) and in the Bibliothéque de l'Arsenal in Paris (ms. 8.314), but their relationship to the 1680 performance is uncertain.

CONCLUSION

For English-speaking students of the Spanish theatre at least, Shergold's *History of the Spanish Stage* remains the one essential reference volume. Here the basic narrative facts are laid out, the evidence carefully noted. But hundreds of Spanish plays, in print and in manuscript, remain to be examined; and archival documents continue to be discovered and published. It is difficult to escape the feeling that we have thus far only scraped the surface, that the details we possess, as important as they undoubtedly are, provide merely a superficial understanding of the Spanish theatre. What was the effect—emotional, intellectual, aesthetic—of a performance of one of Spain's great plays? What role did the theatre play in the social and cultural life of seventeenth-century Madrid? What precisely was the economic and political context for the theatre? The materials on which answers to these questions can be based are becoming available, and we might anticipate more sociological-cultural studies of the theatre such as those of Díez Barque mentioned earlier. But we might hope as well for more experimental performances of Spanish plays—by lesser playwrights as well as by the handful of acknowledged masters—in order to assess more adequately the qualities as well as the quantity of Spanish Golden Age drama.

REFERENCES

Aerssen, Francis van [Antoine de Brunel]. *Voyage d'Espagne*. Paris, 1665.
Alenda y Mira, J. *Relaciones de solemnidades y fiestas públicas de España*. Madrid, 1903.
Arróniz, Othón. *Teatros y escenarios del Siglo de Oro*. Madrid, 1977.
Barrett, L. L. "The Inner Recess on the Public Stages in Renaissance Spain." *Research Opportunities in Renaissance Drama* X (1967), 25–31.

————. "Research in Spanish Comedy: A Personal View." *Research Opportunities in Renaissance Drama*, IX (1966), 8–12.

Barrionuevo, Jerónimo de. *Avisos (1654–1658)*. Ed. A. Paz y Melia. 4 Vols. Madrid, 1892–94.

Brockett, Oscar G. *History of the Theatre*. 3d ed. Boston, 1977.

Cabrera de Córdoba, Luis. *Relaciones de las casas sucedidas en la corte de España, desde 1599 hasta 1614*. Ed. D. Pascual de Gayangos. Madrid, 1857.

Calderón de la Barca, P. *Obras*. Ed. E. Hartzenbusch. Biblioteca de Autores Españoles, vols. VII, IX, XII, XIV. Madrid, 1944–45.

Calvete de Estrella, Juan Christoval. *El felicissimo viaje del muy alto y luy poderoso Príncipe Don Philippo*. Ed. Miguel Artigas. Sociedat de Bibliófilos Españoles. 2 Vols. Madrid, 1930.

————. *Le Trés-Heureux Voyage*. Tr. J. Petit. Publications de la Société des Bibliophiles de Belgique. 5 Vols. Brussels, 1873–84.

Carboneres, Manuel. *Relacion y explication historico de la solemne procesion del Corpus, que annualmente celebra la ciudad de Valencia*. Valencia, 1873.

Clark, Barrett H., ed. *European Theories of the Drama*. Rev. Henry Popkin. New York, 1965.

Cotarelo y Mori, Emilio. *Bibliografía de las controversias sobre la licitud del teatro en España*. Madrid, 1904.

————. *Ensayo sobre la vida y obras de D. Pedro Calderón de la Barca: Parte Primera*. Madrid, 1924.

Crawford, J.P.W. *Spanish Drama before Lope de Vega*. Philadelphia, 1922; rev. ed. 1937.

Cristóbal de Villalón. *Ingeniosa comparación entre lo antiguo y lo presente*. Ed. M. Serravo y Sanz. Madrid, 1898.

Cuervo-Arango y González-Carvajal, Francisco. *Don Francisco Antonio de Bances y López Candamo. Estudio bio-bibliográfico y critico*. Madrid, 1916.

Diaz Rengifo, Juan, *Arte poetica espanõla*. Madrid, 1606. Barcelona, 1759.

Díez Barque, José María. *Sociedad y teatro en la España de Lope de Vega*. Barcelona, 1978.

————. *Sociología de la comedia espanõla del siglo XVII*. Barcelona, 1976.

Farinelli, A. *Viajes por España y Portugal desde la Edad Media hasta el siglo XX*. 3 Vols. Rome, 1942–44.

Iñiguez Almech, F. *Casas reales y jardines de Felipe II*. Madrid, 1952.

Jacquot, Jean, ed. *Le Lieu théâtral à la Renaissance*. Paris, 1964.

Loftis, John. "*The Duchess of Malfi* on the Spanish and English Stages." *Research Opportunities in Renaissance Drama*. XII (1969), 25–31.

López Pinciano, Alonso. *Philosophia antigua poética*. Ed. A. Carballo Picazo. 3 Vols. Madrid, 1953.[1596]

Molina Campuzano, M. *Planos de Madrid de los siglos XVII y XVIII*. Madrid, 1960.

Muret. *Lettres écrites de Madrid en 1666 et 1667*. Ed. A. Morel-Fatio. Paris, 1879.

Pellicer, Casiano. *Tratado histórico sobre el origen y progresos de la comedia y del histrionismo en España*. 2 Vols. Madrid, 1804.

Pérez Pastor, Cristóbal. *Documentos para la biografía de D. Pedro Calderón de la Barca*. Madrid, 1905.

————. *Noticias y documentos relativos a la historia y literatura españolas*. Real Academia Española, *Memorias*, vols. X-XIII. Madrid, 1910–26.

————. *Nuevos datos acerca del histrionismo español en los siglos XVI y XVII.* Primera Serie. Madrid, 1901.

————. *Nuevos datos acerca del histrionismo español en los siglos XVI y XVII.* Segunda Serie. Bordeaux, 1914.

Pinheiro da Veiga, T. *Fastiginia o fastos geniales.* Tr. N. Alonso Cortés. Valladolid, 1916.

Ramírez de Arellano, F., and J. Sancho Rayón, eds. *Comedias inéditas de Frey Lope Felix de Vega Carpa.* Collección Libros Españoles Raros o Curiosos, vol. VI. Madrid, 1873.

Rennert, Hugo Albert. *The Spanish Stage in the Time of Lope de Vega.* New York, 1963.[1909]

Riccoboni, Luigi. *A General History of the Stage.* 2d. ed. London, 1754.

Rojas Villandrando, Agustín de. *El viaje entretenido.* Ed. M. Menéndez y Pelayo. Nueva Biblioteca de Autores Españoles, Vol. XXI. Madrid, 1915.

Rouanet, L. "Un Autographe inédit de Calderón," *Revue Hispanique* VI (1899), 196–200.

Rufo y Gutiérrez, Juan. *Las seyscientas apotegmas.* Ed. A. G. de Amezúa. Sociedad de Bibliófilos Españoles. Madrid, 1923.

Sánchez Arjona, J. *Noticias referentes a los anales del teatro en Sevilla desde Lope de Ruede hasta fines del siglo XVII.* Seville, 1898.

————. *El teatro en Sevilla en los siglos XVI y XVII.* Madrid, 1887.

Schack, Graf von. *Geschicte der Dramatischen Litteratur und Kunst in Spanien.* 3 Vols. Berlin, 1845–46.

Sepúlveda, Ricardo. *El Corral de la Pacheca.* Madrid, 1888.

Shergold, N. D. "Le Dessin de Comba et l'ancien théâtre Espagnol," in *Le Lieu théâtral à la Renaissance,* Ed. Jean Jacquot (Paris, 1964).

————. *A History of the Spanish Stage from Medieval Times until the End of the Seventeenth Century.* Oxford, 1967.

————, and J. E. Varey. *Los autos sacramentales en Madrid en la epoca de Calderón 1637–1681: Estudio y documentos.* Madrid, 1961.

Shoemaker, W. H. *The Multiple Stage in Spain during the Fifteenth and Sixteenth Centuries.* Princeton, 1935.

Somers, John. *A Fourth Collection of Scarce and Valuable Tracts.* 4 Vols. London, 1752.

Stanhope, Alexander. *Spain under Charles the Second; Or, extracts from the Correspondence of the Hon. Alexander Stanhope, British Minister at Madrid, 1690–1699.* Ed. Lord Mahon. 2d ed. London, 1844.

Stern, Charlotte. "The Early Spanish Drama: From Medieval Ritual to Renaissance Art," *Renaissance Drama* n.s. VI (1973), 177–201.

————. "Juan del Encina's Carnival Eclogues and the Spanish Drama of the Renaissance." *Renaissance Drama,* VIII (1965), 181–195.

Valbuena Prat, Angel. *La novela picaresca española.* 2d ed. Madrid, 1946.

Varey, J. E. "Calderón, Cosme Lotti, Velazquez, and the Madrid Festivities of 1636–1637." *Renaissance Drama* n.s. I (1968), 253–282.

————, and N. D. Shergold. *Teatros y comedias en Madrid: 1600–1699. Estudio y documentos.* Fuentes para la historia del teatro en España, vols. III-VI. London, 1971–79.

Vega Carpio, Lope Felix de. *Epistolario*. Ed. A. G. de Amezua. 4 Vols. Madrid, 1935–43.

————. *Obras*. Real Academia Española. 15 Vols. Madrid, 1890–1913.

Wade, G. E. "A Note on a Seventeenth-Century Comedia Performance." *Bulletin of the "Comediantes"* X (1958), 10–12.

Webber, Edwin J. "Hispano-Italian Renaissance Drama: Notes on Opportunities and Problems." *Renaissance Drama* VII (1964), 151–157.

Williams, Ronald B. *The Staging of Plays in the Spanish Peninsula Prior to 1555*. Iowa City, 1935.

Wilson, Margaret. *Spanish Drama of the Golden Age*. Oxford, 1969.

4

THE ELIZABETHAN THEATRE

SCHOLARSHIP

The history of any institution can be written only when there is a need discerned to understand that history and there are facts available for its interpretation. The history of the English theatre before the Restoration in no exception. Until the end of the eighteenth century, little thought was devoted to the theatrical conditions of an age deemed so uncivilized that many of the plays of its greatest playwright were acted in versions "reformed and made fit" in accordance with the more refined sensibilities of the Restoration and eighteenth century. The few discussions of Elizabethan theatrical conditions that did appear tended to cite Shakespeare, Jonson, and Beaumont and Fletcher among the playwrights, and Alleyn, Burbage, and Field among the actors. The period just before the closing of the theatres in 1642 was the most likely to be known by post-Restoration writers. James Wright, in *Historia Histrionica* (1699) discusses the half dozen playhouses in use after 1629: Blackfriars, the Phoenix or Cockpit, Salisbury Court, the Globe, Fortune, and Red Bull. The list is repeated by John Downes in his *Roscius Anglicanus* (1708). The prevailing attitude towards former theatrical conditions was established at a very early date. Writing in 1664, Richard Flecknoe, who professed admiration for Elizabethan dramatists and actors, was moved to condescension when comparing Elizabethan playhouses with those of the Restoration:

Now, for the difference betwixt our Theaters and those of former times, they were but plain and simple, with no other Scenes, nor Decorations of the Stage, but onely old Tapestry, and the Stage strew'd with rushes, (with their Habits accordingly) whereas ours now for cost and ornament are arriv'd to the heighth of Magnificence. . . . [*Love's Kingdom*]

The real founder of Elizabethan theatrical history was Edmond Malone (1741–1812), whose "Historical Account of the Rise and Progress of the English Stage and of the Economy and Usages of our Ancient Theatres" first appeared in his edition of Shakespeare published in 1790. A slightly expanded version was printed in 1821. Malone went about investigating Shakespeare's stage by first consulting printed plays and published materials. He cites Stowe's *Chronicles*, Thomas Heywood's *Apology for Actors*, Wright's *Historia Histrionica*, and various antitheatrical treatises such as William Prynne's *Histriomastix*. But he went further and investigated unpublished documents and records, many of which he quotes. He not only drew attention to the Revels accounts, but his transcription of the Office Book of Henry Herbert, Master of the Revels 1623–73, is our only record of this important lost manuscript. In addition, it was Malone who first recorded "some curious Manuscripts relative to the stage" which were housed at Dulwich College. These documents, associated with the actor Edward Alleyn and his father-in-law, Philip Henslowe, theatrical manager of the Rose and other playhouses, are among the most significant discoveries of English theatrical scholarship. In fact, most of the essential documents were known to Malone, and he was able thereby to expand considerably the current knowledge of the Elizabethan theatre. In addition to the six theatres mentioned by Wright and Downes, he discusses Whitefriars, the Theatre, and the Curtain; and he mentions the Swan, the Rose, and the Hope—although he confines any extended discussion to the two playhouses associated with Shakespeare, that is, the Globe and Blackfriars. Malone knew that the Globe was round or polygonal, that spectators stood in the pit or sat in the galleries, and that scenery was not usually a part of the stage accoutrements. Not surprisingly, he is sometimes unclear as to the distinctions between different kinds of theatre, and in his discussion of them often moves disconcertingly from public to private to court theatres. He was nonetheless meticulous in the marshalling of evidence and argument in his "endeavour to exhibit as accurate a delineation of the internal form and economy of our ancient theatres, as the distance at which we stand, and the obscurity of the subject, will permit." It is indeed difficult to praise Malone too highly. His scholarly credentials rank him with the best of all time, as the following testimonial from a distinguished modern scholar attests:

Malone's honesty, accuracy, and industry were unrivalled in the English studies of his own time, and they have seldom been equalled since. He was not always right, but he had an admirable ability to stay within his evidence, and a rare reluctance to announce his private preferences as established facts." (G. E. Bentley, *Seventeenth Century Stage*, pp. x-xi).

The same could not always be said of the nineteenth-century scholars who continued to search out and publish documentary materials. Malone's "Account" was continued by the competent George Chalmers, who provided more details from Council Registers and Statute Books. But the most notorious, and most puzzling, personality to devote himself to a continuation of Malone's work on the Elizabethan theatre was John Payne Collier (1789–1883), an indefatigible researcher in the great library collections of England, both public and private, and author of *History of English Dramatic Poetry* (1831), for many years a highly regarded and standard work on the subject. Collier obtained admission to the Department of State Papers, to the Office of the Privy Council, and to the Chapter-House at Westminster, where, in his own words, "I soon discovered . . . many valuable original documents." In the British Library, among the Burghley papers, the Harleian, Cottonian, and Royal manuscript collections, "I met," he continues,

with letters from, and concerning, our most notorious poets, the predecessors and contemporaries of Shakespeare; and in a Diary, kept by an intelligent Barrister, who lived while our great dramatist was in the zenith of his popularity I found original and authentic notices and anecdotes of him, Spenser, Jonson, Marston, and other distinguished authors of the time. [*History of English Dramatic Poetry*, I, ix]

Collier was not so meticulous nor so accurate as Malone in the citing, describing, and printing of the documents upon which he based his conclusions, but in this respect he differed little from other amateur scholars of the nineteenth century. What does distinguish Collier is that the legitimate and exciting discoveries that he did make seem not to have satisfied him, and he embarked upon a strange career of forgery that has cast doubt on his legitimate researches and even on those of his associates.

The most famous of Collier's forgeries, and the one that led eventually to his unmasking, was the so-called Perkins Folio, a copy of the 1632 folio of Shakespeare's plays, in which Collier claimed to have discovered thousands of annotations and textual emendations in a seventeenth-century hand—all of them provided by Collier himself. But other documents Collier had supposedly found in libraries and archives also proved, upon examination, to be of dubious authenticity. In addition, some documents cited or quoted by Collier were not to be found in the locations indicated. (The fullest account of the forgeries and the ensuing controversy is provided by Dewey Ganzel in *Fortune and Men's Eyes*, although Ganzel denies Collier's guilt.)

Most scholars are honest. They may be careless, wilful, mistaken; they may be dull, unimaginative, opinionated; but rarely do they attempt to deceive one another. But this is precisely what Collier did, and partly because the reasons for his actions are so obscure, the case has remained a disturbing puzzle to scholars. One reaction—an understandable one—was to suspect everything that Collier touched, and to reject much of it out of hand. Subsequent investigation has shown that mistakes can be made in this direction as well. For instance, a petition from the inhabitants of Blackfriars to the Privy Council (1596?), which Collier ostensibly found in the State Paper Office (*History of English Dramatic Poetry*, I, 297) was suspected to be a forged document but is now generally accepted as genuine. Even more seriously, the revelation of Collier's dishonesty cast a shadow over the activities of one of his associates, Peter Cunningham. In 1842, Cunningham published an edition of the Revels Accounts, most of the originals of which were subsequently deposited in the Public Records Office. In 1868, Cunningham, elderly and alcoholic, offered two of the original Revels documents for sale to the British Museum. They were impounded and kept at the Public Records Office, but the suspicion of forgery hung over them and most scholars assumed they were not genuine. Then in 1911 in *Some Supposed Shakespeare Forgeries*, Ernest Law declared all the Revels documents genuine. Controversy continued through the 1920s, with the attack on the documents reaching a climax in Samuel A. Tannenbaum's *Shakspere Forgeries in the Revels Accounts* (1928). A. E. Stamp, of the Public Records Office, however, in an ingeniously reasoned argument that includes the analysis of the worm holes in the manuscripts, demonstrated their authenticity to the satisfaction of most scholars (*The Disputed Revels Accounts*, 1930). On the other hand, everything that Collier himself published must be treated with scepticism. If it cannot be verified from an independent source, it is wisest not to rely on it.

Fortunately, such episodes in the history of scholarship are not frequent, and nineteenth-century historians proceeded with the task of collecting and publishing documentary materials pertaining to the Elizabethan stage. W. C. Hazlitt printed a large number of documents in *The English Drama and Stage under the Tudor and Stuart Princes 1543–1664* (1832). Although he had no reason at the time to doubt the authenticity of any of the material published by Collier, Hazlitt collated the documents previously printed by Collier with the originals. And he added an unintentionally ironic note: "It is plainly worse than useless, in all cases, to reproduce texts without subjecting them to this process, let the prior Editor's character for precision be what it may" (p. vii). J. O. Halliwell-Phillipps in *Outlines of the Life of Shakespeare* (1883) is mainly concerned with the playwright, but he includes among his "theatrical evidences" documents relating to the Blackfriars and the Globe, and a manuscript attributed to Dr. Simon Forman which contains contemporary accounts of the performances of four plays, three of which are by Shakespeare.

The last of the great Victorian amateur theatre historians was Frederick Gard Fleay (1831–1909), whose erratic scholarship culminated in his *Chronicle History of the London Stage* (1890). An irascible and opinionated man, Fleay fancied himself the apostle of a new "scientific method" in his researches and heaped scorn on the work of Collier and Halliwell-Phillipps, the former for the large number of guesses and forgeries, the latter for "want of accuracy." Of the value of his own work, Fleay had no doubts:

I distinctly claim, firstly, that this is the first treatise that has any just right to be called a history of the Shakespearean stage; and, secondly, that in no stage history whatever are so many intricate problems solved and critical difficulties removed, with such apparently slender resources, as in this one. [p. 5]

Unfortunately, Fleay's personality was at odds with his scientific pretensions, and guess and intuition rather than the sober sifting of data impelled him to his conclusions. Still, we have seen before that historical method is as often dependent upon the speculative imagination as upon data-based pragmatism, and the sometime lack of discipline in the exercise of his imagination did not prevent Fleay from arriving at conclusions that later and more patient scholarship has been able to validate. Men such as Fleay, in the words of G. E. Bentley, "had so much experience with the plays and the theatrical records of the time that at their best they instinctively, or subconsciously, set up for themselves limits of probability more precise and valid than less experienced scholars can set with fully developed arguments" (*Jacobean and Caroline Stage*, III, x).

The scientific method Fleay tried unsuccessfully to introduce into his studies was more systematically exploited by German scholars and by Americans trained in German methods. Facts were held to be demonstrable and immutable, and it was the task of the historian to establish and present historical facts. A firm adherent of this credo was C. W. Wallace, Professor of English at the University of Nebraska, whose patient gathering of materials bore fruit in two note-laden volumes: *The Children of the Chapel at Blackfriars* (1908) and *The Evolution of the English Drama* (1912). Wallace himself indicated in the first volume that the footnotes were his most important contribution to scholarship; and he described the second as "a work of scientific accuracy and reliability" as opposed to "the publications of those who are properly only dilettanti, unrepresentative of scholarship" (*Evolution of the English Drama*, p. xi). The implicit tension in this comparison between scientific and professional (American) scholarship and dilettantish and amateur (English) scholarship was to underlie transatlantic scholarly relations for a couple of generations. As late as 1932 we find the young M. C. Bradbrook making sneering references to "the danger of applying scientific methods in the expectancy of discovering scientific facts, a procedure about as logical as digging with a silver spade in the hope of striking a vein of silver. American scholarship found this type of investigation very much to its taste. . . ." (*Elizabethan Stage Conditions*, pp. 19–20).

Ultimately, of course, most of this is a non-issue: Facts and methods are neither more nor less valid for being called scientific. And scholars in both England and America proceeded with their efforts to survey and publish materials relating to the Elizabethan theatre. In *Early London Theatres* (1894), Thomas Fairman Ordish, long-time member of the New Shakespere Society, provided the first systematic survey of the evidence available for the study of Elizabethan playhouses; and his work was greatly expanded almost a quarter of a century later by the American Joseph Quincey Adams, whose *Shakespearean Playhouses* (1917) treats seventeen regular theatres and five more temporary or projected ones (as opposed to the six discussed by Ordish). Although both books have to a large extent been superseded by the monumental studies of E. K. Chambers and G. E. Bentley, they remain insightful and surprisingly reliable. As far as Chambers and Bentley are concerned, all students of Elizabethan theatre history remain in their debt. *The Elizabethan Stage* (1923) and *The Jaco-*

bean and Caroline Stage (1941–68) are in a sense the culmination of the process begun by Malone and pursued through such eccentric paths in the nineteenth century of exploring and presenting all available documentary material in as useful a form as print would permit. Both works are reference surveys, and while both authors must constantly interpret the meaning and significance of the evidence they cite and present—a necessary process even in the *selection* of material included—neither is given to empty speculation or elaborate theorizing. Bentley is adamant on the point: "Responsible reference books should severely restrict the space given to the weighing of conflicting hypotheses" (*Jacobean and Caroline Stage*, VI, v). The four volumes of *The Elizabethan Stage* and the seven of *The Jacobean and Caroline Stage* represent our most complete source of information concerning playwrights, plays, players, playhouses, performances, acting companies, and the immediate social, political, and economic context for the English theatre between 1500 and 1642.

Throughout the nineteenth century, as scholars laboured in archives and libraries, among public records and private papers, very little attention was focussed on the precise details of an Elizabethan playhouse or on the precise methods of an Elizabethan dramatic performance. The reasons for this neglect of what is for modern theatre historians a central concern are various. The Victorian Age shared the post-Restoration assumption of the crudity of Elizabethan production and the concomitant assumption that it was therefore not worth investigating. Most of the research was carried out by scholars more at home in the library than in the theatre. And what theatrical experience they might have had was limited to contemporary domestic drama performed in a box set, or the "spectacular realism" of adapted Shakespearean plays, complete with casts of thousands and real rabbits. But, most of all, there was little evidence to draw attention to the details of an Elizabethan stage and to force a reconsideration of other evidence, especially the texts of plays, in the light of fresh expectations.

Here and there, it is true, there were experiments that suggested some theatrical producers were fumbling toward a different conception of Elizabethan staging. At the Haymarket theatre in 1844, *The Taming of the Shrew* was presented with two screens and a pair of curtains. In Germany in the 1840s Ludwig Tieck was experimenting with a stage that featured several acting levels connected by stairs, and curtained pillars. At Munich in 1889 the Hungarian producer Jocza Savits staged *King Lear* on a thrust stage backed by a proscenium-framed open stage which in turn featured a rear inner stage. (See Allardyce Nicholl's review of scholarship in *Shakespeare Survey I*, 1948.) Nevertheless, until the last quarter of the nineteenth century, the world of scholarship and the world of theatrical production remained determinedly isolated from one another.

The man who, more than any other, helped to bridge the gap between scholarship and the living theatre was William Poel (1852–1934), founder in 1894 and director of the Elizabethan Stage Society. Poel believed that Shakespearean staging of the late nineteenth century was totally mistaken. He held that it was essential to use a text as close as possible to the original prompt-book, to speak the lines quickly, with "exaggerated naturalness," and to concentrate on a Shakespearean play as something *heard*; and he maintained as a consequence that the stage should be bare of elaborate sets. On April 16, 1881, Poel put these ideas into practice with a production at St. George's Hall of the *Hamlet* of the 1603 Quarto, played on a bare, draped platform. The performance was savagely reviewed, but Shakespearean production was never quite the same after it. Poel worked from the inside; that is, rather than attempting to reconstruct an Elizabethan stage in every detail, he concentrated on what he found through experience to be the essentials of an Elizabethan production. It remained to more conventional scholarship to bring other evidence to bear on the problem. Poel was not always right in his details: He continued to use transverse curtains between two front pillars on his stage, for example; but his general sense of an Elizabethan performance has in fact been shown to be correct. "Poel's work on the Elizabethans," writes his biographer, "was work of technical reconstruction, interesting and debatable always, pursued with a scholarship which was disinterested but rarely quite dispassionate" (Robert Speaight, *William Poel and the Elizabethan Revival*, p. 173).

It is nevertheless unlikely that Poel by himself could have redirected the attention of conservative scholars to the reconstruction of the Elizabethan stage and to Elizabethan staging. Traditional archival research also played its part. In 1888, for the first time, the famous drawing of the interior of the Swan theatre, attributed to the Dutchman Johannes DeWitt and discovered by K. T. Gaedertz in the library of the University of Utrecht in Holland, was published. Discussions of this drawing ushered in what we might call the age of theatrical reconstruction and forced scholars to reconsider the staging requirements of Elizabethan plays. The problem of reconciling the drawing with the resources seemingly required by dramatic texts was and is a formidable one; and in the final analysis, most scholars have been forced either to accept the drawing and to downplay the demands of the texts, or to reject the drawing in favour of the texts. In particular, the absence in the Swan drawing of a curtain and an "inner stage" caused a good deal of consternation. The problem is real enough, but it was made more acute at the time (and in some cases well into the twentieth century) by two fundamental assumptions held concerning the nature of Elizabethan stages and the development of stage architecture.

In the first place, it was assumed that there was a direct line of development from the Elizabethan stage to the proscenium stage of the nineteenth century, and that it was possible therefore to reconstruct the Elizabethan stage on the basis of information available for any part of the evolutionary sequence. Thus Ashley Thorndike in 1916:

We can trace, step by step, the successive changes that have gradually transformed the stage of Shakespeare into that of today. On all questions where direct contemporary information is lacking, we must attempt to reconstruct the Elizabethan stage and its practices from our knowledge either of earlier or later times. Since our knowledge of the Restoration stage is based on abundant information, we are able to apply this with great advantage in our effort to reconstruct the Elizabethan stage [*Shakespeare's Theater*, p. 73]

He writes in a similar vein: "We can reverse the process of evolution and reconstruct the Elizabethan stage from the arrangement and methods of the Restoration theaters" (pp. 77–78). This assumption underlies as well Victor E. Albright's *Shakespearean Stage* (1909) and W. J. Lawrence's *Physical Conditions of the Elizabethan Public Playhouse* (1927). It is central as well to John Cranford Adams' *Globe Playhouse* (1942), perhaps the best known and most influential reconstruction of an Elizabethan playhouse ever done. "The 'picture stage' of today," writes Adams, "is not the offspring solely of the Continental proscenium-type stage; one of its parents assuredly is the Elizabethan inner stage, with its curtained opening . . ." (p. 168). It is easy to see how this assumption led to an insistence on an inner-stage and curtains, and to a rejection of the Swan drawing, which includes neither. (At times, scholarly confidence can be amusing, as in Albright's comment that the lack of curtains in the Swan drawing demonstrates that it must have been done by a man "unacquainted with the art of acting" [p. 40]).

The second assumption is that all Elizabethan playhouses were pretty much alike and therefore that evidence concerning any one of them could be applied in the reconstruction of any other. This idea resulted in the synthetic reconstruction of a "typical" Elizabethan stage. There is, of course, a grain of truth in this. Undoubtedly, Elizabethan playhouses did include some common characteristics; and the fact that the same play could be, and sometimes was, successfully performed at different playhouses suggests that neither dramatic requirements nor theatrical resources were unique to any play or playhouse. But whether this allows for the indiscriminate application of evidence derived from a wide variety of sources over a sixty-five-year period is another matter. The assumption and the method both can be seen as late as 1959 in Leslie Hotson's *Shakespeare's Wooden O*, as well as in Adams' earlier *Globe Playhouse*.

Both of these assumptions have long been recognized as faulty and likely to lead to unacceptable or questionable conclusions, and there has developed over the past forty years a revised methodology for reconstructing Elizabethan playing conditions. This has necessitated a continuing attack on many cherished notions concerning the Elizabethan stage, including Adams' reconstructed Globe. It has also included, of course, a fresh set of assumptions and procedures. Briefly, they are these: that we must look for the origins and sources of many of the characteristics of the Elizabethan stage in medieval staging conventions rather than extrapolating backward from the Restoration stage; that the proper focus of scholarly inquiry is the individual theatre rather than a synthetic "typical" Elizabethan playhouse; and that the dramatic texts used as evidence should not only be identified specifically with the playhouse under consideration, but should as far as possible be playhouse documents (prompt-books) or at least early editions rather than modern edited texts.

J. Isaacs anticipated the revised methodology in some respects in 1933 in *Production and Stage Management at the Blackfriars Theatre*, in which he cited as his chief evidence inductions or acted prologues, literary stage directions, manuscript prompt-copies, and plays printed from prompt-copies. Isaacs examined 150 plays, seventy "undoubtedly" performed at Blackfriars, the remainder "both public and private plays of illustrative interest" (p. 5). Such materials by themselves are not sufficient to provide completely fresh conclusions, however, unless the assumptions according to which they are interpreted are also questioned and revised. William A. Armstrong, for instance, employed Isaacs' method in *Elizabethan Private Theatres* (1958), in which he examined the stage directions of 150 plays written for the private theatres and published before the Restoration. His analysis of possible scenic methods employed at these theatres and his outline in general terms of changing scenic practices over sixty-five years is very valuable. But his assumption of an inner-stage and two doors as constants affects his interpretation of stage directions and contributes to his conclusion that it was the private rather than the public Elizabethan theatre that anticipated the Restoration playhouse. (The conclusion may in fact be true, but its basis on the existence of an inner-stage is suspect.)

The real hero of the revisionists is, however, George F. Reynolds, whose *Staging of Elizabethan Plays at the Red Bull Theatre 1605–1625* (1940) has received belated recognition as a landmark in Elizabethan stage studies. Reynolds was no newcomer to the field: His articles on Elizabethan staging had appeared as early as 1905. But his scholarly method of continually questioning and refining methods and ideas—his own as well as others—kept him from achieving the fame—or the notoriety—of less cautious but more flamboyant scholars. John Cranford Adams' book on the Globe, which appeared two years after Reynolds' volume, almost completely eclipsed the latter's accomplishment. The confident and detailed reconstruction of Shakespeare's theatre left a far more lasting impression than the cautious and tentative discussion of an obscure public theatre with a limited known repertory and a questionable reputation. (The application of Reynolds' methods to the Globe had to wait until the 1962 publication of Bernard Beckerman's *Shakespeare at the Globe 1599–1609*.)

Reynolds begins by remarking on the unanimity concerning Elizabethan staging on the part of scholars like Albright, Thorndike, Chambers, and Lawrence, but he notes that it is a unanimity "in contradiction in some items to probability and in others to the evidence on which we can feel most certain" (p. 1). He goes on to cite the persistence of the inner-stage in reconstructions in spite of its absence from the Swan drawing. "There have also been," he writes,

too many generalizations from a few instances; too many uncontrolled suppositions of what might have been, without any ascertained facts of Elizabethan procedure to support them; too many theories advanced by scholars versed only in books and not acquainted with even amateur dramatic production. [p. 2]

Reynolds goes on to stress two faults of earlier scholarship in particular. First was the tendency to interpret the Elizabethan stage in terms of modern stage conventions, which led to the "invention" of the transverse front curtain, to the finding of an embryonic proscenium stage in a similarly invented inner-stage, to un-Elizabethan aesthetic conceptions of consistency and suitability, to the confusing of Elizabethan dramatic illusion with modern notions of the illusion of reality. (The tendency led as well to bizarre theories of Elizabethan staging, such as that of Cecil Brodmeier, who in 1904 proposed that scenes requiring elaborate properties were performed at the rear of the stage, where they could be arranged behind a curtain, and that "unpropertied" scenes were acted on the bare stage in front of the closed curtain. This, Brodmeier urged, necessitated the alternation of "propertied" and "unpropertied" scenes. Neither common sense nor the texts of plays supported this "alternation" theory which derived more from late-nineteenth-century conceptions of a stage than from contemporary Elizabethan evidence.) Second, Reynolds pointed to the tendency to accept stage-directions both implicit and explicit as literally true, as "statements of fact made in carefully consistent terminology, when inspection shows that the terms are used with little consistency and that the directions are often as dramatically conceived as the text itself" (p. 93).

Reynolds' own method was based on "a more careful skepticism, and stricter discrimination," and he approached his subject "from its own historic backgrounds"—its medieval past and its contemporary European context. He uses three kinds of evidence: contemporary pictures of the exteriors and interiors of theatres; contemporary contracts, descriptions, and allusions; and play texts themselves. He accepts the Swan drawing and therefore rejects an inner-stage and postulates instead a removable curtained framework, not used in all plays and not present on the Swan stage when DeWitt visited the playhouse. Carefully limiting his investigation to a single playhouse and a limited time-span (from the opening of the Red Bull in 1605 to its first reconstruction in 1625), Reynolds is equally careful to limit the play texts to be analyzed. Moreover, he divides the forty-six plays he uses into three categories, based on the closeness of their known connection with the Red Bull. The first category consists of thirteen "unquestionably" Red Bull plays; the second (nineteen plays) of plays "probably" performed at the Red Bull; and the third (fourteen plays) of plays "possibly connected" with the playhouse. And Reynolds is especially cautious in his handling of stage directions, whose nomenclature he finds "various, inexact, even imaginative" (p. 187). Yet for all his care in the selection and treatment of dramatic texts as evidence for staging practices, he pays scant attention to the editions he consults, which range from authentic playhouse documents (*The Two Noble Ladies*, *The Welsh Ambassador*) to a nineteenth-century reprint of Thomas Dekker's play. Indeed, the neglect of bibliographical, textual, and historical evidence with respect to the texts used as evidence remains the most telling criticism of Reynolds' method.

It is worth noting as well that Reynolds' conclusions are basically negative:

He questions whether the stage equipment needed for the presentation of Elizabethan plays was so elaborate or standardized as previous theories had indicated. (This is a conclusion echoed in Beckerman's later study of the Globe, based mainly on the evidence of eleven Shakespearean plays and twelve by contemporary playwrights, all performed at the Globe between 1599 and 1609. Staging, he argues, was determined more by the form of the dramatic text than by the structure of the stage. The stage *was* bare; the spectators were informed more by what they heard than by what they saw. See *Shakespeare at the Globe*, pp. 108, 214.)

In spite of its limited subject and its occasional lapses in methodological rigor, Reynolds' study established the generally accepted method for investigating the staging at specific playhouses. Evidence is selected for its relevance to the particular theatre, for example, the texts of plays known to have been performed at the theatre, references to details and practices identified specifically with the playhouse. When other evidence is introduced, the "neutral" is preferred to the overly specific; for example, a general comment on the nature of performances in a letter or a petition is preferable to a specific reference to a different theatre. In other words, there is not only a careful selecting of evidence, but a ranking of the evidence. And, ultimately, a scholar must choose either to stop at the point where the information stops or to continue the reconstruction on the basis of conjecture; but the line of demarcation must be clearly drawn.

Since the pioneering studies of Isaacs and Reynolds, other playhouses have been investigated along the same lines. Besides Beckerman on the Globe, we have T. J. King on the staging of plays at the Phoenix between 1617 and 1642 (Columbia University dissertation, 1963), and Ernest L. Rhodes' *Henslowe's Rose* (1976). We have never realized the ideal expressed by Allardyce Nicoll in 1948, that "each theatre and its plays should have their appropriate volume" (*Shakespeare Survey* I, 15); but it has generally been taken for granted that the procedure is a valid one and graduate students are regularly enjoined to such studies as a matter of course. Nevertheless, the scholarly instinct to synthesize and generalize is not dead, and there have been renewed efforts to describe a "typical" Elizabethan playhouse and to proceed with generalizations concerning dramaturgy and staging practice based on this synthetic model.

The process by which the typical resources of an Elizabethan theatre are derived, however, differ markedly from the eclecticism of earlier syntheses. We now find scholars concerned with the characteristics common to the individual theatres whose staging has been investigated in terms of evidence rigorously selected for its relevance and applicability. There is an appreciation too of the fact that the years between 1576 and 1642 were years of vigorous theatrical activity and experiment, that the same plays were performed under a variety of conditions, that production methods were changing, that the efforts of stage historians should be directed towards establishing the *limits* of staging possibilities, the *minimum* requirements for the performance of an Elizabethan play.

Thus, J. L. Styan accepts that an Elizabethan public theatre consisted of a symmetrically rounded or square, unroofed auditorium with galleries and an acting platform of generous size. He specifies a tight, enclosing auditorium, a projecting platform about as deep as it was wide, two upstage entrances to the stage, and at least one balcony: "There is no proof that the theatre consisted of more than this. These features are also all that are needed for an adequate Elizabethan performance" (*Shakespeare's Stagecraft*, pp. 12–13). And such staging arrangements fit nicely with what most scholars believe to have been the origins of tbe Elizabethan theatre. Thus Richard Leacroft in *Development of the English Playhouse:*

A rectangular raised stage is backed by a wall containing two doors and a balconey above, an arrangement clearly derived from the rectangular acting area before the hall screens. This stage is set within an amphitheatre of three galleries, a clear development of the timber hall and bear baiting yards. [p. 31]

For the historian interested in the specific details and process of change in theatre architecture and staging practice over the three-quarters of a century that followed the building of the Theatre in 1576, the case is put by Glynne Wickham:

We must assume a fundamental similarity between the arrangements made in all the buildings which we know the actors to have used for the staging of their plays between 1576 and 1660, and then proceed to analyze the variants which both the order of historical events and changing artistic considerations came to impose upon them. [*Early English Stages*, II, ii, 174]

Moreover, this "fundamental similarity," it is insisted, is not limited to the so-called public theatres, but applies to *all* Elizabethan production—in public theatres, in private theatres, at court. This idea challenges the long-held assumption—given almost canonical status in Chambers' *Elizabethan Stage*—that the staging conventions of the private indoor theatres and at court were utterly different from those of the public playhouses. Wickham draws attention to the architectural and pictorial evidence that now allows the historian to trace the variations on what he believes to have been a single set of staging conventions—Tudor halls still standing, DeWitt's sketch of the Swan, drawings by Inigo Jones of the Cockpit-in-Court. And in fact, on the basis of this evidence and some other drawings, D. F. Rowan was moved in 1971 to a perhaps premature expression of confidence in a new era in Elizabethan theatrical studies. "I believe," he wrote, "that on the basis of the primary pictorial evidence one can justifiably speak of *the* English playhouse from 1595 to 1630, and in the absence of evidence to the contrary, I further believe that one can now speak with some measure of confidence of *the* Elizabethan theatre, whether 'public,' 'private,' or 'courtly.' " And he went on to describe how the way was now clear "to build with studies of the ways in which individual dramatists exploited the known resources of their theatre, to move from speculation on the statics of theatre buildings to the dynamics of theatrical production'' (*Renaissance Drama* n.s., IV, 49, 51).

The innate conservatism of academic scholarship has rendered Rowan's vision more pious than prognostic, although studies such as he proposes are being carried out. The problem is that for many scholars and critics, until and unless the details concerning such things as the inner-stage or the number of entrances or the existence of a trap are settled to their satisfaction, the ''dynamics of theatrical production'' remain in the area of subjective speculation. And the situation is not helped by the tendency too often encountered of performance theorists to be forty years out of date concerning the ''statics of theatre buildings,'' to find them, for instance, turning to Adams' *Globe Playhouse* as their authority.

Another line of inquiry concerning the Elizabethan theatre has been pursued intermittently in the twentieth century, that is, its connection with the Continental theatre, particularly with the classically derived scenic practices and theatre architecture of sixteenth-century Italy. Most of the investigations—although not all—have been centred on the Jacobean court masque and the perspective scenes devised by Inigo Jones. In fact, the masque has usually been treated in isolation from the professional theatre and it has generated its own tradition of scholarship and criticism. Yet the distinction between staging at ''public'' and ''private'' theatres, and between this staging and that at court, as we have already noted, has always been but uneasily maintained, and in recent years has begun to break down. In fact, the notion was gently questioned in the book generally considered to be the seminal study of the Renaissance context for the Elizabethan theatre. Lily B. Campbell in *Scenes and Machines on the English Stage during the Renaissance*, published in 1923, admits that the Elizabethan public theatres are ''a matter of secondary importance in this history of Renaissance stage scenery'' (p. 116), but she goes on to offer a little-heeded observation:

Nevertheless no consideration of stage spectacle can ignore the fact that the English theatre was apparently sharing with all of western Europe the affect of the Vitruvian revival, and that the English theatres—both ''private'' and ''public''—were such theatres as resulted everywhere from the new interest in the theatres of the ancients. [p. 121]

She concludes that English playhouses were ''keeping pace with the times'' when theatrical activity was abruptly brought to a stop in 1642 (p. 211).

Campbell's main emphasis, however, is on the academic, scholarly, and courtly nature of the Renaissance treatment of spectacle on the stage. ''In matters of spectacle, at least,'' she concludes, ''the public stage followed after the academic stage and the court stage, which pioneered the way in the scenic representation of the drama'' (p. 293). This yet has the status of received opinion. In fact, the most fruitful studies of the Italian influence on the English stage have generally been confined to the courtly spectacles of James I and Charles I. Allardyce Nicoll, in *Stuart Masques and the Renaissance Stage* (1938), for example, attempts to determine as precisely as possible the methods of staging used in the performance of the Jacobean and Caroline masque. In order to do so he examines English practice in light of contemporary Italian practice. His evidence consists of the texts of the English masques, the extant sketches and designs—mostly by Inigo Jones—for these masques, and—perhaps most significantly—the treatises and manuals produced in connection with Italian experiment and practice (those of Serlio, Sabbattini, Fürttenbach, and Leone de' Sommi).

A provocative work of somewhat broader scope, George Kernodle's *From Art to Theatre* (1944), attempts to place both Italian and English staging practices in the wider context of inherited medieval artistic traditions and contemporary Continental street pageantry. Kernodle suggests that "the greatest problem of the Renaissance stage was the organization of a number of divergent scenic elements into some principle of spatial unity" (p. 7). And of the three possible solutions bequeathed by medieval art—side arches with a clear centre, a centre arch with subordinate side accents, or a flat arcade screen—he argues that the Italians adopted a version of the first (side arches with a central perspective) while stage designers in England and Flanders opted for the central pavilion or arch. The immediate predecessors of the stage in England and Flanders were the street pageants or *tableaux vivants*, of which the Low Countries in particular provide numerous examples: "A comparison [of street pageants and stage drama] will make clear, not only that many particular scenes of Elizabethan drama were derived from the *tableaux vivants* but that they provided the basic pattern of the English stage facade" (p. 134). This façade consists of a central arch, framing a discovery space behind a pair of doors; side arches or doors; and a curtained upper-stage. Various architectural symbols—throne, arbor, arras—could transform this façade into an emblematic representation of a palace, or garden, or room. Kernodle's reconstruction is in fact no more farfetched than most, but it seems generally agreed that his theory of the origins of the stage remain unproved. There is no evidence of the influence of the *tableaux vivants* and Continental street pageantry in England after the third decade of the sixteenth century. On the other hand, the tricky question of influence is probably of less importance than Kernodle's drawing attention to an aesthetic problem common to all Renaissance staging, and to parallels and similarities among the solutions he found. In the final analysis, the question of influence gives way to the larger one of the nature of the Renaissance theatre, and ultimately to the question of the nature of theatrical presentation itself. It is in this respect that *From Art to Theatre* is most valuable.

The most recent attempt to link the Elizabethan theatre building to Continental developments was undertaken by Frances Yates, an art and intellectual historian, who in *Theatre of the World* (1969) expands on Campbell's observation that English playhouses of the late sixteenth and early seventeenth centuries were

associated with the revival of interest in Vitruvius and the classical theatre. Yates
traces the influence of Vitruvius in England mainly through the careers of the
mathematician and astrologer John Dee (1527–1608) and the physician and mystic
Robert Fludd (1574–1637), both of whom she places in sequence with the architect and masque designer Inigo Jones (1573–1652). She draws particular attention to Dee's preface to an English translation of Euclid published in 1570,
Vitruvian in conception and example and addressed specifically to the artisan
class of London, and to an engraving of a stage in the *Microcosm* volume of
Fludd's *History of Two Worlds* (1619), labelled "Theatrum Orbi." A "theatrical undercurrent," Yates argues, underlies the work of both Dee and Fludd,
and a popular Vitruvianism influenced the construction of the Theatre in 1576
and the Globe in 1599 and 1614. Fludd's engraving represents the latter. "I
believe," writes Yates, "that out of Dee's popular Vitruvianism there was evolved
a popular adaptation of the ancient theatre, as described by Vitruvius, Alberti,
and Barbaro, resulting in a new type of building of immense significance . . ."
(p. 41). In general, *Theatre of the World* is a difficult book to judge. It is specific where Campbell is merely suggestive, but it is also filled with irritating
rhetorical questions that often substitute for argument, with numerous conjectural phrases such as "may be," "it seems to me," and it "reads to me as
though." We search in vain for some indication of the distribution and influence of Dee's preface among the joiners and carpenters of London, or for some
evidence that Fludd had access to Dee's papers, as Yates suggests. She herself
admits that her reconstruction of the Globe is "less factual and realistic" than
conventional reconstructions. In spite of the misgivings that must attend any
consideration of the thesis, her theory is internally consistent, imaginative, and
suprisingly convincing. We can no longer afford the luxury of a parochial view
of Elizabethan stage architecture that denies the possibility of Continental influence.

One further possibility for a Continental connection has been advanced by
Richard Hosley, who argues in *The First Public Playhouse* (ed. Herbert Berry,
1979) that Burbage may have found a model for the Theatre in the three-storied
banqueting house built at Calais in 1520 for a meeting between Henry VIII and
the Emperor Charles V. (The two main sources of information concerning the
banqueting house are Turpyn's *Chronicle of Calais*, held in the British Library
and edited in 1846 by J. G. Nichols, and a description by Marino Sanudo in
the *Calendar of State Papers, Venice*, 1520–1526.)

DRAMATIC TEXTS

The texts of Elizabethan plays obviously constitute an important source of
information for the theatre historian. Of the approximately 3,000 plays estimated to have been produced between 1500 and 1642, almost 900 are extant,
about fifty in manuscript, the remainder in printed editions of varying quality.
(The exact number remains approximate, since fresh discoveries continue to be

made from time to time.) Oddly, stage historians have often shown little interest in the historical and bibliographical details concerning the plays they cite,
and they ignore not only chronology and theatrical auspices but also the provenance and nature of the edited texts at their disposal. Even Reynolds, otherwise
so meticulous in his methodology, tended to consult editions close at hand and
made little effort to examine original texts. Yet any edited text, as W. W. Greg,
doyen of bibliographical studies, noted almost sixty years ago, is "merely a
text from which most of the relevant evidence has been carefully removed. To
rely on it is like trying to solve an archaeological problem, not by the study of
the finds *in situ*, but from neatly ticketed specimens in a museum" (quoted by
S. Schoenbaum in *Internal Evidence and Elizabethan Dramatic Authorship*, p.
172). And many of the nineteenth-century editions of Elizabethan playwrights,
which formed the bulk of scholarly references, compounded the error by changing, "regularizing," and even adding stage directions to the texts according to
Victorian principles of stagecraft.

Modern editors are fortunately more scrupulous than this and their editorial
principles more refined and rigorous; but their efforts still leave something to
be desired so far as theatre historians are concerned. The problem is the old
one of the "authority" of a dramatic text which, while the prime evidence for
the work, is technically not the equivalent of the play in performance. There
are in theory at least two versions of any acted play: the version written by the
author (his "foul papers") and the version adapted for performance (the "prompt-
book"). One of these will serve as the basis for the printed editions of the play,
which may incorporate other changes as well, both intentional and uninten-
tional. An editor dealing with Elizabethan drama rarely has either the author's
foul papers or the prompt-book available and must therefore determine as well
as possible which version was used in the preparation of the earliest printed
text. Traditionally, editors have preferred the "authority" of what the playwright actually wrote and their texts have reflected their attempts to reconstruct
the author's intention uncontaminated by playhouse alterations. Theatre historians would prefer a text approximating the playhouse version. For this reason,
it is argued that information concerning stage conditions and performance can
be derived only from original manuscripts and early printed editions, and that
it is necessary as well to distinguish carefully between those texts associated
with production and those whose origin is unknown; that the theatre historian
must make a detailed analysis of the historical and bibliographical evidence
concerning any play used as evidence, that the texts be distinguished on the
basis of their copy source, and that those giving indications of playhouse origin
be considered of most use to the theatre historian. This certainly is the position
championed by T. J. King, who has made the point again and again in his doc-
toral dissertation, in review articles, and especially in *Shakespearean Staging
1599–1642* (1971).

On the face of it, the procedure proposed by King, postulating as it does the
superiority of prompt-book over foul papers and thereby representing a refine-

ment on Reynolds' methodology, seems a reasonable one for a theatre historian to adopt. But the facts of Elizabethan dramatic texts and manuscripts and of Elizabethan publishing and printing practices render it less useful than it appears. In a review of King's book in *Renaissance Drama* n.s. IV (1971), Bernard Beckerman makes three important points. First, be notes that "using bibliographical evidence of playhouse origin as a guide for establishing the provenance of a text . . . is not the same thing as using prompt copy to illuminate staging practice" (p. 239), that playhouse origin does not automatically endow a printed text with special theatrical authority. Second, he asks, "Is not the text of a mature Elizabethan play, whether or not of playhouse origin, likely to reflect staging practice more accurately than the prompt manuscript of a relatively inexperienced author such as Henry Glapthorne?" (p. 240). And finally, concerning the extant prompt-books themselves, he points out that they contain surprisingly few indications of staging practice, that in fact a number of them are totally inadequate as guides to actual production. Not only, then, is the evidence of playhouse origin of a text open to interpretation, but the significance of prompt-copy origin is at best ambiguous. Nevertheless, in theory at any rate, the preference of prompt-copy over foul papers for the purposes of the theatre historian remains valid.

In most instances the existence of either foul papers or a prompt-copy must be inferred from the printed text of a play, and the theatre historian is dependent upon the textual scholar for information about the particular character of a given text. Among the four dozen or so extant dramatic manuscripts, however, are a handful of authentic prompt-books. These, together with half a dozen stage "plots"—skeleton outlines of plays written on large boards for playhouse use—and a single actor's part belonging to Edward Alleyn, are true playhouse or production documents. The existence of most of them has long been known. Edmond Malone printed four of the "plots" in his "Historical Account of the . . . Stage"; Collier discussed them briefly in 1831; and in 1860 Halliwell-Phillipps published *The Theatre Plots of Three Old English Dramas* for private circulation. Neither plots nor prompt-books received any concerted attention, however, until the second decade of the twentieth century. W. J. Lawrence noted their neglect in *Pre-Restoration Stage Studies* (1927), a situation at least partially rectified by the 1931 publication of W. W. Greg's *Dramatic Documents from the Elizabethan Playhouses*, in which the documents are described and some of them reproduced.

Prompt-Books

Greg classifies the extant manuscripts into three groups. Class A consists of true prompt-books, "copies which either bear evidence of having been used in actual performance or at least prepared for such use, or else of being transcripts of such copies preserving their distinctive features or made for official purposes." The second group consists of "manuscripts of a generally similar character but which show no definite evidence of having been used in the playhouse''; and the third group is a miscellaneous collection giving no indication of playhouse origin (*Dramatic Documents*, I, 191). The most important for the theatre historian, of course, are the fifteen manuscripts in Greg's Class A. Of less value but still important are the fifteen belonging to the second group. Thirteen of the thirty plays are found in the same manuscript in the British Library (Egerton 1994); and the Class A manuscript generally deemed to be the most valuable, Philip Massinger's autograph, *Believe as You List*, is to be found in the same collection (Egerton 2828). With four exceptions, the remainder of the manuscripts are also in the British Library. The exceptions are in the Cardiff Public Library, the Huntington Library, the library at Dulwich College, and that at Worcester College, Oxford. These are important documents for the theatre historian, although enthusiasm for what they can tell us has waned somewhat since J. Isaacs' ecstatic claim that ''prompt books with their marginal markings take us as near the tiring-house as anything can, and to handle them is the next best thrill to watching a good performance of the play'' (*Production and Stage-Management at the Blackfriars Theatre*, p. 14). The problem is simply that we possess too few of them, and the directions they contain are too few and too banal to tell us much about staging practice. (A note in the *Times Literary Supplement* for May 2, 1980, indicates that the British Library has acquired the manuscript of a hithero unknown play dating from the second decade of the seventeenth century and evidently intended for performance at the Inns of Court. The text is incomplete, but there are full stage-directions. The significance of the manuscript has not yet been determined.)

Stage Plots

Edmond Malone discovered four ''plats'' among the papers of Edward Alleyn at Dulwich College: *Fredrick and Basilea, The Second Part of the Seven Deadly Sins, The Dead Man's Fortune*, and *The First Part of Tamar Cam*. In 1831 Collier reported that only *The Seven Deadly Sins* was still at Dulwich. There it remains to this day (ms. XIX). Collier indicated that the other three had disappeared but, by whatever route, two of them arrived at the British Library (Add. ms. 10449). *Tamar Cam* is now known only from the Prolegomena to the *Variorum Shakespeare* of 1803, printed from a transcript by George Steevens. British Library Add. ms. 10499 also contains fragmentary ''plots'' of *The Battle of Alcazar, The Second Part of Fortune's Tennis*, and Chettle and Dekker's *Troilus and Cressida*. (See Greg, *Dramatic Documents*, I, 1–169. The plots are reproduced in Volume II.) In general, these plots consist of a record of the successive entrances of the characters, sometimes including information concerning properties and casting, and providing descriptive stage-directions for complicated stage action. They seem to have been intended as back-stage guides for the performers, but the absence of any clear contemporary reference to them leaves their provenance and purpose hazy.

Actors' Parts

The only actor's part that survives from the Elizabethan theatre is a fragment of Edward Alleyn's part in Robert Greene's *Orlando Furioso* (1591). The manuscript, preserved at Dulwich College (ms. 1, item 138) and printed by Greg, consists of 530 lines: Orlando's speeches and cues (two or three words) for about two-thirds of the play. It is impossible to say how typical this sole surviving example was.

The relationship between prompt-books such as those discussed by Greg and the earliest printed editions of plays is not always clear. Descriptive stage-directions in a printed text suggest that the play was specially prepared for publication and in its printed form does not necessarily reflect playhouse practice. In some instances, most notably the *Works* of Ben Jonson, published in 1616, we know that the author deliberately revised his work for publication. On the other hand, the disjointed and "incomplete" nature of some texts (the so-called bad quartos of Shakespeare for instance) indicates the possibility of a "memorial reconstruction" of a text heard in performance or remembered by an actor. That plays were printed directly from prompt-copies in some cases is demonstrated by Massinger's *The City Madam* (printed 1658), which retains a number of anticipatory stage directions in the margins, although other descriptive directions point to the author as well. The orthodox view, given by Chambers, is that the average Elizabethan dramatic text lies somewhere between the extremes of Jonson's *Works* and the short-hand notes of an incompetent reporter, "and is probably derived from a playhouse 'book' handed over by the actors to the printer" (*Elizabethan Stage*, III, 193). It is on the basis of this thesis that Greg argues for the importance of the few prompt-books and plots that have survived. They form, he writes, "an indispensable background to all useful thought, and a framework to which must conform all valid conjecture, concerning the textual phenomena and history of the Elizabethan drama" (*Dramatic Documents*, I, xi). (Full bibliographical information concerning the printed drama is contained in Greg's *Bibliography of the English Printed Drama to the Restoration*.)

Provided the complexity of the "textual phenomena" examined is recognized, the theatre historian can derive a considerable amount of information from play texts. Very often the title-page of a printed play informs us at what theatre and by what company the play was performed. Sometimes too the date of first performance is included. Occasionally a preface or dedication affixed to a printed play will contain a piece of pertinent information. Thomas Heywood notes in the dedication of Marlowe's *Jew of Malta* (published 1633), for example, that "the part of the Jew [was] presented by so unimitable an Actor as Mr. Allin [Edward Alleyn]." In too few instances, printed editions provide actor-lists, and in even fewer cases, cast-lists in which the specific role played by each actor is indicated. Jonson's *Works* contains actor-lists for nine plays, and we discover that William Shakespeare appeared in *Every Man in His Humour* and in *Sejanus*. Shakespeare's First Folio (1623) contains a list of actors, "The Names of the Principall Actors in all these playes." *Fifty Comedies and Tragedies* (1679), the second folio of Beaumont and Fletcher plays, provides actor-lists for twenty-four plays, and in one case an elaborate cast-list. The origin of these lists is unknown. Although they appear to be generally accurate, the cast-list of *The Wild Goose Chase*, since it contains the names of actors who did not join the King's Men until after the date of first performance of the play, cannot represent the original cast. Other than these, actor- or cast-lists are attached to the following quarto editions: John Webster, *The Duchess of Malfi* (1623); John Ford, *The Lover's Melancholy* (1629); James Shirley, *The Wedding* (1629); Lodowick Carlell, *The Deserving Favourite* (1629); Philip Massinger, *The Roman Actor* (1629), *The Picture* (1630), *The Renegado* (1630); Thomas Nabbes, *Hannibal and Scipio* (1637). The 1634 quarto of *The Two Noble Kinsmen* prints two stage-directions that name the actors in minor roles. Of the forty-three lists, thirty-six refer to the King's Men.

Stage-directions, as usual, must be treated circumspectly and, of course, be taken into consideration only if they occur in an early edition. (The history of scholarship is dotted with instances of error whereby editorially inserted directions have been assumed to have the authority of either the playwright or the playhouse.) And even when dealing with early editions, we must constantly be aware that stage-directions may be the work of the author, as he composed the play or as he revised it for publication, or they may represent the work of the prompter, or they may have been inserted by the printer or an editor. They are, moreover, notoriously difficult to interpret, their precise meaning and significance varying with the investigator's conception of what constitutes desirable or "normal" stage practice.

Implicit stage-directions are equally difficult to interpret. Lines spoken by the actors seemingly can indicate settings, designate bodily movements, and specify the use of properties or even scenery. Spatial relationships can sometimes be inferred, and stage movement and the direction of a given speech tentatively determined. But care must be taken to avoid anachronistic notions of "realism," to distinguish between real scenery or properties and "spoken" scenery, to entertain the possibility that some implicit indications of movement or setting are to be interpreted metaphorically rather than literally. It is sometimes advocated that reconstructions of performance should be confined to what is absolutely essential to production rather than allowing speculation on the merely possible. The advice is sound. Unfortunately, the rudimentary state of performance theory rarely allows for agreement as to what is absolutely essential.

One theory concerning what early texts can tell us about the acting of Elizabethan plays has been discredited, but it still pops up occasionally, and it was assumed as valid by John Dover Wilson in The New Cambridge Shakespeare (1921–67), still in print and still used. The theory was proposed by Percy Simpson who in *Shakespearian Punctuation* (1911) argued that the punctuation in Elizabethan dramatic texts was a guide not to syntax, but to pronunciation, that it had a rhetorical rather than a grammatical basis. It provided, in Dover Wilson's words, "stage directions in shorthand." Punctuation marks were held to be guides to intonation, to pauses, to emphasis, even to stage business. To the extent that it freed the punctuation of texts from the absolute tyranny of the modern editor and caused the original pointing to be considered with a new respect, the theory performed a valuable service. But there is little to support its more far-reaching claims of playhouse authority. Even Dover Wilson was finally forced to admit that, "while the original pointing should always receive respectful consideration as being ultimately derived from the playhouse, it is too often overlaid and confused by the high-handed action of compositors" (Introduction to New Cambridge *Hamlet*, pp. xxx-xxxi).

The texts of masques differ in several respects from those of plays. In the first place, a masque was normally performed only once, and its published version was basically a descriptive commemoration of the event. Even so, relatively few texts have come down to us. Of the almost one hundred masques known to have been performed between 1603 and 1642, the texts of fewer than sixty survive, half of them the work of Ben Jonson. (See Allardyce Nicoll, *Stuart Masques*, and W. W. Greg, *List of Masques*.) Secondly, the spectacular nature of the masque is reflected in the sometimes unliterary qualities of the text, devoted as it must be to describing scenic marvels, choreography, and courtly participants. (Texts are often labelled "Descriptions.") Since, except for Jonson's efforts, the masque has little claim to status as a literary art, it has in the past suffered from misunderstanding and neglect on the part of critics and textual scholars alike. The opening sentence of Francis Bacon's essay "Of Masques and Triumphs"—"These things are but Toys"—served as a standard valuation until the end of the nineteenth century. The text was merely a *scenario* or a *libretto*, neither of which was considered worthy of literary analysis.

The central position of music in masque performance would seem to necessitate a consideration of musical notation as part of the text; yet no edition of any masque includes the music that was used. In fact, masque music was seldom published at all, and no complete score for any masque survives. Nevertheless, masque music does exist, and theatre historians have reason to be grateful to Andrew J. Sabol who in *Four Hundred Songs and Dances from the Stuart Masque* (1978) prints virtually all the extant songs (51) and a large number of dances (251) related to over half the masques known to have been performed at court between 1604 and 1640. (A preliminary edition, *Songs and Dances for the Stuart Masque*, containing thirty-eight songs and twenty-five dances related to twenty masques, appeared in 1959.) Sabol found some of the music in printed editions, but most of it exists in manuscripts scattered among at least sixteen libraries in England, Scotland, Ireland, France, and the United States. The most important printed items are the following: John Playford, *Court Ayres* (1655) and *Courtly Masquing Ayres* (1662); Paulus Matthysz, *Uitnemend Kabinet*, printed in Amsterdam in 1646 and 1649; Alfonso Ferrabosco, *Ayres* (1609); John Wilson, *Cheerful Ayres* (1660); and the dance collections, published in Germany, of Thomas Simpson, William Brade, and John Adson. In only three instances is any music included with the printed text of a masque: Thomas Campion's *Lord Hay's Mask* (1607) and *Lord Somerset's Mask* (1614) each contains airs written by Campion; and some copies of *The Masque of Flowers* (1614) contain four-part music for five of the songs. (Incredibly, E.A.J. Honigmann, in his edition of *The Masque of Flowers*, printed in *A Book of Masques*, published in 1967, does not bother to include this music.)

The most significant manuscript collection of masque music is in the British Library (Add. MS. 10444). Once belonging to Sir Nicholas L'Estrange (1603–55), an amateur musicologist, it is composed of two part-books of 129 folios, containing three distinct collections of two-part instrumental music for dance, of which the first two are related to the masque. The manuscript was first recognized as important for the study of the masque by Halliwell-Phillipps in the nineteenth century, and various scholars have since that time extended the identification of the music with specific masques. Other important manuscripts in the British Library include a compilation of lute music (Add. MS. 38539) by John Sturte, who performed in the nuptial masques of 1613–14, and an autograph songbook containing songs for Milton's *Comus* by Henry Lawes (Add. MS. 53723). Henry's brother William has also left us an autograph score for portions of three masques (Bodleian Mu. S.b.2) that provides, in Sabol's words, "a sizable corpus of dramatic music of the 1630's of the utmost importance" (p. 32).

The masque is a complex theatrical form, perhaps ultimately incomprehensible to us in its totality, but until we recognize musical notation as well as description, dialogue, and lyrics as part of the text with which we have to work, no amount of integration of poetry and spectacle is going to rescue these "bungling shews" (Malone's phrase) from eternal misunderstanding.

OFFICIAL AND LEGAL DOCUMENTS

The consultation, collection, and publication of public and legal documents have been central activities of historians of the Elizabethan theatre ever since the time of Malone. National, municipal, and private repositories have been searched—often haphazardly but occasionally with triumphant results—for materials relating to the theatre. We have already noted the early activities of Collier and Cunningham and W. C. Hazlitt. By the last quarter of the nineteenth century the gathering and publishing of material was being undertaken on a more systematic basis, first in *The Shakespeare Society Papers* (1844–49), later in the *Transactions of the New Shakspere Society* (1874–92), and later still in the *Collections* of the Malone Society, which have appeared at irregular intervals since 1907. Continental scholars also contributed to the publication of theatrical documents: Forty-four volumes of *Materialien zur Kunde des alteren Englischen dramas*, under the editorship of Willy Bang, appeared between 1902 and 1914; and the series was continued from 1927 as *Materials for the Study of the Old English Drama*, under Henry Devocht. (Both the Malone Society publications and the *Materialien* include editions of plays—often diplomatic reproductions of manuscripts—that are also of considerable value to theatre historians.) John Tucker Murray's researches in the archives of towns and cities outside London, especially in municipal account-books, Mayors' Court books, and the letter-books of Corporations, provided fresh material for *English Dramatic Companies* (1910). We have the scholarly *compendia* of Chambers and Bentley, supplemented by Glynne Wickham's *Early English Stages*. Fresh material continues on occasion to come to light, but with one notable exception— the accounts of the Office of the Works (see below)—the documents now in print make up the bulk of the relevant evidence.

Government Documents

So far as public records are concerned, theatre historians have been aided in their researches by the fact that investigators from other fields as well as the state itself are interested in recovering them. Since many branches and levels of government at one time or another concerned themselves with theatrical affairs, official acts and proceedings of various kinds are of interest to theatre historians. Ordinances and regulations concerning the Royal Household were published by the Society of Antiquaries in 1790; *Statutes of the Realm* appeared between 1810 and 1828; and *Calendars of State Papers* (Domestic, Foreign, Scottish, Spanish, Venetian) have been published in many volumes since the mid-nineteenth century. The *Journals* of both Houses of Parliament are also accessible. Other reports and calendars are available in 191 volumes of the *Historical Manuscripts Commission Reports*, published between 1871 and 1936. Acts of the Privy Council for the years 1542–1604 are available in an edition prepared by J. R. Dasent; and those records (minutes and letters) from the Privy Council *Register* for 1603–42 relating to the drama have been published in the Malone Society *Collections* for 1911 (I.iv-v). Finally, W. de G. Birch provides *Historical Charters and Constitutional Documents of the City of London* (1887).

Some records are naturally of more interest than others. Those of the Lord Chamberlain's Office, preserved in the Public Records Office in London, contain the registers of warrants, copies of patents, wardrobe accounts for coronations and royal funerals, records of livery allowances—all of which is useful in reconstructing theatrical and para-theatrical activities at court. (These records have been published by the Malone Society in *Collections* I,i [1907], I.iv-v [1911], and II.iii [1931].) Official documents for most of Elizabeth's reign are supplemented by semi-official papers and letters of Sir William Cecil, Lord Burghley, who for forty years served as the Queen's counseller and first minister. The collection was purchased from the Marquis of Lansdowne by the British Museum in 1807, hence the appellation the "Lansdowne Manuscripts"; pertinent parts have been published by the Malone Society in *Collections* I.ii (1908). And finally, the attempts by the City of London to control plays and play-acting are reflected in two principal sources: the *Register* of the Privy Council (noted above) and the City *Remembrancia*, which contains repertories, journals, and letter-books. (An *Analytical Index* to the *Remembrancia* is provided by W. H. and H. C. Overall; and the Malone Society published dramatic records from it in *Collections* I.i [1907], II.iii [1931], and IV [1956].)

Nevertheless, the bulk of the public documents that have come down to us is of no direct interest to the theatre historian. It is often wise, however, when attempting to interpret a document that does concern itself with the theatre to consider the specific political and administrative context in which the particular action was taken. The concerns of law-makers and politicians, after all, are ideally peace, order, and good government, in practice spiced with the very human yearning to exercise power; their concern is rarely to direct the course of theatre history, however much they may affect it.

The relationship between the governments, national and local, and theatres and players traceable in these records has been seen mainly in terms of the attempts of governments to control the drama, to regulate theatrical activities, and to license and censor plays. The earliest—and still standard—account of the laws and regulations that affected the drama during the period is Virginia C. Gildersleeve's *Government Regulation of the Elizabethan Drama* (1908). Chambers provides extracts and summaries of 160 "documents of control" dating between 1531 and 1617 in *The Elizabethan Stage* (IV, Appendix D). The picture that emerges for Elizabeth's reign is summarized by Glynne Wickham:

Government action during the thirty-three years between 1570 and the end of the reign includes the reorganization of the Revels Offices with the establishment of its Master as an official licenser of plays and playhouses, the setting up of a censorship commission on which the Revels Office, the Church and the City of London were all directly represented, action against the stage in Poor Law regulations, Star Chamber orders for the registration of all plays appearing in print and even an Order in Council authorizing the demolition of all theatres in and about London. [*Early English Stages*, II.i.76]

After the accession of James I in 1603, such aggressive measures against the theatre ceased, and for good reason. As Wickham puts it: "Within three or four years of his Coronation James had virtually appropriated into his own hands control of players, plays, playmakers and theatres" (II.i, 90). Opposition to the theatre on religious and moral grounds continued, of course, but with the victory of the court over the city in the struggle for the control of the drama, the opposition lost its legislative voice. When finally it again found a voice in Parliament, however, it sounded as thunder: The first Ordinance against Stage-Plays and Interludes was passed on September 2, 1642; the second on October 22, 1647; and the final Ordinance for Suppression of all Stage-Plays and Interludes on February 9, 1647–48.

Legal Documents

These are generally concerned not with political or governmental matters, but with the legal negotiations, agreements, and disputes undertaken between individuals and the state. They include patents (documents granting some right to an individual or a group), records of lawsuits, leases, contracts, wills, and records of real estate transactions. Documents of this sort are now usually stored in the Public Records Office, although many of them remain uncatalogued and uncalendared. Again, the bulk of them commonly cited by scholars have been published in whole or in part in Chambers and Bentley.

The difficulty of locating a specific record makes it imperative that when new documents are found they be adequately located, described, and preferably published. Unfortunately, either by design or through oversight investigators have from time to time provided elaborate and controversial discussions and theories based on materials they claim to have examined but which they neither locate precisely nor transcribe. Collier is, of course, notorious in this regard, and his colleague Cunningham at times was similarly careless. In *Shakespeare Society Papers* (IV), for example, Cunningham published several documents concerning the granting of a theatre patent to one Richard Heton at the Salisbury Court theatre. He offered no discussion of them and indicated no source for them. (See Bentley, *Jacobean and CarolineStage*, II, 684–687.) But the later and presumably more honest scholars have been equally guilty. C. W. Wallace supposedly discovered some documents concerning the playwright Richard Brome and the Salisbury Court theatre. Included was a contract made in 1635 between Brome and the theatre management for his services as a dramatist. The contract is of primary importance as an indication of customary relations between a playwright and an acting company, and it would merit close and penetrating scrutiny if we could find it. Unfortunately, information about its contents is limited to Wallace's brief commentary in *The Century Magazine* (1910). (See Bentley, *Jacobean and Caroline Stage*, III, 52–54.) Wallace never published his documents, and he died in 1932 without ever revealing their whereabouts. While we have no reason to doubt that Wallace actually saw the documents, or that his description is accurate so far as it goes, the necessity of relying on an inadequate second-hand account renders the evidence less useful than it would otherwise be. A similar neglect of source and context for quotations from documents mars the early work of C. J. Sisson on the Boar's Head Inn, and Leslie Hotson's theorizing in *Shakespeare's Wooden O* (1959). We might hope that in future the location, context, and a transcript of an unpublished document will accompany the discussion or use of it as evidence.

The volume of legal documents available can, nonetheless, sometimes give us a false sense of what we know or are able to learn about the Elizabethan theatre. Patents, leases, and lawsuits comprise an incomplete record at best and the information to be derived from them is often of peripheral interest. The known history of the Theatre, for instance, is largely a matter of legal wrangling over title and rights. Or the large collection of petitions, answers, and judgements between members of the King's Men and the Lord Chamberlain in 1635, known as the *Sharers' Papers*, seems to speak of serious dissension in the principal acting compnay of the time, and yet there is no hint that it affected the troupe's fortunes; and the papers tell us nothing about the theatrical activities of the players.

(*The Sharers' Papers* were discovered in the Lord Chamberlain's books by Halliwell-Phillipps, who published them in the first volume of his *Outlines of the Life of Shakespeare*; the Malone Society published a more accurate transcription in its *Collections*, II, iii [1931]. Also see Bentley's discussion in *The Jacobean and Caroline Stage*, I, 43–47.) And in spite of the large number of such documents concerning the two Blackfriars Playhouses—the most important of which are printed in the Malone Society's *Collections*, II.i (1913)—the structure and appearance of the theatre are still largely unknown.

Similarly, the birth records and wills of Elizabethan and Jacobean actors so assiduously searched out by generations of scholars have yielded disconcertingly little information that is useful in reconstructing their professional lives and stage careers. (See especially Edwin Nungezer, *Dictionary of Actors*, and the second volume of Bentley's *Jacobean and Caroline Stage*.) On the other hand, on the basis of these and other documents, it is possible to determine something of the actors' social and legal status, their relationships with patrons and employers. "Establishing the players' place in the social structure of the age," writes Muriel Bradbrook in *Rise of the Common Player* (1962), reveals that the players represented a new social group, and the opposition they met "is a classic example of social prejudice and of the force of unexamined assumptions" (p. v). In other words, together with similar investigations of the status of playwrights and the composition of audiences, studies such as Bradbrook's can offer a fresh interpretation of the Elizabethan theatre in terms of social structure. And in fact, G. E. Bentley has attempted just this in *Profession of Dramatist in Shakespeare's Time* (1971) and in a forthcoming book on the Elizabethan actor.

The Revels Documents

Documents relating to court entertainments have long been recognized as important for Elizabethan stage history. The existence of a court official to supervise and pay for court entertainments is first mentioned in 1494, and a permanent Master of the Revels as he was called was appointed in 1545. The powers of the office in its early years were limited: Its responsibilities were shared with various other departments of the Royal Household. After the appointment of Sir Edmund Tilney as Master of the Revels in 1579, however, the powers and responsibilities of the office increased. Sir Edmund himself appears to have been singularly inactive, but the competent Clerk of the Revels, Thomas Blagrave, kept the office running smoothly. Two decrees, of 1581 and 1603, extended the powers of the Master of the Revels by granting him the right to license players and censor plays. (The 1581 document is printed in Chambers, *Elizabethan Stage*, IV, Appendix D, no. lvi.) The mastership passed, on Tilney's death in 1610, to Sir George Buck, who was in turn succeeded in 1622 by Sir Henry Herbert, the best-known of the Masters. Herbert held the office until his death in 1673, but the later years of his incumbency and the years of his immediate successors were marked by a steadily decreasing authority, particularly in the area of censorship, which by 1737 had passed directly to the Lord Chamberlain. With the exception of masques, for which the Master of the Revels was not responsible, most of our information concerning staging at court is derived from documents associated with the Office of the Revels. What relevance such staging methods might have for the public theatre is still moot; and the interpretation of court staging has yielded widely divergent theories, from the view that it was essentially Italianate to the opinion that it continued the medieval tradition of mansions.

The records and accounts of the Office of the Revels are nevertheless of considerable interest to the theatre historian, and since the days of Malone numerous scholars have laboured to present the accounts and describe the office. Yet the position has remained a difficult thing to pin down and its evidence difficult to assess. The reasons are succinctly outlined by W. R. Streitberger in *Research Opportunities in Renaissance Drama* (XXI, 1978):

The primary records, in secretary script for the most part, are scattered among several repositories in England and the United States; collections of records used by earlier scholars have since been sold; some records have disappeared entirely and what we know about them derives from excerpts made by earlier scholars; still other records have been printed in obscure editions. Further, scholarship on the office and in some cases on the accounts themselves contain errors of one sort of another, and the project of untangling the errors is a very difficult one. [p. 11]

The student who wishes to evaluate theories based on this evidence, or who must consult it, therefore needs some help in sorting it out.

Few of the early accounts from the period before 1571 have survived. Most of those that have survived were preserved in a private collection at Loseley, the bulk of which is now in the Folger Shakespeare Library. (See A. J. Kempe, *The Loseley Mansucripts*, 1835.) The most important of them were printed by Albert Feuillerat in 1908 and 1914. (Actually, Feuillerat was anticipated by Halliwell-Phillipps' *Collection of Ancient Documents Respecting the Office of Master of the Revels*, which appeared in 1870 in a limited edition of eleven copies.)

The greatest concentration of accounts is for the years 1571–88. Eleven of these accounts, annotated by auditors, are in the Public Records Office (Accounts Various 3, 907; cited by Feuillerat under its former number 1213). They were first printed by Peter Cunningham in 1842; a better edition is that of Feuillerat (1908), who adds one further account for November 1587 to October 1589, found in the British Library. Two further accounts, for 1604–5 and 1611–1612, were also printed by Cunningham. These are the accounts long suspected of being forgeries but now generally accepted as genuine. Further records of the Revels accounts for the reigns of James I and Charles I are rare indeed. In fact, the only surviving original document from the Office of the Revels after 1612 is a scrap of waste paper containing a list of plays evidently being considered for court performance. (See Frank Marcham, *King's Office of the Revels*.)

It is at first glance odd, therefore, that the most famous document from the Revels Office dates from the period of Henry Herbert's mastership (1622–73). The original of Herbert's Office-Book, printed by J. Adams in *Dramatic Records of Sir Henry Herbert* (1917), has long since disappeared. Like those of his predecessors, Tilney and Buck, Herbert's Office-Book contained a record of licensing fees, court performances, titles of plays, and names of playwrights— a valuable source of information on matters theatrical. It has been possible to reconstruct a little of the document's history. At Herbert's death it was left in a chest in his library at Ribbesford, but by 1787 it had turned up in the possession of one Francis Ingram, at whose home it was examined by Edmond Malone and George Chalmers. Malone reported that the book was in a decayed condition as early as 1790, and it is fortunate that substantial extracts from it were printed by Chalmers in *A Supplemental Apology for the Believers in the Shakespeare-Papers* (1799) and by Malone in the third volume of his *Variorum Shakespeare* (1821). An independent transcript of the office-book, done in the nineteenth century, was cut up and pasted in its various pieces in the appropriate places in the scrapbooks of J. O. Halliwell-Phillipps, now in the Folger Shakespeare Library in Washington, D.C. That we can be as sure of the contents of the book as we are is dependent both upon the industry and honesty of Chalmers and Malone and on the fact that we have three copies to collate.

Documents from other departments of the Royal Household complement the Revels documents and thus help to fill in our picture of staging at court. The fragmentary records of the Office of Works in the Public Records Office, for instance, suggest that this department was responsible for the building, the stage, and the seating arrangements for court performances, that is, the "hard" furnishings as opposed to the "soft" furnishings (hangings, cloths, curtains) provided by the Revels Office. Feuillerat prints some extracts from the Works accounts—although not always knowingly—and Glynne Wickham provides accounts relating to the Banquet House at Somerset House in 1632/33 in *Early English Stages* (II.ii, 223–224). (Wickham's promise in II.i to print the Works Accounts in full has not yet been fulfilled; the Malone Society plans an edition in the near future.) The Declared Accounts of the Treasurer of the Chamber are similarly valuable, recording payments made to all players and entertainers appearing at court. They thus provide a catalogue of court entertainments from 1558 to 1642. Many of the accounts are included by Chambers in his chronological table of entries in the Chamber and Revels Accounts in *The Elizabethan Stage* (IV, Appendix B). But the complete records were not published until the Malone Society provided them in its *Collections* (VI, 1961).

WRITTEN EVIDENCE

Written documents other than official and legal records include the kind of material we have encountered previously in our surveys of evidence for the theatres of Italy and Spain: critical treaties; a miscellaneous collection of newsletters and pamphlets, correspondence, diaries, and letters; and visitors' accounts of the Elizabethan theatre. A standard chronicle is still Stow's *Annals*, continued by Edmund Howes and published in 1631. (Some manuscript notes to a copy of this edition, written about 1656–1658 and now in the Folger Shakespeare Library [Phillipps MS. 11613] record the pulling down of the Globe theatre on April 15, 1644, "to make tennements in the roome of it." See Bentley, VI, 200.) But we have in addition an invaluable collection of manuscripts once belonging to the actor Edward Alleyn and held at Dulwich Colloge.

Critical Documents

English critical documents of the Renaissance that touch upon matters dramatic or theatrical were for the most part written as replies to Puritan attacks on literature and the stage. These attacks began in earnest in 1577 with John Northbrooke's *Treatise against Dicing, Dancing, Plays and Interludes*. Critical documents outside the controversy over the stage are of interest only as providing some of the critical framework for the specific defenses written by apologists for the theatre. Some of them, such as Leonard Coxe's *Art or Craft of Rhetoric* (ca. 1524), Thomas Wilson's *Art of Rhetoric* (1553), or Roger Ascham's *The Scholemaster* (1570), are rhetorical studies of literature; others, such as William Webbe's *Discourse of English Poetry* (1586) and George Puttenham's *Art of English Poesy* (1589), are devoted to the classification of kinds and the study of metrics. The point to bear in mind is that in spite of an occasional glimmer of an independent spirit, these Englishmen were part of the European Renaissance, and the assumptions, procedures, and theories they brought to bear on their subjects were in general derived from classical practice through the medium of Italian critical theory. And in spite of the achievements of the non-classical Elizabethan theatre, and in spite of the fact that the attacks on the stage that prompted the critical responses were directed specifically at the popular stage, English dramatic theory and criticism of the sixteenth and seventeenth centuries remained classically oriented. (The standard collection of sixteenth-century critical documents is G. Gregory Smith's *Elizabethan Critical Essays*, 1904.)

The first flurry of attack and response that followed Northbrooke's treatise, featuring principally Stephen Gosson on the attack and Thomas Lodge for the defense, culminated in one of the two most important critical documents of the Elizabethan period. Sir Philip Sidney's *Defense of Poesy* was written about 1583, although it was not printed until 1595. Sidney upholds the classical ideals of dramaturgy and staging, and he derives his classicism principally from Italy. He defends and justifies an ideal stage, not the Elizabethan stage; and viewed from this point of view, he actually does not answer the Puritan objections to the lewdness and social destructiveness of the London playhouses. Certainly he did not put an end to the attacks, which continued throughout the period, reaching a weighty climax in William Prynne's *Histriomastix* (1633). (Nearly all the relevant documents concerning the controversy are collected in the fifty volumes of *The English Stage: Attack and Defense 1577–1730*, published 1973–74.)

Nor were the men of the theatre concerned to answer their critics. The dramatists, we find, have disconcertingly little to say about their craft or their profession. We have about a dozen dedications and prefaces to printed plays, and we have Ben Jonson's *Timber, or Discoveries* (1641). Moreover, Jonson's work, the second most important critical document of the period, is directed just as firmly against contemporary playwrighting practices as Sidney's work had been. Elizabethan England did not produce a champion of the "new way of writing plays" as had the Spain of Lope de Vega. The entire period, then, is framed by two classically inspired theoretical documents.

This marked gap in England between theory and practice means that information concerning the Elizabethan stage can be gained only incidentally from the documents, and that most of what there is derives from diatribes against the theatre and must be interpreted in that light. It also affirms the importance of considering both theory and practice when analyzing or evaluating either. For the theatre historian, the relationship between the two represents a significant phenomenon. At the risk of oversimplification, for instance, we can characterize that relationship for the various theatres of the Renaissance this way. In Italy, critical theory was part and parcel of theatrical activity: theory and practice interacted on one another. In Spain, critical treatises tended to reflect playhouse practice rather than lead it. In France, as we shall see, the opposite is true: Dramatic theory determined theatrical practice. Finally, in England, as we have seen, there was no direct relationship between critical theory and the stage.

Occasional Treatises, Pamphlets, and Newsletters

Although as producers of critical and theoretical commentary playwrights are something of a disappointment, some of their other writings have proved more fruitful. Thomas Heywood (ca. 1574–1641) was the author of a long series of pamphlets on various subjects; the most significant for our purposes is *An Apology for Actors* (1612), one of the best of the contemporary replies to Puritan attacks. It differs from the replies of ivory-towered critics like Sidney mainly in its being a defense of the actor's profession as Heywood had practised it for fifteen years. Like his learned brethren, Heywood adheres to convention by arguing on the analogy with classical antiquity, but in the process he manages to allude significantly to the contemporary theatre. Coming as it does from the pen of a true man of the theatre, *An Apology for Actors* is an important document.

Another frequently cited discussion of the contemporary theatre by a man with direct acquaintance with it is *The Gull's Hornbook* (1609) by Thomas Dekker. Chapter 6, "How a Gallant Should Behave Himself in a Play-house," is of particular interest. Ben Jonson's comments in the Induction to *Bartholomew Fair* (1614), like the discussions of Heywood and Dekker, refer to conditions in the public theatres. The author of the Praeludium for *The Careless Shepherd* (published 1656) is concerned almost exclusively with staging practices at the private Salisbury Court theatre in the 1630s. (All four documents are represented in *The Seventeenth-Century Stage* edited by G. E. Bentley.)

Occasional pamphlets and weekly newsletters, some of them the productions of well-known figures such as Robert Greene, Thomas Nashe, and John Harington, also provide odd pieces of information concerning the theatre. (The bulk of such references are cited in Chamber's *Elizabethan Stage* and in Bentley's *Jacobean and Caroline Stage*.) The newsletters, both Puritan and Royalist, appeared under such intriguing titles as *Perfect Occurrences*, *Mercurius Pragmaticus*, and *The Kingdom's Weekly Intelligencer*. The pamphlets of John Taylor the Water Poet, writer of doggerel verse and Thames waterman, are typical of the genre, although possibly more diverting. For example, in 1613 the building of the Fortune theatre in the western suburbs of London made that area rather than the Bankside the main theatre district, with the result that the watermen, who had previously ferried playgoers across the river, were suddenly without customers. Taylor rose to the occasion with a pamphlet titled *The True Cause of the Watermen's Suit concerning Players, and the reasons that their playing on London side is their extreme hindrances. With a Relation how farre that suit was proceeded in, and the occasions that it was not affected*. Similarly tantalizing but ultimately disappointing items include Henry Fitz-Geoffrey's *Notes from Black-Fryers* (1617), constituting, in the words of G. E. Bentley, who prints it (VI, 42–44), "the longest extant contemporary passage on the theatre, as well as the least intelligible"; and *The Stage-players Complaint* (1641), a dialogue in which the times and the plague are equally lamented, but which is otherwise unhelpful.

Although not strictly a pamphlet, Francis Meres' famous literary commonplace-book may well be included here. *Palladis Tamia: Wits Treasury* (1598) has been too often cited and consequently its value too often overestimated. It does provide some evidence for the dating of plays, and in one instance at least— that of Shakespeare's *Love's Labours Won*—for the existence of an otherwise unknown play. But as representative of the taste of his day—the reason he is most often referred to—Meres cannot be trusted. He presents his evaluations in a series of parallels between classical and Elizabethan literature, an extreme example of what has been called the "Euphuistic mood," and must therefore stretch or constrict the Elizabethans to fit the pattern he establishes for the ancients: "As there are . . . so there. . . ." (*Palladis Tamia* is printed by G. Gregory Smith in *Elizabethan Critical Essays*, II, 308–324.)

The art of rhetorical delivery, as taught in schools and practised by lawyers, preachers, and other public speakers, was set forth in various books, and on the premise—supported by contemporary references—that the actor and the orator performed according to the same rules, these works have been used as evidence for discussions of Elizabethan acting. John Bulwer's *Chirologia* and *Chironomio*, published together in 1644, provide one of the main sources of information for B. L. Joseph's analysis of the player's craft in *Elizabethan Acting* (1951; revised 1964).

Letters and Diaries

Letters and diaries, normally not written for publication, add yet another dimension to the picture we have of the Elizabethan theatre. (Again, most theatrical references in the correspondence of the period are noted by Chambers and Bentley.) The originals of letters are, of course, scattered throughout libraries, public and private; but those of public figures are far more likely to have been preserved and in some instances published. Thus letters to Sir Dudley Carleton, at times ambassador to various countries, are listed in the *Calander of State Papers, Domestic*, and those of John Chamberlain (1553–1627), one of the most prolific letter-writers of the time and cited on numerous occasions by both Chambers and Bentley, are available in a collection edited by Norman Egbert McClure and in *The Court and Times of James I*, edited by R. F. Williams. A more general collection is *Original Letters Illustrative of English History*, edited by H. Ellis in eleven volumes.

The principal diaries of the period that have provided information concerning the theatre are the following.

Henry Machym's manuscript diary for the years 1550–63 is preserved in the British Library (MS. Cotton, Vitellius F. V.). Machym briefly records his attendance at several performances of Passion plays, of plays by the Children of Pauls, of plays at Court. His references to the times of day indicate artificial lighting and therefore indoor performances. (The diary has been edited for the Camden Society by J. G. Nichols.)

Simon Forman's *Booke of Plaies* (Bodleian MS. Ashmole 208), which records the astrologer's visits to the theatre 1610–11, was at one time considered of doubtful authenticity but now appears to be accepted as genuine. Forman's entries are largely plot summaries, but he does occasionally hint at stage business. (Extracts from Forman's *Booke of Plaies* are printed in Gāmini Salgādo, *Eyewitnesses of Shakespeare*, pp. 31–33.) The diary of Thomas Crosfield (edited by F. S. Boas, 1935) contains an interview with Richard Kendall, wardrobe keeper of the Salisbury Court players, dated July 18, 1634. (The significant entries are also printed in Bentley, II, 688–689.)

By far the most significant diary for our purposes, however, is that of Sir Humphrey Mildmay (British Library Harl. MS. 454), which consists of accounts for the period from January 21, 1631/32 to July 22, 1652, and a diary covering the period from July 3, 1633, to July 9, 1652. Of most importance is the fact that Mildmay records about six visits per year to the theatre over a ten-year period from 1633 to 1643. Bentley, who prints the relevant details in *The Jacobean and Caroline Stage*, III, 673–681), calls the diary "the most complete account of any individual's theatre attendance which exists for any ·Englishman before Pepys" (II, 673). The reference to Pepys is perhaps unfortunate, for the student who envisages a Pepys-like description of theatre attendance will be disappointed by Mildmay's bland records, which offer us little information concerning the play seen or the author's reaction to it.

Accounts of Foreign Observers

Yet a further perspective is provided by accounts of foreign observers of the theatrical scene. Many of these observations and comments are contained in the correspondence of diplomats, and most of the material is occasional in nature. We find, for instance, Orazio Busino, Chaplain to the Venetian Embassy in London, in a letter dated December 8, 1617, describing a visit to a theatre—possibly Blackfriars, almost certainly *not* the Fortune as has sometimes been maintained—in which he remarks on the costumes and interludes of music (he was ignorant of English) and the "nobility in such excellent array" in the audience, including a "richly dressed" young lady who importuned the chaplain for a rendezvous (Bentley, VI, 151). Busino is also responsible for the detailed account of the performance in January 1617 of Jonson's *Pleasure Reconciled to Virtue*. (The account is printed in Italian in Herford and Simpson, *Ben Jonson*, X, 580–584, summarized with long quotations in English in Mary Sullivan, *Court Masques of James I*, pp. 114–117; excerpts are translated in Chambers, I, 202n., and in Bentley, VI, 257–258.)

It is in a letter from the Spanish ambassador sent home to Madrid concerning the performance of Thomas Middleton's *A Game at Chess* at the Globe theatre in August 1624 that we find one of the two known contemporary estimates of the capacity of an Elizabethan playhouse. The play, in which the Spanish were ridiculed, ran for an unprecedented nine days, and the indignant ambassador points out that there were "more than 3000 persons there on the day that the audience was smallest," and that "during these last four days more than 12,000 persons have all heard the play" (Bentley, IV, 871–872). (A similar figure is given by Johannes DeWitt for the Swan theatre in 1596. See below.) Some scholars have found these figures too high, but Elizabethan audiences were not limited by fire regulations and were likely more tolerant than we of overcrowding. And it does seem unlikely that both the Spanish ambassador and DeWitt would err so precisely in accord with one another.

Other diplomatic documents admittedly yield less direct information concerning theatrical affairs. The dispatches and correspondence of the ambassadors of France, Spain, Venice, Flanders, and Florence, even when they touch upon theatrical affairs, are often concerned mainly with court intrigue and diplomatic oneupmanship. Much of our information about this activity, including extracts from the correspondence, is to be found in *Finetti Philoxenis* (1656) by Sir John Finett, from 1612 first assistant to the Master of Ceremonies and then himself Master, the official charged with ensuring the well-being of ambassadors and with protocol. Although correspondence associated with the Venetian embassy is particularly rich in theatrical allusion (see *Calendar of State Papers, Venice*, and Bentley, *passim*), recent work by John Orrell in the State Archives of Florence and Turin has revealed that regular weekly newsletters from agents in London to Florence and Savoy contain a substantial number of references to the theatre. Extracts and translations of pertinent parts of the Florentine correspondence are provided by Orrell in articles in *Theatre Research International* n.s., III (1978) and *Theatre Survey* XX (1979); extracts from the Savory material is found in *Theatre Research International*, n.s., IV (1979).

Like the letters of Busino and the Spanish ambassador, the accounts of foreign travellers to London sometimes provide details of theatre architecture or practise that native observers seem to have considered too obvious to mention. Chambers (II, 358–369) notes the comments of the following visitors:

a. Samuel Kiechel (1585), who refers to theatrical performances "nearly every day of the week" in "peculiar houses, which are so made to have about three galleries over one another. . . .";

b. Prince Louis of Anhalt-Cothen (1596), who found four playhouses in London, presumably the Theatre, the Curtain, the Rose, and the Swan;

c. Johannes DeWitt (1596), who left us not only a description of London theatres, but a drawing of the interior of the Swan (see below);

d. Paul Hentzner (1598), who also provides a brief description of the Swan;

e. Thomas Platter (1599), who describes the system of fees for entrance to an unnamed Elizabethan playhouse;

f. Frederic Gerschow (1602), who records in his journal the visits of Philipp Julius, Duke of Stettin-Pomerania, to several dramatic performances, including a *kinder-comoedia* at the Blackfriars on September 18,

g. Prince Otto of Hesse-Cassel (1611), who notes the existence of seven theatres, of which the Globe is the most important; but he also notes of the children's company at Whitefriars that they "are the best company in London."

Little enough; but the fact that these men were impressed sufficiently by the number, size, and nature of London's theatres to offer any comment at all is significant.

Hundreds of disparate pieces of information are provided by this plethora of written evidence, and historians have used it to piece together a picture of the Elizabethan theatre and its development over a sixty-year period. This kind of evidence can in fact be useful in establishing a date, providing a name, suggesting a context, or indicating an attitude. On rare occasions it offers a fleeting glimpse of a performance or a theatre. At times, nonetheless, it seems more honoured in the collection than in the interpretation. It would, it is true, require a truly creative act of synthesis on the part of an historian to provide what is— or some day may be—the sociology of the Elizabethan theatrical world towards which such documents point. Thus far most scholars have been content to draw on such information in order to answer specific rather than general questions.

The Dulwich Manuscripts

In 1592, Edward Alleyn (1566–1626), at the time the leading actor of Strange's Men and destined to achieve distinction as one of the two greatest actors of the period (the other was Richard Burbage), married Joan Woodward, the step-daughter of Philip Henslowe, owner and manager of the Rose theatre. Alleyn and Henslowe subsequently formed a business partnership which lasted until Henslowe's death in 1616, and which became possibly the most potent single force in the theatrical life of the time. Fortunately for the theatre historian, the details of many of Alleyn and Henslowe's business transactions are available in a remarkable collection of manuscripts preserved in the College of God's Gift at Dulwich, an institution begun by Alleyn in 1613 and officially founded by him in 1619. It is no exaggeration to say that these Dulwich manuscripts are the single most important body of theatrical material, exclusive of play texts, to have come down to us from the Elizabethan and Jacobean periods.

Edmund Malone, in Additions to his "Historical Account of the Rise and Progress of the English Stage" (1790), notes "some curious Manuscripts relative to the stage" at Dulwich College, indicating that among them were Henslowe's account-book and diary for the years 1597–1603, as well as a bundle of loose papers consisting of an inventory of the wardrobe and playbooks. Malone published portions of the material, and his transcript of the diary now forms part of the collection at Dulwich. It is fortunate that he printed what he did, for Collier reported in 1831 that nearly all the inventories that Malone quoted had disappeared. (The lost inventories are printed by Foakes and Rickert, *Henslowe's Diary*, Appendix 2, pp. 316–325.) Collier continued the task of publishing the material, and produced three volumes for the Shakespeare Society: *Memoires of Edward Alleyn* (1841), *A Collection of Original Documents illustrative of the life and times of Edward Alleyn* (1843), and *Henslowe's Diary* (1845). The unmasking of Collier as a forger of documents necessitated the re-editing of this material however, and W. W. Greg published *Henslowe's Diary* in two volumes in 1904 and 1908, and *Henslowe's Papers* in 1907. (Greg reproduces in *Dramatic Documents* the four "plots" reported by Malone, but only one remains at Dulwich. See above.) The diary was edited once again by R. A. Foakes and R. T. Rickert in 1961; and Foakes is also responsible for a valuable facsimile edition of *Henslowe Papers* (1977).

The Dulwich manuscripts are gathered in a series of volumes, three of which are of special relevance to the theatre. Volume I contains 144 items, mainly letters and papers relating to the stage and particularly to the Fortune theatre. Volume II has forty-two items relating to the activities of Alleyn and Henslowe as Masters of the Royal Game of Bears, Bulls, and Mastiff-Dogs. Volume VII contains the famous diary. (All of this material is reproduced in facsimile by Foakes.) When the material was catalogued by G. F. Warner in 1881, it was divided into muniments (public documents such as deeds and contracts) and manuscripts (private records, letters, memoranda, Henslowe's diary). The numbering of the documents is based on this division.

Among the important manuscripts and muniments are the following:

a. A letter from Henslowe to Alleyn, dated September 28, 1593, containing a rough sketch (approximately 12.5 cm. x 8 cm.) of what appears to be a proscenium stage

(MS. I. Art. 14). (The rudimentary nature of the sketch is indicated by Ernest Rhodes' understandable error in printing it wrong way up in *Henslowe's Rose*.)

b. A dramatic dialogue, with stage directions (MS. I. Art. 139).

c. Orlando's part from Robert Greene's *Orlando Furioso* (MS. I. Art. 138), usually assumed to have been used by Alleyn.

d. An inventory of theatrical costumes from the years 1590–1600 (MS. I. Art. 30).

e. A series of documents relating to the building of the first Fortune theatre in 1600 (MS. I. Arts. 27–29), its conveyance to Alleyn in March 1610 (Art. 56), the sales of shares (Arts. 58–62), the renting out of the second Fortune by Dulwich College between 1637 and 1649 (Arts. 114–122), the report of a survey of the Fortune in 1656 (Art. 124), and the leasing and final sale of the property between 1659 and 1662 (Arts. 124–134).

f. Deed of partnership in the Rose theatre between Philip Henslowe and John Cholmley, dated January 10, 1586/87 (Muniment 16).

Of even more importance, however, is a contract between Peter Streete and Henslowe and Alleyn for the erection of the Fortune theatre, dated January 8, 1599/1600 (Muniment 22). The contract seems at first glance to be specific enough to allow for an accurate reconstruction. Indeed, in 1907 Walter H. Godfrey, with the advice of William Archer, constructed a scale model of the Fortune based on the specifications of the contract. But in spite of the many details of size and construction contained in the contract, at certain crucial points we find that arrangements are to be made as they were at the Globe: In particular, we find the frustrating direction, "And the saide Stadge to be in all other proporcions contryved and fashioned like unto the Stage of the saide Plaiehowse called the Globe." Since, unlike Peter Streete, we are ignorant of the "contritions, conveyances, fashions, thinge and things effected" at the Globe, we remain in similar ignorance of them at the Fortune. The contract also refers to a "Plott thereof drawen," which is no longer extant. We ought nevertheless to be grateful for what we do have. (A sketch limited to the known specifics of the contract appears in C. Walter Hodges, *Globe Restored*, p. 188).

A similar difficulty attends the interpretation of the so-called Hope contract of August 29, 1613 (Muniment 49). The contract calls for the demolition of the Bear Garden and for the erection of a new building modelled on the Swan. (The contract contains four references to the older playhouse.) We do, however, possess a sketch of the Swan, and Glynne Wickham, for one, believes that the four references to the Swan in the Hope contract corroborate DeWitt's drawing (*Early English Stages*, II.ii, 72–73). The desirability of consulting either the originals or facsimiles of Elizabethan documents is also demonstrated by an error made by W. W. Greg in his transcription of the contract printed in his *Henslowe Papers*. In two places, the contract refers to "Game place or house" and "Game place or Plaiehouse." Greg misread the *G* as *S*, and his error was for years repeated, even in Bentley's authoritative *Jacobean and Caroline Stage* (VI, 201). The erroneous reading, of course, tends to downplay the dual nature of both the early Bear Garden and the new Hope.

Henslowe's Diary and Account-Book (MS VII) is the most famous document among the Dulwich manuscripts. Originally used by John Henslowe to record accounts relating to mining during the years 1576–78, the book passed to his brother Philip some time before 1592. Philip Henslowe used the book regularly between 1591 and 1597, intermittently until 1604, and occasionally until 1609. While various private matters are noted, together with some non-theatrical accounts (not to mention John's original mining accounts), the bulk of the diary is in fact given over to theatrical affairs, to Henslowe's financial relationships with players and playwrights, and to accounts relating to the building and maintenance of playhouses. Of most interest is a set of detailed accounts of daily receipts that Henslowe realized from performances at his theatres between February 1591/92 and November 1597. The document is not easy to decipher. It is not clear precisely why Henslowe kept the accounts or what he meant by some of the entries. Although his spelling is eccentric even by eclectic Elizabethan standards, and although business matters are the principal concerns of the diary, it is unlikely that Henslowe was in fact the illiterate Philistine capitalist painted by Greg, or that his practices were necessarily different from those obtaining at other playhouses.

PICTORIAL AND GRAPHIC EVIDENCE

Pictorial and graphic material relating to the Elizabethan stage includes maps and long views of London, sketches of theatre interiors, ground plans and elevations of theatres, scene and costume designs for court masques. But the impression of a wealth of information is soon dispelled by the disputed relevance of some of the pictures and sketches, by the difficulties of interpreting others, and by what appears to be the continuing reluctance of scholars to credit graphic evidence over the inner picture, laboriously built up from play texts, assumption, and conjecture, in their mind's eye. To an extent, of course, scepticism is both healthy and necessary. The worth of any piece of pictorial evidence must be judged according to rigorously applied criteria, and the limits of its possible relevance established. (This is true of evidence of any kind.) We need to establish the date and the authenticity of the material; we need to know what it purports to represent or to be; we need to understand its purpose; and we should like to determine the identity and competence of the artist or draftsmen.

Maps and Long Views of London

Well over thirty maps or long views of London dating from before the middle of the sixteenth century to the eighteenth century have been used by theatre historians to locate Elizabethan theatres and to determine something of their exterior appearance. Most of these maps have been reproduced by the London Topographical Society. (A good number are also included in C. Walter Hodges, *The Globe Restored*, Irwin Smith, *Shakespeare's Globe Playhouse*, and Glynne Wickham, *Early English Stages*, II, ii. Guides to the maps are provided by

Chambers in *The Elizabethan Stage*, II, 353–355, by James Stinson in *Studies in the Elizabethan Theatre*, ed. C. T. Prouty, pp. 107–111, and by I. A. Shapiro in *Shakespeare Survey* I, 1948.) The most frequently cited are the following:

Hoefnagel

The so-called Hoefnagel map was first published in G. Braun and F. Hohenberg, *Civitates Orbis Terrarum* (Cologne, 1582), from a survey of 1554–57. The view features a bull-baiting ring and a bear-baiting ring. The animals are shown. (*Early English Stages*, II.ii, Plate IV.4).

Agas

This map, attributed to Ralph Agas, possibly from the same survey as the Hoefnagel view but with a more accurate perspective, was drawn some time after 1561 and depicts the same two baiting rings. Here they are clearly two-story circular structures. (*Early English Stages*, II.ii. Plate V.5.) There also exists in the British Library (Sloane MS. 2596) a coloured drawing by William Smith, dated 1588, which is probably based on Hoefnagel or Agas or both. (*Early English Stages*, II.ii, Plate VI.6.)

The Norden Engravings

In 1593 there appeared in John Norden's *Speculum Britanniae* an engraving of London and Westminster signed by Pieter Van den Keere, presumably from a survey of the same date. (*Early English Stages*, II, ii, Plate VII.8.) The earlier baiting rings are here replaced by a rebuilt bear-baiting house of three tiers and, south-east of it, a structure labelled "The play howse," most likely to be identified with the Rose. Revised drawings of Norden's London and Westminster maps appeared a few years later in a large panorama of London called *Civitas Londini* (1600). (The map exists in a unique copy in the Royal Library, Stockholm. See *Early English Stages*, II.ii, Plate VII.9.) The Rose is now labelled "The Stare," and "The Beare howse" has become the "Beargarden": Both are outfitted with a loft and a flag. And added to the scene are "the Globe" and "The Swane."

Visscher

J. C. Visscher's *View of London* (1616) exists in two copies, the first in the British Library and a second, imperfect copy in the Folger Shakespeare Library. Once widely accepted and reproduced, the Visscher engraving has been shown by Shapiro to be inaccurate and derivative.

Hollar's Sketch and Long View of London

Wenceslaus Hollar's *Long View of London* was published in 1647 and is generally considered to be the most accurate of the maps of London that we possess. (For a discussion of Hollar's reliability as an observer and draftsman, see

Hodges' *Shakespeare's Second Globe*, pp. 20–32: for a reproduction of the entire panorama see the same author's *Globe Restored*, Plate 4.) We possess as well a pencil sketch by Hollar of the Bankside, partially inked over (reproduced by Hodges in *Shakespeare's Second Globe*, fig. 12). The etching contains features not shown in the sketch, and it has therefore been postulated that while the sketch is undoubtedly the source of the etched version, Hollar elaborated the latter from memory. The fallibility of his memory may account too for the fact that the labels attached to the two playhouses in the Long View ("The Globe" and "Beere bayting h")—neither of which occurs in the sketch—have been accidentally interchanged. (The actual bear-baiting house was the dual-purpose Hope.) It is important to note this cross-labelling, for the error has not always been recognized. The first edition of John Cranford Adams' *Globe Playhouse*, for example, reproduces the wrong playhouse as the Globe. The error was corrected in the second edition in 1961.

The View of the City of London from the North towards the South

This engraving, preserved in the library of the University of Utrecht, depicts a theatre variously identified as either the Theatre or the Curtain. (The engraving is reproduced in *Early English Stages*, II.ii, Plate XXXII; also in *First Public Playhouse*, ed. Herbert Berry, figs. 1, 2.) In either case the engraving is significant in that it is the only known depiction of any of the earliest Elizabethan theatres, which were built north of the city rather than on the south bank.

While the evidence just outlined seems clear enough, a thorough examination and analysis of all the extant maps can be both difficult and confusing. Many of them have been assigned varying titles, artists, and dates; their sources are often obscure; and reproductions of them are sometimes imperfect. Their interpretation is complicated as well by their pictorial character. E. K. Chambers' observations are still to the point:

> They are not strict plans in two dimensions . . . but either drawings in full perspective, or bird's eye views in diminished perspective. The imaginary standpoint is always in the south [with the exception of the last example], and the pictorial aspect is emphasized in the foreground, with the result that, while the Bankside theatres, but not those north of the river, are generally indicated, this is rarely with a precision which renders it possible to locate them in relation to the thoroughfares amongst which they stand. This is more particularly the case since . . . it is probable that the details are often both conventionally represented and out of scale. [*Elizabethan Stage*, II, 353]

We ought not underestimate, nonetheless, what the maps and long views do tell us about the location, shape, and nature of the Bankside playhouses.

Theatre Interiors

The difficulties and controversies attending the exterior views of London theatres pale in comparison with those surrounding the very few extant illustra-

tions of the interior acting areas of Elizabethan theatres. One drawing in particular, DeWitt's drawing of the Swan theatre, stands at the centre of scholarly
debate over the reconstruction of the Elizabethan stage. Once we discard the
obviously irrelevant (see Chambers, II, 519–520), we are left with a total of
five drawings purporting to be of an Elizabethan stage: (*a*) DeWitt's drawing
of the Swan (1596), (*b*) a small vignette on the title-page of William Alabas-
ter's *Roxana* (1632), (*c*) another vignette on the title-page of Nathaniel Rich-
ards' *Messalina* (1640), (*d*) an engraved frontispiece to a collection of drolls
(short skits fashioned from comic scenes in older plays) by Francis Kirkman,
entitled *The Wits* (1672), and (*e*) an engraving of a stage in the *Microcosm* volume of Robert Fludd's *History of Two Worlds* (1619). All of them have served
as guides for the reconstruction of Elizabethan theatres, usually with little reason advanced why one was selected over another.

Both the *Roxana* vignette and the *Messalina* vignette feature a rear curtain
and a tapered stage bordered on three sides by a low railing. *Roxana* includes
figures of actors on the stage and in the balcony above what are evidently members of the audience. (Both vignettes, greatly enlarged, are included in *Early
English Stages*, II.ii, figs. 7, 8.) The tendency early in this century to overvalue
these two pieces of pictorial evidence has given way to the realization that the
only theatres of the period with which they could possibly correspond were those
converted from cockpits, that is, the Royal Cockpit before its conversion to a
regular theatre by Inigo Jones in 1629, and the Phoenix or Cockpit in Drury
Lane. (See Wickham, *Early English Stages*, II.ii, 82.) But there is no positive
evidence to indicate what they are supposed to represent.

The frontispiece to *The Wits* is equally puzzling. Again, there is no indication of what stage the picture is supposed to depict. In the 1673 edition of *The
Wits* Kirkman mentions that the Red Bull was a popular theatre for the performance of drolls, and this remark has sometimes been taken as evidence that the
engraving shows the stage of the Red Bull. We again find a thrust stage, un-
tapered this time, a rear curtain, and members of the audience in a balcony
above the rear stage. Characters from several different plays are shown on the
stage. But the presence of footlights and candelabra clearly suggests an indoor
stage and therefore that the Red Bull is not a likely candidate for the model. In
point of fact, it seems likely that the picture of the stage is as much a composite
as is the scene shown on the stage.

The foremost champion of the Fludd engraving and its relevance to the Elizabethan stage is Frances Yates, who first suggested it as a possible solution to
the problem of Shakespearean staging in *The Art of Memory* (1966) and elaborated her argument in *Theatre of the World* (1969). The drawing, which is
labelled "Theatrum Orbi," was first discussed in *Shakespeare Quarterly* (IX,
1958) by Richard Bernheimer, who suggested that it had little to do with Fludd's
text and actually represents a German building given some English characteristics for the use of English players. I. A. Shapiro, on the other hand, argues
that the drawing is of the Blackfriars theatre (*Shakespeare Studies* II, 1966).

Yates, whose treatment of Fludd and the Vitruvian tradition is most thorough (see above), believes that the label on the engraving means exactly what it translates to mean, and that it is the Globe that is represented:

Here [is] . . . a large central opening flanked by two other entrances. Here can be seen a terrace on the upper level. And here also is an upper chamber with windows. . . . We now see that the upper chamber with its windows was in the centre of the terrace, and that there were two entrances on to this terrace, symmetrically placed directly above the two side entrances to the main stage below. [*Theatre of the World*, pp. 137–138]

Yates is nevertheless too careful a scholar and too iconologically sophisticated to interpret the engraving out of context. "The Fludd theatre engraving," she writes,

can yield priceless information about the Elizabethan and Jacobean theatre, but only on its own terms. It forms part of a memory system, and an astral or magical memory system, and what it has to contribute of real information about the stage must be carefully sifted from the distortions due to the strange context in which it appears. [pp. 150–151]

Although there are issues to be raised with respect to Yates' interpretation of the engraving, it clearly represents a piece of pictorial evidence that must be accounted for.

The most frequently reproduced and discussed drawing of the interior of an Elizabethan theatre is that attributed to Johannes DeWitt, a Dutch visitor to London in 1596. DeWitt's manuscript *Observationes Londinenses*, to which was attached a sketch of the Swan theatre, is lost; and we are indebted for an extract from its contents and a copy of the drawing to the author's friend Arend van Buchell, who entered the material into a commonplace book now in the Utrecht University library (MS. Var. 355). The extract and the sketch were first published by K. T. Gaedertz in 1888. The drawing was published with an English commentary in the same year by Henry Benjamin Wheatley and reissued in the *Transactions* of the New Shakspere Society (No. 12, 1887—92, Pt. II). (The drawing has often been reproduced. The Latin text is provided by Chambers in *Elizabethan Stage*, II, 361–362; an English translation by Joseph Quincey Adams is printed in his *Shakespearean Playhouses*, pp. 167–168, and in Nagler's *Source Book in Theatrical History*, pp. 116–117.)

The significance of the find was not at first apparent, and even after its import began to be realized, the reaction of many scholars was to dismiss the drawing on the grounds that it could not be reconciled with their conceptions of the Elizabethan theatre. Ashley Thorndike in *Shakespeare's Theater* (1916), for example, writes:

It [the drawing] is of uncertain date, based on hearsay evidence, drawn from description and not from direct observation. . . . It is . . . self-contradictory . . . there is no sign of curtains such as appear in other pictures of Elizabethan stages. . . . It should be adjudged as a hasty and self-contradictory drawing on hearsay evidence of the interior of a playhouse that was virtually abandoned for plays within a few years after it was built. [pp. 53–54]

The sceptical note continues in a slightly more cautious tone in John Cranford Adams: "The Swan sketch . . . must always be approached with reservations, for it abounds in so many contradictions, omissions, and obvious errors that no reliance can be placed upon any detail unless that detail is sustained by evidence from other sources" (*The Globe Playhouse*, p. 49). Bernard Beckerman also has reservations: "However plausible the suggestions for additions [to the drawing] may be, they cannot still the doubt with which one is obliged to regard the sketch, and though DeWitt's testimony cannot be ignored, it cannot be accepted without corroboration" (*Shakespeare at the Globe*, p. 100).

Against this negative response has been a growing opinion that the Swan drawing represents prime evidence and that the burden of proof lies on the sceptics. This line was taken by Chambers in *The Elizabethan Stage*. "The Swan drawing is our one contemporary picture of the interior of a public playhouse," he writes, "and it is a dangerous business to explain away its evidence by an assumption of inaccurate observation on the part of DeWitt, merely because that evidence conflicts with subjective interpretations of stage-directions, arrived at in the course of the pursuit of a 'typical' stage" (II, 526). G. E. Bentley echoes the viewpoint: "Contradiction of any of the features of this sketch . . . should be received with scepticism unless accompanied by overwhelming evidence" (*Jacobean and Caroline Stage*, VI, 250). And in what is without doubt the most thorough survey of architectural precedents for the design of the Elizabethan playhouse, Glynne Wickham provides a context for an interpretation of the Swan drawing which, he argues, "has the advantage . . . of allowing us now to accept DeWitt's sketch of the Swan Theatre at its face value without modification, interpolation or any other unwarranted change" (*Early English Stages*, II.i, 204). It is unlikely that Wickham's theory of the dumping of the actors' scaffold, screen, and "houses" into the standard three-tiered Tudor game-house as the principle underlying the structure of the Elizabethan public theatre will be universally accepted, but it does solve many of the problems associated with the Swan drawing.

DeWitt's sketch does present problems of interpretation. Specifically, scholars have found it difficult to explain the following features: (*a*) the two shaded shapes under the stage on each side; (*b*) the presence of human figures in the balcony behind the stage (actors? spectators?); and (*c*) the absence of anything resembling an "inner stage." To these areas of concern may be added the question of how the wall of the tiring house is joined to the adjacent galleries: Does it stand out from the curve or is it flush with the galleries? The seeming shortcomings of DeWitt's sketch have been variously explained: The picture represents a composite impression of the theatre (Beckerman); DeWitt simply did not bother with all the details (Hosley); the drawing in fact represents the Swan stage as DeWitt saw it (Wickham). The most persuasive explanation, however, is that the drawing follows the conventions of "simultaneous representation" and was intended to show how the theatre worked. (See John B. Gleason, *Shakespeare Quarterly* XXXII [1981], 324–338).

Even if we are inclined to accept Wickman's view, of course, we are not bound to assume that the Swan features were typical of any playhouse other than the Swan. It may in fact be true that the Swan represents a unique experiment that failed. On the other hand, we ought also to remember that of the four playhouses he saw (the Theatre, Curtain, Rose, and Swan) DeWitt considered the Swan "the largest and the most magnificent." It is difficult to believe that its magnificence was a function of the paucity of its facilities. Whatever the truth of the matter, we are unlikely to be able to reconstruct the essence of an Elizabethan public stage without taking this single most important piece of evidence into account.

Ground Plans and Elevations

Most of these are late, related to court theatres, and are attributed in the main to the architect and scene designer Inigo Jones (1573–1652) and his pupil John Webb (1611–72). Recent reinterpretations of some of the plans have, nevertheless, suggested wider implications concerning the general development of Elizabethan theatre architecture.

In the library of Worcester College, Oxford, are several manuscript drawings attributed to Jones and Webb, including the following:

a. Two drawings, one above the other, each representing a *frons scaenae* and a section of the auditorium, evidently copied from Palladio's original design for the Teatro Olimpico, which Jones had procured on a visit to Vicenza in 1613.

b. The left-hand side of the same sheets (the Palladio copies are on the right side) contains the plan of a theatre and the elevation of a *frons scaenae*. (The drawings are reproduced in Leacroft, *Development of the English Playhouse*, fig. 45.) Unfortunately, there is nothing to indicate what theatre the drawings were intended to represent.

In the same collection of drawings are two further sheets, catalogued under "Barber-Surgeons' Hall." they consist of (1) a drawing of an elliptical "amphitheatrum," (2) an elevation and plan, and (3) two cross-sections of a theatre. An anatomy theatre was in fact designed and built by Jones for the Livery Company of Barber-Surgeons between 1635 and 1639, and little attention was paid to the drawings until D. F. Rowan of the University of New Brunswick published them with an interpretive commentary in *New Theatre Magazine* (1969). The elevation and plan and the two cross-sections bear little resemblance to the amphitheatrum, or to other drawings of the hall, and it is now generally agreed that they were incorrectly catalogued. (See Leacroft, fig. 47–50; Wickham, *Early*

English Stages, II.ii, Plates XXIV, XXV.) Rowan and others have noted the stylistic resemblance between the Barber-Surgeon drawings and Jones' plans for the Cockpit-in-Court (see below). And Rowan argues that the drawings, which seem to combine the Swan and the Teatro Olimpico, represent a theatrical missing-link between the Swan and the Cockpit-in-Court and thus serve to fill in our picture of the Elizabethan stage. (See his article in *Renaissance Drama* n.s., IV, 1971.) It is still not clear, however, whether the plans were for a proposed or an executed structure. Rowan offers no suggestions, although Wickham postulates in *Early English Stages* (II.ii, 145–147) that the two sets of drawings fit the specifications for the Salisbury Court theatre, erected in 1629.

The most discussed of the drawings in the Worcester College collection are those of the Cockpit-in-Court. (They are reproduced in Leacroft, fig. 21; Bentley, VI, 276–277; Wickham, II, ii, Plates XIX-XXI; Orgel and Strong, *Inigo Jones*, I, fig. III.) The drawings have been known since 1901, but it has not always been clear whether they were the work of Jones or of his pupil, Webb. They were originally believed to have been by Jones and to depict the new theatre built in Whitehall, it was thought, about 1622. This was the position of Joseph Quincey Adams in *Shakespearean Playhouses* (1917) and of Chambers in *Elizabethan Stage*. The attribution was challenged, however, and several scholars—Lily B. Campbell in *Scenes and Machines on the English Stage* (1923), Eleanore Boswell in *Restoration Court Stage* (1932), Allardyce Nicoll in *Stuart Masques* (1938)—either argued or assumed that the plan and elevation were by Webb and depicted the Cockpit-in-Court as renovated in November 1660. Accounts for that year in the Office of the Works (quoted in Boswell, *Restoration Court Stage*, p. 239) seem to support the theory. Further work in the accounts by F. P. Wilson uncovered records relating to building activities within the Cockpit playhouse in Whitehall between 1629 and 1632, which help to demonstrate that the drawings were in fact by Jones, and that they refer to the conversion of the Cockpit-in-Court to a proper theatre in 1629–30. (The accounts are printed by Bentley in *Jacobean and Caroline Stage*, VI, 271–273.) The identification of the drawings with the theatre of the 1629–32 accounts makes the Cockpit-in-Court the best documented playhouse of the period. And the significance of the theatre and the plans for it is enhanced by the possibility that the theatre was intended for professional rather than amateur actors, and that it reflects traditional Elizabethan stage architecture in its essentials. (See Wickham, *Shakespeare's Dramatic Heritage*, pp. 151–162, and Rowan in *Elizabethan Theatre*, ed. D. Galloway, pp. 89–102).

Other drawings by Jones or Webb in the collection of the Duke of Devonshire at Chatworth include a sketch of a proscenium arch and perspective scene labelled "for yė cokpitt for my lo Chaberalen 1639." It is uncertain what Cockpit is being referred to, the Cockpit-in-Court, the Phoenix, or another. A drawing closely resembling this "cokpitt" sketch is preserved in the Wren collection at All Souls, Oxford, catalogued as a "Lecture Theatre Repository for the College of Physicians." Again, its provenance and purpose are uncertain. It is sometimes taken as a preliminary sketch for Thomas Killigrew's first Theatre Royal in Drury Lane (1663); but Leacroft thinks it may be a sketch for an adaptation of the Great Hall at Whitehall. (See Leacroft's *Development of the English Playhouse*, fig. 58.) A final drawing from the collection are the plan and section of a stage at Whitehall, done by Webb for a production of Roger Boyle's *Mustapha* (1665). (See Leacroft, fig. 55.)

The Banqueting House at Whitehall, at least the one in use between 1606 and 1619, is represented in a ground floor plan prepared by Robert Smythson in 1618 (reproduced in Orgel and Strong, fig. B) and in a plan, elevation, and section in the British Library (Lansdowne 1171) for the auditorium and stage for the performance in 1635 of *Florimene* (Orgel and Strong, figs. 321–324). Lansdowne 1171 also contains a drawing of the stage for William Davenant's *Salmacida Spolia*, performed in 1640 in a temporary masquing room at Whitehall. (See Nicoll, *Stuart Masques*, figs. 78, 79.) An unidentified plan, also in the British Library, perhaps intended for a specially designed masque theatre, shows a T-shaped hall, but little else can be said about it (Leacroft, fig. 40). Finally, in the Huntington Library in Pasadena, California, is a rough drawing of a ground plan and stage for Mildmay Fane's *Candy Restored* (1641), performed at Fane's home at Apthorpe. The scenic arrangements are interesting, but the private nature of the performance does not suggest any far-reaching significance. (See the edition of *Candy Restored* by Clifford Leech, and Nicoll, *Stuart Masques*, fig. 40.)

Masques: Scene and Costume Designs

The designs of Inigo Jones for the masques performed at the Court of James I and Charles I during the years 1605–40 represent almost the entirety of extant scene and costume designs of the period. The great bulk of them are preserved in the Duke of Devonshire's library at Chatsworth, catalogued in 1924 by Percy Simpson and C. F. Bell in *Designs by Inigo Jones for Masques and Plays at Court*. Simpson and Bell identified and reproduced many of the designs, but their work has to a large extent been superseded by that of Stephen Orgel and Roy Strong, whose *Inigo Jones: The Theatre of the Stuart Court* appeared in 1973. They include a total of 482 drawings, ten of them originally executed in colour, representing the designs for twenty-three masques, three pastorals, and two plays. Designs for two masques are complete: William Davenant's *Britannia Triumphans* (1638) and *Salmacida Spolia* (1640). Orgel and Strong point out as well that the scenes for these masques, as for almost every scene done between 1630 and 1640, were copied in detail from the Parigi designs for Florentine *intermezzi*.

John Webb continued to design for dramatic productions, and several of his drawings are in the Chatsworth collection as well, including five scenes for Davenant's *Siege of Rhodes* (1656) and four scenes for *Mustapha* (1665). Two others were probably intended for the same production.

We saw in our previous considerations of scene designs that a certain amount of caution is essential to their proper interpretation as production documents. Jones' designs are no exception to this rule. Most of them are original drawings and not engravings, but a true appreciation of their theatrical value depends still on a knowledge of stage mechanics in the seventeenth century. Earlier, we considered some of the sources for such knowledge, and it is in the light of Italian theatre practise that Allardyce Nicoll attempts to interpret English scene designs in *Stuart Masques*. He offers an appropriate warning:

A scenic artist's sketch is at best nothing but the basis for a setting, and to interpret it, to translate its vague terms into actual stage proportions, demands more than simple aesthetic appreciation. A canvas or a mural painting is complete in itself; its destiny is achieved when it leaves the painter's hands. Not so a scenic design, which exists for an ultimate purpose not yet realized when it itself is completed; its intent must always presuppose the creation of some other thing guided by its directions. To judge these designs rightly, therefore, we must know the precise methods by which the artist intended his primal conception to become transmogrified into the theatrical scene. [*Stuart Masques*, pp. 25–26]

Miscellaneous Pictorial Evidence

Four unrelated pieces of graphic evidence complete our present survey:

a. Henslowe's sketch of a proscenium stage (Dulwich College MS. I. 14) remains an enigma. We do not know what it is supposed to represent.

b. Leslie Hotson, in *Shakespeare's Wooden O*, draws attention to an undated engraving found in a manuscript journal of a Dutch East India Company agent who was in London during the years 1629–36, which he insists shows the Fortune theatre under construction some time before the autumn of 1600 (Appendix C, pp. 310–313). Bentley dismisses the identification as "most ingenious but scarcely convincing" (*Jacobean and Caroline Stage*, VI, 145).

c. Among the manuscripts in the library of the Marquess of Bath at Longleat is to be found a drawing of a scene from Shakespeare's *Titus Andronicus*, evidently showing Tamora pleading with Titus to spare her two sons, kneeling behind her. Behind the sons is the black figure of Aaron the Moor, and at Titus' back are two Roman soldiers. On a separate page is the endorsement, "Henrye Peachams Hande 1595." E. K. Chambers first published the sketch in in *The Library* (March, 1925) and since that time it has been reproduced a multitude of times and cited as the earliest known illustration of a Shakespearean scene. The costumes in particular—a mixture of "Roman" dress on the principals and decidedly Elizabethan garb on the soldiers—have prompted discussion of Elizabethan costuming of historical plays. Actually, it is not certain which Peacham is supposed to be responsible for the drawing, the father or the son; and the details of the sketch do not coincide with details of the play. Some scholars have doubted the drawing's authenticity.

d. The 1615 edition of Thomas Kyd's *The Spanish Tragedy* incorporates on its title-page a woodcut depicting the murder of Horatio. The young man's body is shown hanging in the "arbour," a trellis-work arch adorned with leaves. This has sometimes been taken as an alternative to a curtained inner-stage as a method of "discovering" something.

There has been little enough pictorial evidence concerning the Elizabethan theatre to come down to us, and even among the material that has survived there are relatively few instances of unquestionable authenticity and import. We can point to Hollar's *Long View*, DeWitt's drawings of the Swan, and Jones' plans for the Cockpit-in-Court and his masque designs. We are on less sure ground with the Fludd engraving, the Barber-Surgeon drawings, and the *Titus* sketch. Other pictures either must be used in the context of other evidence or must remain in limbo until or unless their meaning can be established.

CONCLUSION

In spite of the vast amounts of effort and erudition expended on the Elizabethan theatre, and in spite of the staggering amount of information we have concerning it, in one crucial respect we are still floundering. We still cannot agree on the facilities of Elizabethan theatres or on the essentials of an Elizabethan performance. This uncertainty is reflected in the on-going emphasis on reconstructions of the various Elizabethan theatres; and it helps to explain too the never-ending wrangling over the DeWitt drawing of the Swan theatre. In fact, the Swan drawing is both literally and symbolically at the centre of Elizabethan stage studies. For not only do reconstructions differ principally on the basis of acceptance or non-acceptance of the sketch, but the questions it raises are central to the understanding of Elizabethan dramaturgy, to an appreciation of the dynamics of Elizabethan theatrical performance, to the interpretation of Elizabethan dramatic texts, and to a determination of the relationship of the Elizabethan theatre to the medieval theatre and to the Restoration theatre. Until these issues are clarified, we cannot be sure of our answers to the broader questions of the intellectual, social, and cultural significance of the Elizabethan theatre. There are few clearer examples of the way in which, however far afield a theatre historian might legitimately be led, studies must in the final analysis center on the primary styles and conditions of performance.

REFERENCES

Adams, John Cranford. *The Globe Playhouse*. 2d ed. New York, 1961.[1942]
Adams, Joseph Quincey. *The Dramatic Records of Sir Henry Herbert*. New Haven, 1917.
———. *Shakespearean Playhouses*. Boston, 1917.
Albright, Victor E. *The Shakespearean Stage*. New York, 1909.
Armstrong, William A. *The Elizabethan Private Theatres: Facts and Problems*. Society for Theatre Research Pamphlet no. 6. London, 1958.
Beckerman, Bernard. Review of T. J. King. *Shakespearean Staging 1599–1642*. In *Renaissance Drama* n.s. IV (1971), 237–244.
———. *Shakespeare at the Globe 1599–1609*. New York, 1962.

Bentley, Gerald Eades. *The Jacobean and Caroline Stage*. 7 Vols. Oxford, 1941–68.
———. *The Profession of Dramatist in Shakespeare's Time 1590–1642*. Princeton, 1971.
———, ed. *The Seventeenth-Century Stage: A Collection of Critical Essays*. Chicago, 1968.
Berry, Herbert, ed. *The First Public Playhouse: The Theatre in Shoreditch 1576–1598*. Montreal, 1979.
Birch, W. de G., ed. *Historical Charters and Constitutional Documents of the City of London*. London, 1887.
Boswell, Eleanore. *The Restoration Court Stage*. Cambridge, Mass., 1932.
Bradbrook, M. C. *Elizabethan Stage Conditions*. Cambridge, 1932.
———. *The Rise of the Common Player*. London, 1962.
Brodmeier, Cecil. *Die Shakespeare-Bühne Nache den Alten Buhnenweisungen*. Weimar, 1904.
Campbell, Lily B. *Scenes and Machines on the English Stage during the Renaissance: A Classical Revival*. New York, 1923.
Chalmers, George. *An Apology for Believers in the Shakespeare-Papers*. London, 1799.
———. *A Supplemental Apology for the Believers in the Shakespeare-Papers*. London, 1799.
Chambers, E. K. *The Elizabethan Stage*. 4 Vols. Oxford, 1923.
Collier, John Payne. *The History of English Dramatic Poetry to the Time of Shakespeare: And Annals of the Stage to the Restoration*. 3 Vols. London, 1831.
Crosfield, Thomas. *The Diary of Thomas Crosfield*. Ed. F. S. Boas. Oxford, 1935.
Dasent, J. R., ed. *Acts of the Privy Council of England*. 32 Vols. London, 1890–1907.
Downes, John. *Roscius Anglicanus: Or an Historical Review of the Stage*. Ed. Arthur Freeman. New York and London, 1974.[1708]
The English Stage: Attack and Defense 1577–1730. Prefaces by Arthur Freeman. 50 Vols. New York and London, 1973–74.
Evans, H. A. *English Masques*. London, 1897.
Ewbank, Inga-Stina. " 'The Eloquence of Masques': A Retrospective View of Masque Criticism." *Renaissance Drama* n.s. I (1968), 307–327.
Felver, Charles S. "The *Commedia Dell' Arte* and English Drama in the Sixteenth and Early Seventeenth Centuries." *Research Opportunities in Renaissance Drama* VI (1963), 24–34.
Feuillerat, A. *Documents Relating to the Office of the Revels in the Time of Queen Elizabeth*. Materialien zur kunde des alteren Englischen Dramas XXI. Louvain, 1908.
———. *Documents Relating to the Revels at Court in the Time of King Edward VI and Queen Mary*. Materialien zur kunde des alteren Englischen Dramas XLIV. Louvain, 1914.
Fleay, Frederick Gard. *A Chronicle History of the London Stage 1559–1642*. London, 1890.
Flecknoe, Richard. *Love's Kingdom, A Pastoral Trage-Comedy with a Short Treatise of the English Stage*. Preface by Arthur Freeman. New York and London, 1973.[1664]
Foakes, R. A., ed. *The Henslowe Papers*. [Facsimile] 2 Vols. London, 1977.
Foakes, R. A., and R. T. Rickert, eds. *Henslowe's Diary*. Cambridge, 1961.
Galloway, David, ed. *The Elizabethan Theatre*. Toronto, 1969.
Ganzel, Dewey. *Fortune and Men's Eyes: The Career of John Payne Collier*. Oxford, 1982.
Gildersleeve, Virginia C. *Government Regulation of the Elizabethan Drama*. New York, 1908.

Gildon, Charles. "Essay on the Art, Rise and Progress of the English Stage." In *The Works of Mr. William Shakespear*. Ed. Nicholas Rowe. London, 1709.

Gleason, John B. "The Dutch Humanist Origins of the De Witt Drawing of the Swan Theatre." *Shakespeare Quarterly* XXXII (1981), 324–338.

Greg, W. W. *A Bibliography of the English Printed Drama to the Restoration.* 4 Vols. London, 1939–59.

————. *Dramatic Documents from the Elizabethan Playhouses.* 2 Vols. Oxford, 1931.

————. *A List of Masques, Pageants, etc. Supplementary to a List of English Plays.* London, 1902.

————. *The Shakespeare First Folio: Its Bibliographical and Textual History.* Oxford, 1955.

————, ed. *Henslowe's Diary.* 2 Vols. London, 1904-08.

————, ed. *Henslowe's Papers.* London, 1907.

Griffin, Alice V. *Pageantry on the Shakespearean Stage.* New Haven, 1951.

Gurr, Andrew. *The Shakespearean Stage 1574–1642.* Cambridge, 1970.

Halliday, F. E. *The Cult of Shakespeare.* New York, 1957.

Halliwell-Phillipps, J. O. *Outlines of the Life of Shakespeare.* 3d ed. London, 1883.

Harbage, Alfred, and S. Schoenbaum. *Annals of English Drama 975–1700.* Rev. ed. London, 1964.

Hazlitt, W. C. *The English Drama and Stage under the Tudor and Stuart Princes 1543–1664.* Bath, 1832.

Herford, C. H. *A Sketch of Recent Shakespearean Investigation 1893–1923.* London, 1923.

Herford, C. H., and Percy Simpson, eds. *Ben Jonson.* 11 Vols. Oxford, 1925–52.

Hodges, C. Walter. *The Globe Restored.* 2d ed. London, 1968.

————. *Shakespeare's Second Globe: The Missing Monument.* Oxford, 1973.

————, Leonard Leone, and S. Schoenbaum, eds. *The Third Globe: Symposium for the Reconstruction of the Globe Playhouse.* Detroit, 1981.

Honigmann, E. A. J., ed. *The Masque of Flowers.* In *A Book of Masques in Honour of Allardyce Nicoll.* Ed. T. J. B. Spencer. Cambridge, 1967.

Hosley, Richard. "The Discovery-Space in Shakespeare's Globe." *Shakespeare Survey* XII (1959), 35–46.

————. "An Elizabethan Tiring-House Facade." *Shakespeare Quarterly* IX (1958), 588.

————. "The Gallery over the Stage in the Public Playhouse of Shakespeare's Time." *Shakespeare Quarterly*, VIII (1957), 15–31.

————. "The Origins of the Shakespearean Playhouse." *Shakespeare Quarterly* XV (1964), 29–40.

————. "The Playhouses and the Stage." In *A New Companion to Shakespeare Studies.* Ed. Kenneth Muir and S. Schoenbaum. Cambridge, 1971.

————. "The Theatre and the Tradition of Playhouse Design." In *The First Public Playhouse.* Ed. Herbert Berry. Montreal, 1979.

Hotson, Leslie. *The First Night of Twelfth Night.* London, 1954.

————. *Shakespeare's Wooden O.* New York, 1959.

Ingleby, C. M. *A Complete View of the Shakspere Controversy.* London, 1861.

Isaacs, J. *Production and Stage-Management at the Blackfriars Theatre.* London, 1933.

Joseph, B. L. *Elizabethan Acting.* Rev. ed. London, 1964.

Kempe, A. J. *The Loseley Manuscripts. Manuscripts and Other Rare Documents . . . Preserved at Loseley House.* London, 1835.

Kernodle, George R. *From Art to Theatre: Form and Convention in the Renaissance*. Chicago, 1944.

King, Thomas James. "Production of Plays at the Phoenix, 1617–42." Columbia University Dissertation, 1963.

————. Review of Irwin Smith, *Shakespeare's Blackfriars Playhouse*. In *Renaissance Drama* IX (1966), 291–309.

————. *Shakespearean Staging 1599–1642*. Cambridge, Mass., 1971.

————. "The Stage in the Time of Shakespeare: A Survey of Major Scholarship." *Renaissance Drama* n.s. IV (1971), 199–235.

Kolin, Philip C. Review of Ernest L. Rhodes, *Henslowe's Rose*. In *Educational Theatre Journal* XXIX (1977), 433–434.

————, and R. O. Wyatt II. "A Bibliography of Scholarship on the Elizabethan Stage since Chambers." *Research Opportunities in Renaissance Drama* XV-XVI (1972–73), 33–59.

Langbaine, Gerard. *An Account of the English Dramatick Poets*. Preface by Arthur Freeman. New York, 1973.[1691]

Lawrence, W. J. *The Physical Conditions of the Elizabethan Public Playhouse*. Cambridge, Mass., 1927.

————. *Pre-Restoration Stage Studies*. Cambridge, Mass., 1927.

Leacroft, Richard. *The Development of the English Playhouse*. London, 1973.

Leech, Clifford, ed. *Mildmay Fane's Raguaillo D'Oceano 1640, and Candy Restored 1641*. Materials for the Study of the Old English Drama n.s. XV. Louvain, 1938.

McGee, C. E., and John Meagher. "Preliminary Checklist of Tudor and Stuart Entertainments: 1558–1603." *Research Opportunities in Renaissance Drama* XXIV (1981), 51–155.

Machym, Henry. *The Diary*. Ed. John Gough Nichols. Camden Society. London, 1842.

Malone, Edmond. "An Historical Account of the Rise and Progress of the English Stage and of the Economy and Usages of our Ancient Theatres." In his *Plays and Poems of William Shakespeare* (London, 1790, 1803) vol. I. Also in *The Plays and Poems of William Shakespeare, with Corrections and Illustrations of Various Commentators: Comprehending a Life of the Poet, and an Enlarged History of the Stage, by the Late Edmond Malone*, ed. James Boswell (London, 1921), vol. III. [Malone's edition is commonly referred to as his *Variorum Shakespeare*.]

Malone Society. *Collections I-XI*. Oxford, 1907–1980.

Marcham, Frank. *The King's Office of the Revels 1610–1622*. London, 1925.

Muir, Kenneth, and S. Schoenbaum, eds. *A New Companion to Shakespeare Studies*. Cambridge, 1971.

Mullin, Donald C. *The Development of the Playhouse: A Survey of Theatre Architecture from the Renaissance to the Present*. Berkeley and Los Angeles, 1970.

Murray, John Tucker. *English Dramatic Companies 1558–1642*. 2 vols. London, 1910.

Nagler, A. M. *Shakespeare's Stage*. New Haven and London, 1958.

————, ed. *A Source Book in Theatrical History*. New York, 1959.[1952]

Nicoll, Allardyce. *Stuart Masques and the Renaissance Stage*. London, 1938.

————. "Studies in the Elizabethan Stage since 1900." *Shakespeare Survey* I (1948), 1–16.

Nungezer, Edwin. *A Dictionary of Actors*. New Haven, 1929.

Ordish, Thomas Fairman. *Early London Theatres (in the Fields)*. Foreword C. Walter Hodges. London, 1971.[1894]

Orgel, Stephen. "What Is a Text?" *Research Opportunities in Renaissance Drama* XXIV (1981), 3–6.

Orgel, Stephen, and Roy Strong. *Inigo Jones: The Theatre of the Stuart Court.* 2 Vols. London, 1973.

Orrell, John. "Amerigo Salvetti and the London Court Theatre, 1616–1640." *Theatre Survey* XX (1979), 1–26.

———. "The London Court Stage in the Savoy Correspondence, 1613–1675." *Theatre Research International* n.s. IV (1979), 79–94.

———. "The London Stage in the Florentine Correspondence, 1604–1618." *Theatre Research International* n.s. III (1978), 157–176.

Overall, W. H., and H. C., Overall, eds. *Analytical Index to the Series of Records Known as the Remembrancia, Preserved among the Archives of the City of London A.D. 1579–1664,* London, 1878.

Palme, Per. *Triumph of Peace: A Study of the Whitehall Banqueting House.* London, 1957.

Paterson, Morton. "The Stagecraft of the Revels Office during the Reign of Elizabeth as Suggested by Documents Relating to the Office." In *Studies in the Elizabethan Theatre.* Ed. Charles T. Prouty. Hamden, Conn., 1961.

Prouty, Charles T., ed. *Studies in the Elizabethan Theatre.* Hamden, Conn., 1961.

Reynolds, George F. Review of John Cranford Adams, "*The Globe Playhouse.*" In *Journal of English and Germanic Philology* XLII (1943), 124–126.

———. *The Staging of Elizabethan Plays at the Red Bull Theatre 1605–1625.* New York, 1940.

Rhodes, Ernest L. *Henslowe's Rose: The Stage and Staging.* Lexington, Kentucky, 1976.

Rowan, D. F. "The Cockpit-in-Court." In *The Elizabethan Theatre.* Ed. David Galloway. Toronto, 1969.

———. "The English Playhouse: 1595–1630." *Renaissance Drama* n.s. IV (1971), 37–51.

———. "A Neglected Jones/Webb Theatre Project: 'Barber-Surgeons' Hall Writ Large.' " *New Theatre Magazine* IX (1969), 6–15.

———. "A Neglected Jones/Webb Theatre Project, Part II: A Theatrical Missing Link." In *The Elizabethan Theatre II.* Ed. David Galloway. Toronto, 1970.

Rymer, Thomas. *A Short View of Tragedy.* London, 1693.

Sabol, Andrew J. *Four Hundred Songs and Dances from the Stuart Masque.* Providence, Rhode Island, 1978.

Salgādo, Gāmini, ed. *Eyewitnesses of Shakespeare: First Hand Accounts of Performances 1590–1890.* London and Toronto, 1975.

Salomon, Brownell. "Visual and Aural Signs in the Performed English Renaissance Play." *Renaissance Drama* n.s. V (1972), 143–169.

Schoenbaum, S. *Internal Evidence and Elizabethan Dramatic Authorship.* Evanston, Ill., 1966.

Seltzer, Daniel. "The Actors and Staging." In *A New Companion to Shakespeare Studies.* Ed. Kenneth Muir and S. Schoenbaum. Cambridge, 1971.

Shakespeare Society Papers. 4 vols. London, 1844–49.

Shapiro, I. A. "The Bankside Theatres: Early Engravings." *Shakespeare Survey* I (1948), 25–37.

———. "An Original Drawing of the Globe Theatre." *Shakespeare Survey* II (1949), 21–23.

———. "Robert Fludd's Stage-Illustration." *Shakespeare Studies* II (1966), 192–209.

Shapiro, Michael. "Annotated Bibliography on Original Staging in Elizabethan Plays." *Research Opportunities in Renaissance Drama* XXIV (1981), 23–49.

Simpson, Percy. *Shakespearian Punctuation*. London, 1911.

Simpson, Percy, and C. F. Bell. *Designs by Inigo Jones for Masques and Plays at Court*. New York, 1966.[1924]

Sisson, C. J. *The Boars Head Theatre: An Inn-Yard Theatre of the Elizabethan Age*. Ed. Stanley Wells. London, 1972.

Smith, G. Gregory, ed. *Elizabethan Critical Essays*. 2 Vols. Oxford, 1904.

Smith, Irwin. *Shakespeare's Globe Playhouse: A Modern Reconstruction*. New York, 1964.

———. *Shakespeare's Globe Playhouse: A Modern Reconstruction*. New York, 1956.

Southern, Richard. *The Staging of Plays before Shakespeare*. London, 1973.

Speaight, Robert. *Shakespeare on the Stage*. London, 1973.

———. *William Poel and the Elizabethan Revival*. Cambridge, Mass., 1954.

Stamp, A. E. *The Disputed Revels Accounts*. Oxford, 1930.

State Papers. *Calendar of State Papers and Manuscripts, Relating to English Affairs, Existing in the Archives and Collections of Venice, and in other Libraries of Northern Italy (1202–1668)*. Ed. Rawdon Brown, G. C. Bentinck, H. F. Brown, and A. B. Hinds. 35 Vols. London, 1864–1935.

———. *Calendar of State Papers, Domestic Series, during the Commonwealth, 1649–1660*. Ed. M. A. E. Green. 13 Vols. London, 1875–1886.

———. *Calendar of State Papers, Domestic Series, of the Reign of Charles I, 1625–1649*. Ed. J. Bruce and W. D. Hamilton. 23 Vols. London, 1858–97.

———. *Calendar of State Papers, Domestic Series, of Edward VI, Mary, Elizabeth and James I, 1547–1625*. Ed. R. Lemon and M. A. E. Green. 12 Vols. London, 1856–72.

———. *Calendar of Letters and Papers, Foreign and Domestic, of the Reign of Henry VIII*. Ed. J. S. Brewer, J. Gairdner, and R. H. Brodie. London, 1862.

Statutes of the Realm. Record Commission. 11 Vols. in 12. London, 1963.[1810–28]

Steele, Mary S. *Plays and Masques at Court during the Reigns of Elizabeth, James, and Charles*. New Haven, 1926.

Stevens, David. *English Renaissance Theatre History: A Reference Guide*. Boston, 1982.

Stinson, James. "Reconstructions of Elizabethan Playhouses." In *Studies in the Elizabethan Theatre*. Ed. Charles T. Prouty. Hamden, Conn., 1961.

Streitburger, W. R. "Renaissance Revels Documents, 1485–1642." *Research Opportunities in Renaissance Drama* XXI (1978), 11–16.

Sturgess, Keith. Review of Ernest L. Rhodes, *Henslowe's Rose*. In *Theatre Research International* III (1978), 216–218.

Styan, J. L. *Shakespeare's Stagecraft*. Cambridge, 1967.

Sullivan, Mary A. *Court Masques of James I*. Lincoln, Nebraska, 1913.

Tannenbaum, Samuel A. *Shakspere Forgeries in the Revels Accounts*. New York, 1928.

———. *Shakspere Studies*. New York, n.d.

Thorndike, Ashley H. *Shakespeare's Theater*. New York, 1916.

Turpyn., Richard (?). *Chronicle of Calais*. Ed. J. G. Nichols. London, 1846.

Wallace, Charles W. *The Children of the Chapel at Blackfriars, 1597–1603*. Lincoln, Nebraska, 1908.

———. *The Evolution of the English Drama up to Shakespeare*. Berlin, 1912.

Warner, G. F. *Catalogue of Manuscripts and Muniments of Alleyn's College of God's Gift*. London, 1881. [Vol. II by F. B. Bickley, 1903.]

Warner, Rebecca. *Epistolary Curiosities, Consisting of Unpublished Letters of the Seventeenth Century Illustrative of the Herbert Family*. Bath, 1818.

Welsford, Enid. *The Court Masque*. New York, 1927.

Wickham, Glynne. *Early English Stages 1300–1600*. 3 Vols. in 4. London, 1959–81.

———. *Shakespeare's Dramatic Heritage*. London, 1969.

Wilson, J. Dover. " 'Titus Andronicus' on the Stage in 1595." *Shakespeare Survey* I (1948), 17–22.

Wilson, John Dover, ed. *Hamlet*. The New Shakespeare. 2d ed. Cambridge, 1936.

Wright, James. *Historia Histrionica*. Ed. Arthur Freeman. New York and London, 1974.[1699]

Yates, Frances. *The Art of Memory*. London and Chicago, 1966.

———. *Theatre of the World*. Chicago, 1969.

5

THE CLASSICAL THEATRE OF FRANCE

SCHOLARSHIP

Historians of the theatre traditionally date the advent of the French classical theatre from the 1630s, when the early plays of Pierre Corneille and especially the quarrel over *Le Cid* helped to establish the dramatic unities as the *sine qua non* of the French drama. French classicism is deemed to have reached a zenith in the work of Molière and Racine, but it continued to dominate European theatrical practice throughout the eighteenth century and even later. Italian precept became French practice, and thus the last of the Renaissance theatres became the first of the neoclassical theatres. It is from such a perspective that the theatre of the sixteenth and early seventeenth centuries is normally interpreted. Efforts are made to trace the influence of Italian theorists on French writers and to chart the gradual development of French classical theatre away from the passion plays, *sotties*, *moralités*, and farces of the medieval stage. The period prior to 1635 can be divided roughly into three segments: pre–1550, ca. 1550–ca. 1600, and ca. 1600–ca. 1635.

The sixteenth century before 1552, the date of Etienne Jodelle's *Cléopâtre captive* (usually considered to mark the beginning of regular French tragedy), is a period during which the normal humanist activities sowed the seeds of a new theatre: Greek plays were translated into Latin and then French; original plays, especially tragedies, were composed in Latin (e.g. George Buchanan's *Jephthes*, ca. 1540). At the same time theatrical performance was dominated by medieval staging practice. In Paris, the Confraternité de la Passion, a guild of amateur actors formed in 1402, staged productions of religious plays in various large halls. In 1548, the year in which the Confraternité built its own hall, the Hôtel de Bourgogne, it was also forbidden by the Parlement of Paris to perform religious plays. Thus, it is argued, the secular drama was free to de-

velop. During these years too a close relationship with Italy was encouraged by
Francis I (reigned 1515–47).

The period bweeen 1552 and the end of the sixteenth century is a period in
which, on the surface at least, the drama that was written most closely resem-
bles the academic and scholarly drama of sixteenth-century Italy. By 1600, semi-
professional companies were performing at the Hôtel de Bourgogne and at other
locations as well, such as *jeux de paume* (tennis courts). An edict of 1595
allowing actors to perform at the fairs of Saint-Germain and Saint-Laurent in
the suburbs of Paris also opened the way for companies to perform at other
places. Performance details during this half century—if indeed many of the plays
were in fact performed—are for the most part unclear, and the dramas of Jodelle, Grévin, La Taille, Garnier, Larivey, and Montchrestien have until fairly
recently been treated more as literary curiosities than as theatrical documents,
important only as evidence of the break in France with its medieval past and as
precursors of the true classicism which was to flourish in the seventeenth century. Several studies, however, have contributed to a somewhat revised view
of the period: Brian Jeffrey, *French Renaissance Comedy* (1969); Richard Griffiths, *Dramatic Technique of Antoine de Montchrestien* (1970): and Donald Stone,
Jr., *French Humanist Tragedy* (1974).

Stone, for instance, argues that

> Our analyses must lose much of their value as accurate accounts of the past if we accept
> *a priori* that the notion France in the sixteenth century broke with the Middle Ages to
> accomplish a Renaissance . . . which in turn prepared French Classicism. Can we be
> sure that the traits of French Classical Drama, so carefully tracked down in the early
> tragedies, were of any consequence to those authors who seem to have used them very
> sparingly? [pp. 3–4]

He points out that the oft-cited Italian influence is notoriously difficult to document, and that a comparison of dramatic treatments of similar subjects reveals
more differences than similarities. Freed from its earlier role as channel through
which Italian theory and practice were transmuted into French classicism, sixteenth-century French tragedy is able to speak for itself, in accents more in tune
with the fifteenth century than with the seventeenth. "Where we have been taught
to expect only inferior literature," writes Stone in his conclusion, "we discovered a vital aesthetic, consistent with what the period knew about tragedy and
about literature's purpose" (p. 210).

The last pre-classical period (ca. 1600–ca. 1635) is characterized by lively
professional activity at the Hôtel de Bourgogne, at the fairs, and at various *jeux
de paume*. (For a useful list of secondary playing places in Paris, see S. Wilma
Deierkauf-Holsboer, *L'Histoire de la mise en scène*, pp. 23–24.) It is the period of the theatre manager Valleran Le Comte (fl. 1590–ca. 1613), of the actress Marie Venier (fl. 1590–1619), and of the famous trio of farce actors, Turlupin, Gaultier-Garguille, and Gros-Guillaume. Above all, it is the period of
Alexandre Hardy (ca. 1575-ca. 1631), one of the earliest known professional

playwrights, as prolific as he was indifferent to the classical rules. Earlier estimates of Hardy's importance have been shown to have been exaggerated, but the rambling tragicomedies he wrote are nevertheless characteristic of these years. Yet during these same years, it is urged, dramatists and audiences alike were slowly being educated in the finer points of classical refinement and decorum in anticipation of Corneille, Molière, and Racine. A concomitant notion, attacked but not destroyed in 1957 by John Lough in *Paris Theatre Audiences*, has been that the impetus to "regular" drama was blocked during these years by the crude and plebiean nature of the audience, that it was not until 1625–35 that a new aristocratic audience emerged capable of appreciating the new, regular drama of Jean Mairet (*Sophonisbe*) and Pierre Corneille (*Le Cid*). The period has, nonetheless, proved difficult to assess: It has taken years of patient archival research to uncover the documents that have finally shed light on these eventful years.

The classical period itself is usually assumed to have peaked by 1677 with the production of Racine's *Phèdre*, but a less value-laden judgment might bring it to the end of the century with Racine's death in 1699, or even to 1715, the year that Louis XIV died. Whatever date we choose, it is true that by the end of the seventeenth century, French classical theatre had settled into competent mediocrity, and the form that had freed the genius of Moliére and Racine had rigidified into the dramatic rules and theatrical conventions that had defined that form.

We should note too that we are here concerned principally if not exclusively with Parisian theatre. The political, intellectual, and cultural centre of France, the city was the goal and the home of the greatest playwrights and actors of the classical period. It has certainly been the focus of historians of the French stage. Although for the years 1590–1710 well over 400 theatre companies outside Paris have been documented, we still know almost nothing of their repertory, their finances, their audiences, or the theatres they played in. The attention of scholars has centered almost exclusively on the five theatres and seven companies of Paris. This fact does not, of course, conflict with the practice of historians of the Spanish or English stages, who have concentrated with equal purpose on Madrid and London. What is remarkable in the case of France is the very late date (1629) at which an acting company was permanently established at the Hôtel de Bourgogne. Both Madrid and London had by this time had a flourishing theatrical life for half a century; London's theatre had in fact only a dozen years to run.

Historians of the ballet and dance, on the other hand, are able to trace the *ballet de cour* from the year 1553, when this courtly entertainment—a combination of the Italian *intermedii* and *trionfi* and ballroom dancing—was imported for the wedding of Catherine de'Medici and Henri II. The new form was given a literary pedigree by the humanist dramatist Etienne Jodelle, who wrote his *Mascarade des Argonautes* in 1558. This first phase culminated in the well-documented *Ballet comique de la reine* (1581), in which poetry, music, and dance were united into a complex dramatic whole. While the dramatic and spectacular elements of the *Ballet comique* were never again so elaborately exploited, court ballets or *mascarades*, in several forms—*ballets melodramatiques, ballets à entrées*—continued through the reign of Henri IV (1589–1610) and during the first part of the reign of Louis XIII. The *ballet de cour* reached new heights of elegance, and developed significant variations, during the long reign of Louis XIV (1643–1715). Of most importance was the shift away from an entertainment featuring amateur participation and ballroom dancing to a "stage" ballet in which the line between professional performer and audience was clearly drawn. Once this occurred, the way was clear for the development of the *comédie-ballet*, a combination of stage-play and ballet, and the *opéra-ballet*, in which dramatic content was reduced in favour of dancing, singing, and spectacle. (The best and best-known of the *comédie-ballets*, of course, were the product of collaboration between Molière and the Italian-born Jean Baptiste Lully.)

From the beginning, the presentation of ballet was influenced by Italians and Italian practice. The form had Italian antecedents. The director of the *Ballet comique de la reine* was Baltazarini di Belgiojoso, known in France as Balthasar de Beaujoyeulx, court valet to Catherine de'Medici. The ballets performed during the early years of Louis XIII's reign were supervised by the Italian machinist-designer Tomaso Francini (1571–1648), who provided the French court with increasingly elaborate perspective scenes. In 1645, Giacomo Torelli began his French career, which spanned the next sixteen years. He was finally replaced by Gaspare Vigarani and later by Carlo Vigarani, who continued as court *machiniste-décorateur* until he was replaced in 1680 by the French Jean Berain. For one hundred years, then, Italian designers supervised court entertainments.

Italianate staging at a royal court in the seventeenth century is to be expected. What is important to realize in the case of the seventeenth-century French theatre is that the practice of court and public stages became so intertwined that tracing the development of French staging becomes to a certain extent a matter of analyzing the interaction among old-fashioned medieval staging techniques, the new Italian perspectives and spectacles, and the strong classical ideal that so strongly informed the regular drama. The Hôtel de Bourgogne and the Théâtre du Marais could claim no direct royal connection (although the company at the Bourgogne styled itself the *Comédiens du Roi* and as the royal troupe was given a pension in 1641 by Louis XIII); but the theatres in the Palais-Cardinal, built by Richelieu in 1641 and renamed the Palais-Royal after the Cardinal's death in 1642, and in the Petit Bourbon, located in a palace next to the Louvre, served not only as court theatres that only invited guests might attend, but also as public playhouses. When Molière returned to Paris from the provinces in 1658, he was granted the use of the Petit Bourbon for public performances; when that theatre was torn down, he was given the use of the Palais-Royal. Both theatres had been remodelled by Torelli in the Italian manner, the

Petit Bourbon in 1645, the Palais-Royal in 1646. Moreover, even before Molière's use of the court theatres, the public theatres had been forced to reckon
with the attractions of court staging. When in 1650 Corneille's *Andromède* was
performed at the Petit Bourbon with the same elaborate machinery and spectacular scenery used three years previously at the Palais-Royal for Torelli's production of *Orphée*, it started a vogue for these so-called machine plays, which
the Théâtre du Marais attempted to follow, eventually to its financial ruin.

Given this close connection between court and public performances, it seems
only fitting that the famous Comédie Française, the world's first national theatre and a continuing French institution, should come into being through two
royal edicts by Louis XIV, the first ordering the merging of Molière's troupe
with the troupe at the Marais after Molière's death in 1673, the second de-
creeing the amalgamation of this company with the Bourgogne company in 1680.
The Comédie Française was given a monopoly on spoken drama in French.
(An exception was made for the Italian troupe, which was allowed to continue
until 1697 at the Hôtel de Bourgogne.) Until 1689 the Comédie Française performed at the Théâtre Guenégard, built for opera in 1670 and first used for plays
in 1673; in 1689 it was given its own theatre. The Palais-Royal continued to
be used for the performance of *opéra-ballet*. By the end of the century, then,
what distinguished "court" and "public" performances was merely the theatrical form in which each specialized.

These events and these concerns provide the foci for the study of French theatre history between 1500 and 1700. Obviously the forty years following 1635,
graced with what is acknowledged to be the greatest drama ever produced in
France, have received the bulk of scholarly attention. There exists, moreover,
far more evidence concerning this period than there is for the sixteenth or even
the early seventeenth century. Under Louis XIV especially, the arts, literature,
and the theatre became closely associated with royal patronage and royal taste,
and both the creation and the consumption of the arts depended upon a cultivated aristocracy and an increasingly literate and sophisticated middle class as-
piring to court favour. Cultural and intellectual institutions were established as
ways of organizing creative endeavor. Cardinal Richelieu chartered the French
Academy in 1637, to which was appended in 1663 the Academy of Inscriptions
and Belles-Lettres, intended to record the events of Louis XIV's reign. The Royal
Academy of Dance was founded in 1661, to be combined in 1671 with the Royal
Academy of Music to form the Royal Academy of Music and Dance, in ac-
tuality Lully's opera company. The royal creation of the Comédie Française has
already been noted. The proceedings of these organizations form part of the
archival and public record and provide historians with valuable information.

Louis XIV's direct support of scholarship and letters was remarkable, and it
undoubtedly encouraged the production of treatises on the drama and on ballet,
but the theatre historian is equally indebted to memoires and personal (often
slanted) observation on the one hand and to semi-popular journalism on the other.
We find a growing number of newspapers, journals, and pamphlets reporting

on the literary and theatrical affairs of the day. Published "news" in this sense had never before provided so much material for the historian's analysis.

As we might expect, the earliest attempts to document and describe the theatre of seventeenth-century France consisted mainly of lists of plays and dates, together with biographical information on the playwrights. On occasion, a rudimentary dramatic analysis was included. Such, for instance, are the volumes of Pierre-François Beauchamps' *Recherches sur les théâtres de France*, published in 1735, and the anonymous *Bibliothèque du théâtre français*, printed in Dresden in 1768. Recognition of the classical period is incipient in the fact that the latter work lists and analyzes only plays by men who wrote after 1636. The first historians to offer more than a catalogue of titles and dates, and to include information on actors and theatres as well as on dramatists, were the brothers Parfaict, whose *Histoire du théâtre français* (1734–49) we have noted before. These eighteenth-century works are often inaccurate, but they also contain information not available elsewhere, and for this reason continue to be consulted.

The nineteenth century saw the continuation of the biographical emphasis, with an important innovation in presentation. Auguste Jal's *Dictionnaire critique de biographie et d'histoire* (1867), for instance, is a mine of documentary information concerning dramatists and actors, containing transcripts of records of baptisms, marriages, and funerals. This admirable practice of printing the relevant documentary evidence was continued in works devoted exclusively to the theatre as well. Eudore Soulié published leases and legal papers together with other relevant documents in *Recherches sur Molière et sa famille* (1863). And between 1870 and 1880 Emile Campardon's researches in the Archives Nationales resulted in half a dozen volumes of hitherto unpublished material concerning Molière, entertainments and spectacles at the fairs of Saint-Germain and Saint-Larent, and French and Italian players. It was in the nineteenth century too that the memoires, journals, and letters of a multitude of seventeenth-century figures were edited and published. Study of the court ballet received a real impetus with the publication in 1868–70 of the six volumes of Paul Lacroix' *Ballets et Mascarades de Cour de Henri III à Louis XIV,* and Louis L' Eclercq's *(Ludovic Celler) Les Origines de l'opéra et le Ballet de la reine* (1581) Lacroix' collection of "texts" is still indispensable for the study of the ballet, and Leclercq's analysis of the *Ballet comique* as the first intentional union of poetry, music, dance, décor, and machines, and the subsequent history of the court ballet as a return to the simpler forms of *mascarade* and *entrée* remains the standard view of the subject.

The collection and publication of archival materials, the printing of memoirs and correspondence, the gathering of facts—these are the expected activities of nineteenth-century scholarship. But the attention paid to the non-literary ballet by Lacroix and expecially Leclercq is illustrative of a fresh perspective on the seventeenth-century French theatre. Scholarly concern was turning not only to non-literary theatrical forms, but to the details of stage presentation, to the *mise en scène*, costume, setting, and theatre architecture. Leclercq in fact published *Les Décors, les costumes et la mise en scène au XVIIe siècle* in 1869; and Germain Bapst's *Essai sur l'histoire du théâtre* appeared in 1893. As we noted earlier, these works mark the beginnings of modern theatre history. When Eugène Rigal turned his attention to the theatre of the sixteenth and early seventeenth centuries, especially in *Alexandre Hardy* (1889) and *Le Théâtre français avant la période classique* (1901), he completed a necessary shift in emphasis among some scholars at least from the study of dramatic literature to the study of theatre history. Hardy's plays would not warrant a second look as literature, but as historical-theatrical phenomena they require a historical explanation.

The growing interest in theatre history as opposed to literary history and the publication of archival material and theatricalia that provided evidence for it went hand-in-hand in the late nineteenth century, and the process has continued into the twentieth century. The Dutch theatre historian S. Wilma Deierkauf-Holsboer has provided authoritative volumes on the Hôtel de Bourgogne (1968–70) and the Théâtre du Marais (1954–58), as well as a study of Alexandre Hardy (1947, rev. 1972). While her work depends to some extent on the memoires and correspondence of the period, it reflects even more the author's years of patient archival research. Mme. Deierkauf-Holsboer continues the French practice of listing and printing the unpublished materials she has found. The procedure is followed as well by Pierre Mélèse, whose *Répertoire analytique des documents contemporains* accompanies his study, *Le Théâtre et le public à Paris sous Louis XIV* (1934). In their citation and use of evidence, Deierkauf-Holsboer and Mélèse are in fact model historians, and their works serve as valuable resources for other researchers. (See especially Mélèse's discussion of evidence in *Le Théâtre et le public*, pp. 6–23.) They also serve to illustrate the two main lines of inquiry in the twentieth century. Mme. Deierkauf-Holsboer is concerned primarily with theatre architecture, stage settings, mise en scène, the performers; Mélèse's concern is to provide a kind of sociology of the theatre based solely on contemporary documents, to determine the way in which contemporary audiences understood and appreciated the theatre of the last half of the seventeenth century. Thus T. E. Lawrenson traces the development of the stage in *The French Stage in the XVIIth Century* (1957), arguing that it was the Italian influence that caused the unnatural cleavage between stage and auditorium that characterized theatre buildings for 200 years. On the other hand, two studies that in general follow Mélèse's lead are John Lough's *Paris Theatre Audiences in the Seventeenth and Eighteenth Centuries* (1957) and W. L. Wiley's *Early Public Theatre in France* (1960). Both authors make use of contemporary plays and prefaces, memoires, journals and diaries, leases and contracts, and seventeenth-century published commentary. While noting that the collection of contemporary documents he offers is probably the most valuable part of his investigation, Lough is equally careful to note that the evidence is incomplete and fragmentary, and that many of the letters and diaries commonly cited actually can provide very little insight into audience reactions to the theatre.

(He offers a similar warning concerning evidence and the conjectural nature of some documents and theories in *Seventeenth-Century French Drama*, an introduction to the social and material conditions of the theatre published in 1979.)
It would be foolish to suggest that these few works of modern scholarship represent more than a small fraction of the studies regularly produced by students of the French classical theatre, but together with H. C. Lancaster's multi-volume *History of French Dramatic Literature in the Seventeenth Century* (1929–42), they are the volumes most likely to be consulted in the first instance.

TEXTS

Play Texts

Consideration of sixteenth-century French dramatic texts inevitably gives rise to the question always asked of plays of an academic or scholarly cast: Were they performed or were they merely armchair exercises? The question is rendered more difficult by the fact that there is almost no external evidence concerning the staging of these plays between 1570 and 1624, and we are therefore thrown back on the internal evidence of the texts themselves. But testimony concerning the performance of Pléiade plays before 1570, usually in an academic or university milieu, has prompted most scholars now to accept the likelihood of performance or at least intended performance for the humanist drama. The playwrights themselves occasionally refer to performance, but there is little hint of where or when. Stage directions, whether incorporated into the dialogue or printed in the margin, can actually be misleading. The genre—drama—called for stage directions, and the writers were prone to provide them even if there was no likelihood of performance and even if they had no particular playing place in mind. In the British Library copy of Pierre Larivey's *Les six premières comédies facecieuses* (1579), the *dramatis personae* is accompanied by a list of actors in a late sixteenth- or early seventeenth-century hand. Although the actors are well-nigh impossible to identify, their names are testimony to the play's being acted. Explicit stage directions are very rare. An intriguing exception is pointed to by Brian Jeffrey in *French Renaissance Comedy* (p. 93). An edition of Gerard de Vivre's *Comédie de la Fidélité nuptiale*, published in Antwerp in 1577, not only contains many stage-directions, some of them in full, but also provides a detailed list of signs used to indicate stage-directions in the text of this and Vivre's other two plays. (See Jeffrey, Plate X.) Most of the instructions are intended to guide the actor in the delivery of his speeches, an understandable concern to a schoolmaster, which Vivre was. Other than this, we are left on our own when we attempt to analyse humanist dramatic texts as production documents. That the texts offer few details of staging indicates perhaps that the playwrights were little concerned about the specifics of stage presentation. Attempts to reconstruct their performance based on the principles of *décor simultané* or unity of place or *récitation dialoguée* have not proved very satisfactory. Perhaps the best solution is that offered by Richard Griffiths for the tragedies of Montchrestien: a neutral stage allowing a swift change of locale in the Elizabethan manner (*Dramatic Technique of Antoine de Montchrestien*, pp. 146–148).

Seventeenth-century French dramatic texts represent acted plays, but they present the usual problems for a theatre historian dealing with a period in which the drama was and is considered to have been a literary as well as a theatrical art. The historian must balance the knowledge that the printed text may well have been altered for publication with the realization that most of this drama was written by experienced playwrights whose success depended upon their acute awareness of the conditions prevailing in a very circumscribed theatrical milieu. It is usually possible to assign classical French plays to a particular theatre and company, and this fact, coupled with a dramaturgy based on the unities, has given rise to fewer controversial interpretations of French theatre practice than we find, for instance, in Jacobean England. Nevertheless, if the evidence of these is to be properly evaluated, some knowledge of the publication process is desirable.

Before about 1610 there was evidently little thought given to the editing or printing of plays written for professional performance. (We are here concerned mainly with the work of Alexandre Hardy.) It is unlikely that anyone considered them "literature," and upon publication they were considered to be in the public domain and could therefore legally be performed by anyone, with no benefits to either author or original company of actors. Moreover, it was not until the 1620s that Hardy, for example, was able to wrest publication rights from Bellerose, the *chef du troupe*, and to bring out his five volumes of *Théâtre* between 1624 and 1628. While publication could provide revenue for dramatists, it is unlikely that a play still profitable in repertory would be printed. It is in fact possible to estimate the success of a play by noting the interval between its first performance and its publication. There is evidence, particularly during the early years of the century, that publication and sales could be difficult and slow, but as the reputations of dramatists grew during the reign of Louis XIV, the demand for reading texts increased, particularly outside Paris.

It is important to remind ourselves that we are dealing with reading texts that may well have been revised for publication. We know too from contemporary newsletters that revivals of old plays were often done with revised texts or revised staging and decor. The author could alter even a published text as he saw fit, and "original" texts could therefore vary considerably from playhouse scripts. The possible relationships between published and performed texts can be seen in the following diagram:

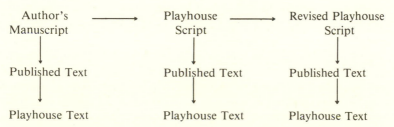

Wherever there is an arrow, there is the possibility of revision. Sorting out these possibilities with respect to any given play can be a time-consuming task, and few modern editors have found it profitable to do so. But theatre historians ought to be aware of the potential complexity of the evidence they cite.

Published play texts are usually accompanied by the dates of *privilège* (theatrical license) and *achevé d'imprimer* (publication), by a dedication, a note to the reader, and often commendatory verses—all grist to the historian's mill. The standard treatment of French plays between 1610 and 1700 is H. C. Lancaster's *History of French Dramatic Literature*, which provides a survey of nearly 1,200 plays.

Ballet Texts

The *ballets de cour* always included music and dancing, of course, but they could include as well songs, recitative, pantomime, acrobatics, spectacle, and dramatic verse. Needless to say, the printed versions of these entertainments, like those of Italian *intermezzi* or the English masque, are inadequate records of the original—and only—performance. Our principal sources of information are the *livrets* or festival books containing a detailed description of the representation and an explanation of its meaning, which began to be published during the reign of Louis XIII. Before 1610 we have only incomplete *livrets*. During the performance itself, members of the audience were in possession of printed booklets which allowed them to follow the events depicted by the ballet (*cf.* Italian *argumenti*). (The largest and most convenient collection of ballet *livrets* is that found in Paul Lacroix' *Ballets et Mascarades* which contains almost 150 ballets performed between 1581 and 1652.) A chronology of published ballets is to be found in the Bibliothèque Nationale (mss. 24352–24357)—a large collection of ballets, operas, pastorals, and tragedies performed at court. These manuscripts, together with ms. fr. 15057, also contain a list of ballet poetry, composed mainly of published poetic works of the period. (Complete lists of ballets, together with sources of information for each ballet, are provided by Margaret M. McGowan in *L'Art du ballet de cour en France* and by Marie-Françoise Christout in *Ballet de cour de Louis XIV*, which continues the record to 1672. Charles Silin records Isaac Benserade's ballets, produced between 1651 and 1681, in *Benserade and His Ballets de Cour*, pp. 205–400.)

An important component of a ballet "text" is the music, but rarely has the music for a specific ballet been preserved. An exception is the famous *Ballet comique de la reine*, which was published with music and engravings in 1582. (A facsimile was published by G. A. Caula in 1962.) We must rely otherwise on collections of instrumental music and airs of varying relevance to ballet. Two collections are of particular significance:

Michel Henry Collection

Part of the manuscript collection in the Bibliothèque Nationale noted above (ms. 24357) was prepared by the Duc de la Vallière and is entitled "Table of

Ballets for 3, 4 and 5 parts which is found in a collection made in 1600 by Michel Henry.'' Henry's collection is unfortunately no longer extant. According to P. F. Godard de Beauchamp, who used it for his *Recherches sur les théâtres de France* (1735), it had been discovered two years previously at Mons. Its subsequent loss is only partially offset by La Vallière's analysis. Although the manuscript in the Bibliotheque Nationale mentions the date 1600, the last entry is dated 1620. (The manuscript and the Henry Collection are discussed by François Lesure in *Fêtes de la Renaissance*, I, 205–219.)

Philidor Collection

A large collection of seventeenth-century music compiled by André Philidor (ca. 1647–1730) is preserved in the library of the Paris Conservatory and in St. Michael's College in Tenbury, England; a transcript is also available in the Library of Congress. It contains a great many dance tunes and airs (upper and lower parts only), all the ballets and operas of Lully, and all the music used at the French court chapel.

In addition, a great many collections of airs possibly used in ballets were published between 1602 and 1643 by Robert Ballard, Pierre Ballard, Gabriel Bataille, Antoine Boesset, and Pierre Guédron. The last named was ''surintendant de la musique du roi'' in the early years of the century, and he and Boesset at least are known to have contributed music to the *ballet de cour*. (See Margaret McGowan, *L'Art du ballet de cour en France*, pp. 318–320, for a list of these published collections.)

Like the Italian *intermezzi* and opera, and the English masque, the French *ballet de cour* presents serious difficulties of historical reconstruction, and not the least of these difficulties is that of finding and integrating the appropriate music, of overcoming past negligence of musical notation as a part of the text.

THEATRICAL DOCUMENTS

Archival materials of interest to the theatre historian, including the usual array of legal documents and institutional records, are dealt with in a later section. Here we are concerned with a few documents of such significance for the study of seventeenth century French theatre that it seems wise to isolate them for special discussion. We have a memoir concerning the rebuilding of the Théâtre du Marais in 1644 and a contract for the renovation of the Hôtel de Bourgogne in 1647. We have a number of *registres* recording the business activities of Molière's company and the Comédie Française. We have a collection of documents concerning the relationship between the actors at the Hôtel de Bourgone and the Confrérie itself in 1632. And, most important of all, we have the famous *Mémoire de Mahelot*, an illustrated record of set design at the Hôtel de Bourgone from about 1630 to 1680. (To these we might conceivably add the theatre posters which appear to have increased in importance as the century wore on, but the half dozen extant *affiches* are too small a sample on which to base any conclusions. See Deierkauf-Holsboer, *L'Histoire de la mise en scène*, pp. 113–115.)

Théâtre du Marais Mémoire (1644)

We owe our knowledge of this important document to Wilma Deierkauf-Holsboer. Scholars had long reconciled themselves to a necessary ignorance concerning the Théâtre du Marais, for in 1872 Auguste Jal had reported in the second edition of his *Dictionnaire* that all the legal documents concerning the theatre and its actors had been destroyed by fire. While searching the Archives Nationales for information on Alexandre Hardy, however, Mme. Deierkauf-Holsboer discovered over one hundred documents relating to the theatre. Jal had been only partially correct: Most of the documents for the years following 1665 had indeed been burnt. The specific document in question, the "Mémoire de ce qu'ill Fault Faire au Jeu de Paulme des Marets," is dated June 3, 1644, and contains instructions for the rebuilding of the theatre after the original had been destroyed by fire. (Deierkauf-Holsboer prints the document in *Le Théâtre du Marais*, I, 194–198.) The document is not always easy to interpret, but there is agreement that the overall dimensions of the structure were 34.5 metres long, 11.5 metres wide, and 15.5 metres high; that the pit measured approximately 18 metres × 11.5 metres; that the raked stage was raised about 2 metres above the pit and featured a proscenium opening of 7.5 metres; that there were three side galleries and a gallery and amphitheatre at the rear; and that the capacity of the theatre was probably about 1,500 persons. What remains in dispute is the exact size of the main stage, and the size and placement of the *théâtre supérieure*, specified in the *Mémoire* as resting on ten pillars about four metres above the main stage and curving upstage two metres at the centre. (See Deierkauf-Holsboer's reconstruction in *Le Théâtre du Marais*, I, Plates VII-X; and also Per Bjürstrom, *Giacomo Torelli*, for an alternative reconstruction.)

Hôtel de Bourgogne Contract (1647)

The "Devis et Marche de Divers Travaux a executer au théâtre de l'Hôtel de Bourgogne," dated April 17, 1647, is also found in the Archives Nationales. (The document is printed by Deierkauf-Holsboer in *Le Théâtre de l'Hôtel de Bourgogne*, II, 183–186.) Again, from our point of view the instructions are somewhat imprecise, although the discovery of the memoir concerning the Theatre du Marais has at least allowed us to make some sense out of the specification that the renovated theatre was to be modelled on "la salle du théâtre du Marais." The raked stage was to be 13.5 metres deep and as wide as the building. (The building has been estimated from other sources to have been either 18.5 metres or 12 metres in width, depending upon the investigator. Deierkauf-Holsboer favours the larger dimension, but most scholars seem to prefer the smaller.) References to the installation of beams at the front of the stage and to the raising of the curtain suggest the presence of a proscenium arch and a curtain. It is usually assumed that neither feature was present in the Hôtel de Bourgogne before 1647.

Theatrical Registers

From the latter part of the seventeenth century we are fortunate to have *registres*, records of performances, receipts, and expenses, for Molière's company for the years 1659–85, and for the Comédie Française from 1680 onwards. The theatres involved are the Petit Bourbon (1659–60), the Palais-Royal (1660–73), the Hôtel Guénégard (1673–89), and the new home of the Comédie Française in the rue Neuve-des-Fosses (1689–1770). While the records are far from complete—especially for the years prior to 1680—they provide valuable information concerning theatrical activities and financial affairs during the last third of the century. All of the extant *registres* are in the archives of the Comédie Française.

Registres from the Petit Bourbon and the Palais-Royal include two ascribed to the actor La Thorillière, covering the periods April 6, 1663-January 6, 1664, and January 11, 1664- January 6, 1665, and one by A. Hubert for the period April 29, 1672-March 21, 1673. (Hubert's *Registre* is printed in the *Revue d'Histoire du Théâtre* 25, 1973, pp. 1–132.) But the best-known set of records is that kept by the actor Charles Varlet, known as La Grange (ca. 1639–92), who joined Molière's company in 1659 to play young lovers, became a mainstay of the troupe, and wrote the only contemporary biography of Molière, published as a preface to the first edition of Molière's works in 1682. La Grange's *Registre*, which begins on April 28, 1659, and ends on August 31, 1683, lists the plays presented and the receipts from each, interspersed with comments on the internal affairs of the company. It is in fact our main source of information concerning Molière's troupe and the early years of the Comédie Française. (The *Registre* was edited in 1947 by B. E. and G. P. Young; and a facsimile edition was published in 1973, with notes by Sylvie Chevalley, archivist of the Comédie Française.)

The archives of the Comédie Française also contain a very large collection of *registres* that provide a nearly unbroken record from 1680 to the present. The records for the last twenty years of the seventeenth century are treated by H. C. Lancaster in *Comédie Française, 1680–1701* (1941). Lancaster does not attempt a literal transcription of the records but provides instead "the names of the actors and the shares they received at the various dates, and indicate[s] the days they played, the general nature of their expenses, charges, profits, and method of paying authors" (p. 7). For the rest, Lancaster lists plays, dates, paid admissions, receipts, and shares.

Collection of Principal Papers

This is a much abbreviated English version of a French title of nearly 150 words referring to a seventy-one page brochure prepared and published by the

Confrérie de la Passion in 1632 and providing a recital of actor-Confrérie struggles through the years. (A copy of the brochure still exists in the Bibliothèque Nationale, but it has unfortunately not been reprinted. A good analysis of the contents is provided by Wiley in *Early Public Theatres of France*, pp. 143–156.) The collection consists essentially of a series of accusations and defenses, and provides evidence for the history of the property and its ownership, and of its use by actors. The *Collection of Principal Papers*, then, supplemented by the archival documents found by Mme. Deierkauf-Holsboer and others, is invaluable in helping us reconstruct the history of this important theatre.

Le Mémoire de Mahelot

The complete title of this manuscript (Bibliothèque Nationale, ms. fr. 24330) is "Mémoire de plusiers decorations qui serve aux piece contenus en ce present livres, commance par Laurent Mahelot et continué par Michel Laurent en l'année 1673." The frontispiece gives the date as 1673. The manuscript was found in the eighteenth century in the library of the Duc de la Vallière by Beauchamps, who used it for his *Recherches sur les théâtres de France*, and it was described in 1783 in the catalogue of the Duke's library. It was purchased for the Bibliothèque Royale, later the Bibliothèque Nationale, in 1784. The first modern scholar to make use of it was Alphonse Royer in *Histoire universelle du théâtre* (1869–78). In 1920, the complete manuscript, including the drawings, was edited by H. C. Lancaster.

The ninety-four sheets of the manuscript were prepared by several hands, and the document is in fact clearly divisible into three parts, widely dispersed in time. The first section, the work either of Mahelot or of Georges Buffequin, a well-known scene designer, consists of *notices* (summaries of décor and occasionally of costume as well) for seventy-one plays, together with sketches of forty-seven set designs for forty-five of the plays. Of the seventy-one plays noted, forty-seven are extant, although not all of these are favoured with designs. Of the eleven plays by Hardy that are represented in thirteen sketches, for example, only three—*La Bell Egyptienne*, *Félismène*, and *Cornélie*—are extant. In those instances where we have *notice*, sketch, and text we may count ourselves fortunate indeed. Among them are four plays by Pierre Du Ryer (*Amarillis*, *Arétaphile*, *Clitophon*, *Vendanges de Suresnes*) and three each by Jean de Rotrou (*La Bague de l'Oubli*, *l'Hypocondriaque*, *Ménechimes*) and Jean Mairet (*Silvanire*, *Sylvie*, *Chriséide et Arimand*). Lancaster was of the opinion that this first section was completed by Mahelot between early 1633 and February 1634, and represents the complete repertory of the Hôtel de Bourgogne at the time. Deierkauf-Holsboer, on the other hand, argues that Hardy's plays mentioned in the *Mémoire* can be dated between 1622 and 1627, and that the last play is Benserade's *Iphis et Iante*, which can be dated shortly before 1637. She therefore postulates that the *Mémoire* presents a list of plays, but not all the plays, performed at the Hôtel de Bourgogne between 1622 and 1635, although not in chronological order. (See *L'Histoire de la mise en scène*, pp. 39–54.)

The second section, whose author is not known, consists merely of seventy-one titles, given without *notices* or sketches and probably representative of the repertory of the Bourgogne 1646–47. The final section, assumed to be the work of Michel Laurent, provides *notices* of fifty-three plays performed at the Hôtel de Bourgogne between 1678 and 1680 and sixty-nine *notices* and two titles without *notices* of plays performed at the rue Guénégard after the union of the troupes in 1680. The terminal date is 1686.

A fifty-year record, however interrupted, of staging practices at a single seventeenth-century theatre is indeed a precious source of information. The descriptions and especially the drawings are true documents of production, the work of theatre professionals who intended their work to be realized in theatrical sets, rather than pictorial art. What has intrigued historians the most about the *Mémoire* is the progression it seems to chart from the *décor simultané* of the medieval stage to the *décor unique* of the neoclassical stage. Scenic wings were arranged as on a perspective stage, but each represented a different locale in the manner of a medieval "mansion." As Lawrenson puts the case: "This theatre is Italian in disposition, the curve of its separate items tending naturally towards a perspective scene. But it is largely mediaeval in function, and this function will be hard-lived" (*French Stage in the XVIIth Century*, pp. 113–114). Actually, such a hybrid stage was not unknown in the seventeenth century. An engraving in Johan Amos Comenius' *Orbis sensualium pictus*, published in London in 1658, suggests a similar practice (reproduced in Nicoll, *Stuart Masques*, fig. 113). And an engraving of the stage of the Schouwburg in Amsterdam, built in 1638 by the Italian-trained Jacob von Campen, shows a setting that reflects a staging practice clearly similar to that employed at the Hôtel de Bourgogne. (The engraving, executed by S. Savry in 1658, is reproduced in Hodges, *The Globe Restored*, Plates 52–54.)

WRITTEN EVIDENCE

Criticism and Controversy

If the theatre historian is to come to grips with the forces that produced the French classical theatre, included must be a consideration of documents of dramatic and critical theory. More importantly, the relationship between the ideas expressed and the drama described in these treatises and actual theatre practice must be determined. There is often a temptation to treat dramatic theory independently of the "real" theatrical world, as a sub-species of the history of ideas rather than as an element contributing to the history of events, of performance. This is, of course, a perfectly legitimate endeavor, but for the theatre historian the ideas contained in theoretical documents, unless they affect or reflect theatrical performance, must remain on the periphery of the main concern. In France, critical theory emerged by the early years of the seventeenth century as central to the theatrical enterprise, both helping to determine principles of dramaturgy and stagecraft, and reflecting and summarizing theatrical practice: The history of dramatic theory and the history of the theatre are in this instance closely interrelated.

The evidence consists of the documents themselves, and although it is possible to find the kind of attacks on the immorality of the stage and answering defenses we saw in England (see C. Urbain and E. Levesque, *L'Eglise et le théâtre*), the main thrust of French criticism was towards "regularity" in the drama, a regularity ensured by the neoclassical rules of dramatic art derived from classical practice and Italian precept, and dedicated to the preservation of *vraisemblance* (verisimilitude) and *les bienséances* (the proprieties). Acceptance of these precepts was not, as we might expect, achieved overnight, and in fact the history of French theatrical criticism and practice, rather, is a long conflict which was finally resolved in favour of regularity.

The first phase in the debate lasted roughly from the middle of the sixteenth century, when Thomas Sebillet's *Art poétique* (1548) provides the first hint of Aristotle or the Italian critics (the precise influence is impossible to determine), to the 1620s, when François Ogier, in the preface to Jean de Schelandre's *Tyr et Sidon* (1628), contributes a clear and well-argued case for ignoring the rules. (The pertinent exerpts from critical writings from Sebillet to Ogier are collected by H. W. Lawton in *Handbook of French Renaissance Dramatic Theory*.) Contemporaneous with and slightly later than Sebillet were the members of *Pléiade*, a group of seven humanists who spoke in the name of a specifically French classicism, which would produce works in French based on classical example and classically derived rules of art. (Selections from Joachim du Bellay, Lazare de Baïf, Pierre Ronsard, and Etienne Jodelle are printed by Lawton, who also offers an excerpt from Jean Vauquelin's *Art poétique*, in essence a summary of Pléiade theories.) Although among the members of the Pléiade only Jodelle was a dramatist, and relatively few of the group's writings were devoted specifically to the drama, the general theories they express, particularly those concerning language and the rules of versification, had a profound influence on French critical theory and ultimately on French dramaturgy. It was the Pléiade's principles that, in a rigidly codified form, underlay the criticism of François de Malherbe (1555–1628), the dominant literary critic in France during the first quarter of the seventeenth century. Malherbe thought the Pléiade too frivolous; he stressed *lucidité, volonté, calcul*—clarity, intellect, calculation—and to ensure these qualities argued forcibly on behalf of rigid rules.

So far as the theatre was concerned, these rules took the form of the three dramatic unities of action—plot, place, and time. The three unities were in fact discussed in France almost simultaneously with Castelvetro's famous promulgation in Italy. Jean de la Taille's *Art de la tragédie*, published as a preface to his play *Saül le furieux* (1572), while showing the influence of Aristotle and especially Horace in its insistence on off-stage violent action, five acts, a chorus, and the necessity of beginning towards the middle or end of the story, also includes the injunction: "The story, or play must always be presented as oc-

curring on the same day, in the same time, and in the same place.'' La Taille
was himself a playwright, but many years were to pass before other playwrights
and critics accepted the confines of the unities. Pierre de Laudun d'Aigalier
protested the unity of time in his *Art poétique* (1598); Hardy paid scant attention to any of the unities; Ogier argued on behalf of an irregular drama in 1628;
Corneille's handling of the unities was central to the quarrel concerning *Le Cid*
in the late 1630s. Corneille eventually accepted the rules but felt compelled to
point out the difficulties and constraints they impose on the playwright. In his
Discourse on the Three Unities, published in 1660 in the collected edition of
his works, he writes:

It is easy for the speculative critics to be severe, but if they would give ten or twelve
dramatic poems to the public, they might perhaps enlarge their rules even more than I
have done, as soon as they realized by experience what constraint their precision required and how many beauties it banned from the stage. [Gilbert, *Literary Criticism*, p.
579]

The whole issue of regularity reached its inevitable climax—for historians of
the theatre at least—in the celebrated "Quarrel of the Cid." Corneille's *Cid*,
produced in 1636, represents from our point of view an astonishingly successful attempt to compress a vast amount of material into the confines of the rules
as they were then understood. In spite of its remaining irregularities, it was also
a very successful play—a fact Corneille stressed in a boastful poem, which may
have been intended to spark controversy. Corneille was answered in a poem by
Jean Mairet, author of the "regular" *Sophonisbe* (1634), who accused the author of *Le Cid* of being merely a translator. Others took up the quarrel, both
for and against Corneille. (Thirty-six of the most important documents are printed
in Armand Gasté, *La Querelle du Cid*). One of the most important of the attacks
was Georges de Scudéry's *Observations sur le Cid*, published in June 1637.
Scudéry's role as champion of the rules indicates the polemical nature and basis
of the quarrel. Not only was Scudéry undoubtedly a third-rate writer, he had
only a few years before, in the preface to his tragicomedy *Ligdamon et Lidias*
(1631), specifically rejected the rules. (His later *Apologie du théâtre*, which appeared in 1639, is of little interest as a critical document, although it does provide some information on the contemporary theatre.) Ultimately, nevertheless,
Scudéry's *Observations*, together with the text of *Le Cid*, was submitted to the
newly founded French Academy for judgement. The author of *Les Sentiments
de l'Académie française sur la tragicomédie du Cid*, published in December
1637, was Jean Chapelain (1595–1674), considered to have been a leading ex-
ponent of dogmatic criticism, which was founded on Ancient Authority and
nurtured by Good Sense and Reason. Chapelain had long advocated classical
form and the three unities: His *Lettre sur la règle des vingt-quatre heures et
Réfutations des objections* had appeared in 1630. Not surprisingly, then, he faulted
Le Cid for its failure to adhere to the unities, although he also acknowledged

some good things about the play as well. Whatever its genesis, there is little doubt that as the epitome of an attitude that was to shape French drama for many years *Les Sentiments* is an important document of the French theatre.

D'Aubignac and Chappuzeau

A treatise that had its origins in the Quarrel of the Cid is *La Pratique du théâtre*, by François Hédelin, Abbé d'Aubignac (1604–76), translated in 1684 as *The Whole Art of the Stage*. Although written about 1640 and informed by ideas current at the time of the Quarrel, d'Aubignac's book was not published in France until 1657. It is in effect a summary of the rules of dramatic art as they had been worked out by theorists and adopted by playwrights during the first half of the seventeenth century; and as such it is an indispensable reference for the study of the French classical theatre. *La Pratique du théâtre* is divided into four books: The first is devoted to general considerations of authors' intenions, the rules of the ancients, the audience, and so on; the second provides a discussion of the rules, the principle of verisimilitude, and the dramatic unities; the third is a detailed analysis of the parts of tragedy; and the last book deals with, among other things, spectacle, décor, and machinery. For theatre historians some of d'Aubignac's most interesting material relates to stage presentation. For even when discussing the ancient theatre he is bound by the practices of his own day and describes contemporary scenic devices. He mentions specifically three types of stage machinery (for Heaven, for Hell, and for the sea), three types of landscape (a garden, the wilderness, and a forest), and two city scenes (a temple and a palace). As a practical handbook, *La Pratique du théâtre* was studied by many dramatists, including Racine, whose annotated copy is still in existence. (The annotations are printed in Charles Arnaud, *Les Théories dramatiques au XVIIe siècle*, 1887.) And it may well have been what prompted Corneille to publish his three *Discourses* in 1660. There is much that is pedantic and absurd in d'Aubignac, but he deserves recognition for having been one of the few theorists in the seventeenth century to follow Castelvetro's lead in stressing the relationship between dramaturgy and theatrical performance.

La pratique du théâtre, then, is one of two basic references for the study of the seventeenth-century French stage. The other is Samuel Chappuzeau's *Théâtre français* (1674). The original edition is very rare, and there was no attempt to reprint the work until 1867, when 106 copies were printed in Brussels. (The 1867 edition was used by A. M. Nagler in preparing an English translation of parts of Chappuzeau's book for inclusion in *Source Book in Theatrical History*, pp. 180–185.) Another, corrected version was prepared in 1875 by Georges Monval. (Monval noted that the autograph manuscript of *Théâtre français*, dated 1673, was in the Romanoff library in Moscow, now part of the State Lenin Library, the national library of the U.S.S.R.) Chappuzeau (1625–1701) was a traveller, a dilettante, and a prolific if mediocre writer, whose most engaging characteristic seems to have been his uncritical curiosity and enthusiasm for whatever engaged his attention. He wrote plays, travel books, and dictionaries, translated Erasmus, and at his death was preparing a history of the royal house of Savoy. Nevertheless, he is now remembered only for his little book on the French theatre, which is divided into three parts: a defense of the theatre, a dictionary of dramatists, and a section describing the lives and organization of the players. He describes the process by which an author got his play produced; comments on rehearsals and the fact that a full-length play could be memorized in eight days; describes the functions of the *orateur*; outlines the duties of musicians, ushers, prompters, and decorators; and explains the distribution of roles. Chappuzeau's conception of the theatre is one with which many modern scholars could readily agree:

I understand that drama demands not only an author who composes it, but also an actor who performs it, and a theatre where it may be represented with the embellishments which it can give it. But the poet's invention is the soul which animates the entire body, and it is from thence mainly that the public derives the pleasure it looks for in the theatre. [Monval's edition, p. 54]

Untainted by special pleading and innocent of empty theorizing, *Théâtre français* remains an important source for students of the theatre.

Ballet and Opera

Since the *ballet de cour* and the later opera of Lully naturally involved dancing, theatre historians have turned to early treatises and handbooks in order to reconstruct the details of dances that in the ballet or opera texts are named but not described. Fabritio Caroso's *Il Ballarino* (1581) provides an extensive vocabulary of contemporary steps and instructions for over one hundred ballroom dances. (An extract is printed in Selma Jeanne Cohen, *Dance as a Theatre Art*, pp. 10–18.) A better known handbook, although still devoted to ballroom dancing, is Jehan Tabourot's (or Thoinot Arbeau's) *Orchésographie* (1589), a detailed account of the social dances in vogue throughout the sixteenth century. Here is contained, in fact, nearly all the exact knowledge we have of sixteenth-century dance: practical instructions for over a dozen specifically named dances (Basse Danse, Pavone, Gaillarde, Volte, Courante, Allemande, Gavotte, Canaries, Bouffons, Morisque, Pavane d'Espagne, and twenty-three varieties of Branle); and the first specific definitions of the proper placing of the dancer's feet at the beginning of steps, the basis of the five positions of classical ballet. (*Orchésographie* is available in English translations by Cyril Beaumont and by Mary Stewart Evans.) Although other treatises continued to be written—Cesare Negri's *Nuove Inventioni di Balli* (1604) for instance—*Orchésographie* remains the single most important source of information concerning the early dance. A later work, François de Lauze's *Apologie de la danse* (1623; translated by Jean Wildeblood in 1952) is a much simplified guide to dance for ladies and gentlemen. We may assume that what Lauze describes was in fact what courtiers learned, or that it at least reflects their general practice.

Lauze also felt compelled to legitimize the dance by referring to the authority of the ancient writers, but he was still concerned with ballroom dancing. It was left to still later writers to treat the ballet as a dramatic genre conforming to the classical rules of dramatic art. However, they did so, as Charles Silin points out in his study of the librettist Isaac de Benserade, only after the ballet had in fact given up its dramatic pretensions and reverted to the *ballet à entrée* (*Benserade and His Ballets de Cour,* p. 179). Such attention began in 1641 with the publication of M. de Saint-Hubert's *Manière de composer et faire réussir les ballets* (Cohen, pp. 31–37), and the theme is continued in the *Mémoires* of Michel de Marolles, Abbé de Villeloin, published in 1656, and in Guillaume Dumanoir's *Mariage de la musique avec la danse* (1664).

A more substantial theoretical position is elaborated by l'Abbé Michel de Pure in his *Idées des spectacles anciens et nouveau* (1668) which, in spite of its title, is more concerned with the rules governing the structure of ballet than with the tracing of its origin and history. Although the rules formulated by Pure were developed from first principles rather than based on actual practice, his work constitutes a valuable commentary on ballet technique and the attendant difficulties of appreciating the aesthetics of the form. (For a fuller discussion, see Christout, *Le Ballet de cour de Louis XIV*, pp. 137ff.)

By far the most important of the seventeenth-century writers on the ballet, however, is Claude-François Ménestrier (1631–1705), who also concerned himself with heraldry and opera. "Remarques pour la conduite de Ballets" appeared in his *Autel de Lyon* in 1658. But his more important *Des Ballets anciens et modernes selon les règles du théâtre* was published in 1682. Ménestrier is the first historian of the ballet and takes great pains to find its origin among the Greeks and Romans, impelled as was Lauze to justify contemporary practice by ancient precedent. His treatment of contemporary ballet-style entertainments is remarkably detailed insofar as choreography is concerned, but like many theorists he is often given to offering advice rather than discussing practice. (An English translation of his comments on ballet costumes is printed in Nagler, *Source Book*, pp. 187–192.)

In *Des Representations en musique anciennes et modernes* (1681) Ménestrier made what is possibly the first attempt in the seventeenth century to systematize theatrical décor and equipment. He notes that the musical theatre (the opera) is better suited for entertainment than for instruction, that we seek in it the marvelous rather than the realistic, and that elaborate machinery and scenic effects are therefore particularly appropriate to the form. Basing his observations on the productions of Lully's opera, Ménestrier categorizes possible stage settings into eleven types, which are capable of being infinitely varied: celestial scenes, sacred scenes, military scenes, rustic or pastoral scenes, maritime settings, royal scenes, civil scenes, historical scenes, poetic settings, magic scenes, and academic scenes.

Correspondence

In a self-contained and highly literate society such as that of the French capital in the seventeenth century, letters were not only written in large numbers, but they also tended to be semi-public expressions of informed individual opinion. Pierre Mélèse attaches great weight to the evidence of private correspondence—"veritable private newspapers"—which he categorizes as generally sincere, spontaneous, and varied (*Le Théâtre et le public à Paris sous Louis XIV*, pp. 21–22). Letter writers are nonetheless not always interested in what we are interested in, and even more rarely do they write with theatre historians in mind. Not surprisingly, the most frequently consulted correspondence is by those with a special claim to fame in the world of *belles lettres*. The letters of Jean Chapelain are sources of information on matters of critical theory and dogmatic opinion. Those of Roger de Bussy-Rabutin (1618–93) reflect their author's caustic wit. Jean Louis Guez de Balzac (1597–1654) achieved fame in his own lifetime by publishing his letters at intervals between 1624 and his death, a practice that in effect turned private opinion into public discussion in the manner of a periodical. Charles Saint-Evrémond (1613–1703) and Mme. de Sévigné (1626–96) provide rich sources of information in their letters concerning the literary, intellectual, and social life of the Paris of Louis XIV. Mme. de Sévigné presents a particularly lively picture. We may add to this list the letters of the remarkable Mme. de Maintenon, wife of the writer Paul Scarron in the 1660s, after his death governess to Louis XIV's illegitimate children, later still partner in a morganatic union with the king himself. While these letters can provide us with some idea of the nature of the theatrical milieu of the time, they are neither detailed enough nor comprehensive enough to serve as prime evidence for the conditions of performance.

Memoirs

Memoirs and journals are similarly defective as historical evidence and, often composed long after the events they describe, they tend to lack the spontaneity of some correspondence. They are more likely as well to be apologetic and self-conscious. The most valuable are actually journals, regularly recorded and not necessarily intended for publication.

Jean Héroard's *Journal sur l'enfance et la jeunesse de Louis XIII*, is in the Bibliothèque Nationale (mss. fr. 4022–4027); substantial extracts were published in 1868 by E. Soulié and E. de Barthélemy. The journal contains brief references to performances at court, but buried as they are in great masses of tedious detail, few scholars have been tempted to go beyond the published extracts to examine the manuscript. In the nineteenth century Arnaud Baschet consulted the manuscript for *Les Comédiens italiens à la cour de France sous Charles IX, Henri III, Henri IV et Louis XIII* (1882), but since that time only John Lough in *Paris Theatre Audiences* (1957) claims to have made a similar effort.

Pierre de l'Estoile (1546–16ll) recorded on a monthly basis the events he found memorable during the reigns of Henri III and Henri IV (1574–1610). His *Mémoires-journaux* are of considerable interest and importance for the light they shed on the happenings of these years. L'Estoile is sometimes referred to as the French Pepys.

The *Historiettes* of Tallemant des Réaux (1619–92), 376 in number, are a collection of short, anecdotal *mémoires*, arranged under the names of notable persons. Never published during their author's lifetime, the *Historiettes* were evidently completed about 1659. At one time Tallemant was considered to have been merely a scandal monger and the *Historiettes* little more than unreliable gossip. There is no doubt that Tallemant enlivened his accounts with scandalous detail and indecency (concerning, for example, Louis XIII's homosexuality), but research among other sources has verified much of his information, and more tolerant scholars have found him an accurate and important observer of the social and political scene. Certainly little got by him: he records, for instance, that a young man named Molière left the Sorbonne to follow Madeleine Béjart, joined her acting troupe, and eventually married her. While the reference to Moliére's being at the Sorbonne and his marrying Madeleine are certainly wrong, they are probably accurate reflections of contemporary opinion. (The *Historiettes* were edited 1932–34 by Georges Mongrédien.)

Philippe de Dangeau (1638–1720) also kept a journal in which he recorded in great detail incidents at the court of Louis XIV from 1684 to about 1714. His unpublished *Journal* was used by Louis de Rouvroy, Duc de Saint-Simon (1675–1755), together with his own notes and a prodigious memory, to compose a voluminous record from 1692 through the 1720s. (Dangeau's *Journal* was edited by E. Soulié 1854–60; Saint-Simon's *Mémoires* 1876–1930 by A. de Boislisle in 43 volumes.)

Jean-Nicolas de Tralage, nephew of the Queen, left a long series of memoires in manuscript, now preserved in the Bibliothèque de l'Arsenal (mss. 6541–44). (They have been partially printed in *Notes et documents sur l'histoire des théâtres de Paris*, edited Paul Lacroix, 1880.)

Other accounts regularly consulted include *Journal de ma vie* by Maréchal de Bassompierre (1646); the *Mémoires* of Michel de Marolles (1681); the *Mémoires* of the Abbé de Choisy (1724); and the *Mémoires* of Pierre de Bourdeilles de Brantôme (d. 1614).

Correspondence and memoirs are seldom detailed about theatrical affairs and especially theatrical performances in a way that fulfills the hopes of theatre historians. Too, they represent limited and spotty records of a theatrical world that for the most part flourished without attracting any particular interest on the part of their authors. In other words, however rich these sources might appear to be, they reveal a great deal more about the writer and his circle than they do directly about the theatre. In this repect, of course, they are in fact valuable as reflections of contemporary theatrical taste. The heart of their matter is the considered opinion of a cultivated audience, and they therefore contribute to the sociology of the theatre.

Literary Journals, Gazettes, and Newsletters

Nothing indicates a shift in the theatre historian's task more than the rise of weekly or monthly periodicals in the seventeenth century. For the first time, regularly published commentary on politics, literature, and the theatre becomes available. We have the beginnings of the literary and theatrical review, destined to provide historians of the eighteenth-, nineteenth-, and twentieth-century theatres sometimes with too much rather than with too little material. Broadsides, newsletters, and pamphlets were common in Elizabethan and Jacobean England, and in Spain, but they were occasional and non-sequential in nature. The new publications in France, the products of middle-class entrepreneurship, herald in a sense the commercialization of the personal journal and memoir (*cf.* the letters of Guez de Balzac, discussed above), a process that was ultimately to include correspondence and autobiography as well. In a broad sense, too, such publications were used for purposes of publicity. As Mélèse points out, the *gazettes* carried announcements and communications, undoubtedly paid for, concerning theatrical creations, the success of plays in performance, and the publication of dramatic works (*Le Théâtre et le public à Paris sous Louis XIV*, p. 20). This is a new world, and by the end of the seventeenth century, however much we might argue over its beginning and direction, it is safe to hazard that the civilization of the Renaissance had run its course.

Mélèse, who in *Le Théâtre et le public* offers a very useful discussion of periodical publications in seventeenth-century France (pp. 7–16), distinguishes three categories: (a) *journaux*, literary magazines which announced new books, provided some idea of their content, and noted new discoveries in the sciences; (b) *gazettes* which were far more political in their orientation; and (c) *la petite presse*, the products of what he calls gossips and newsmongers. The *journaux* considered the theatre only insofar as plays were published as books. They consequently tell us very little about theatrical presentation. Their commentary, by gentlemen of taste, was uninfluenced by the circumstances of production, by the acting, or the *mises-en-scéne*. For this kind of information it is necessary to turn to the *gazettes* and *la petite presse*. Some journalists in fact specialized in theatrical affairs, announcing and commenting on new plays, reviewing the performances of specific actors, keeping the public informed of the behind-the-scenes theatrical gossip, and so on. Unfortunately, much of this material has disappeared.

The most important *journaux* of the seventeenth century are the following: (a) the *Journal des Scavans*, founded in 1665 by Denis de Salle and continued under several editors through 1714, and considered to have been the premier literary journal in France; (b) *Nouvelles de la République des Lettres*, published in Amsterdam by Pierre Bayle from 1689 to 1689 and continued by Henri Besnage de Beauval in Rotterdam as *Histoire des Ouvrages de Scavans* (1687–1709); and (c) *Bibliothéque Universelle*, edited 1686–93 by Jean le Clerc.

The honour of founding the first French newspaper, *La Gazette*, in 1631 belongs to Theophraste Renaudot (1586–1653), a physician and publicist who operated under the patronage of both Cardinal Richelieu and his successor, Mazarin. Renaudot published collections of the *gazettes*, together with supplements, in yearly *Recueils des gazettes* between 1633 and 1653. *La Gazette* continued after his death and in 1762 became *La Gazette de France*. Nearly a dozen other newspapers, mostly from the last quarter of the century, were published outside France—in The Hague, in Amsterdam, and Utrecht in Holland; in Hamburg and in Brussels. (These publications are found in parts in the Bibliothèque Nationale, the Archives Nationales, the British Library, and the Bibliothèque Royale in Brussels. See Mélèse, *Le Théâtre*, pp. 9–12.) We have in addition two short-lived rivals of *La Gazette*: François' Colletet's *Journals de la Ville de Paris* (1676) and Sandras de Courtilz's *Annales de la Cour et de Paris pour les années 1697 et 1698* (1702).

Although the publications of *la petite presse* have been sadly depleted over the years, there are several manuscript collections extant, including *Lettres historiques et anecdotiques* for the years 1682–87, in the Bibliothéque Nationale (mss. fr. 10265). But in several instances *la petite presse* achieved a prominence that merited a more permanent form. *La Muze Royale* (1656–60), begun in 1655 as *La Muze heroï-comique au Roy*, probably the work of Charles Robinet de Saint-Jean, and *La Muze historique* (1658–59) by Jean La Gravette de Mayolas are available for consultation. More important sources are the weekly letters or *gazettes* in burlesque verse published by Jean Loret between 1650 and 1665. Loret began with single copies, then collected these in a series of about a dozen volumes, the entire project culminating in the three volumes of *La Muze historique* published between 1650 and 1665. (*La Muze historique* has been edited by Ch. L. Livet, 1857–78.) Loret reported the events of the day, including the publication of new books and the performances of new plays, enthusiastically and indiscriminately, and for this very reason remains a valuable source of information for historians. And finally, we have *Le Mercure galant*, founded on an irregular basis in 1672 by Jean Donneau de Visé (1638–1710) and appearing monthly from 1678. (It was known as *Le Mercure galant* until 1714; *Le Nouveau Mercure* 1714–21; *Le Mercure* 1721–24. In 1724 it became *Le Mercure de France* and so continued until 1791.) Mélèse calls *Le Mercure galant* ''the most important, and also the most characteristic of the 'reviews' of worldly information'' (*Le Théâtre*, p. 15). And like most of the periodical sources, it is especially valuable for the last quarter of the century.

Drama and Fiction

The baroque spirit of the seventeenth century encouraged a self-reflective examination of the illusion of the theatre itself, and several French plays feature

a play-within-a-play, represent a performance or a rehearsal, or name characters after the actors portraying them. Occasionally, these plays reveal details of
contemporary theatrical performance otherwise denied us. *Le Comédie des comédiens* (ca. 1631) by Le Sieur Gaugenot and a play of the same name by
Georges de Scudéry (1632) depict rehearsals at the Hôtel de Bourgogne and at
the Théâtre du Marais respectively. Corneille's *Illusion comique* (1636) has a
play-within-a-play; and the characters in Philippe Quinault's *La Comédie sans
comédie* (1655) bear the names of the actors playing the parts. But the most
famous group of plays dealing with the theatre form part of the comic war of
1663, which followed the production in December 1662 of Molière's *L'Ecole
des femmes*. Molière wrote two plays in his own defense: *La Critique d'Ecole
des Femmes*, in which "critics" discuss the play; and *l'Impromptu de Versailles*, which portrays a rehearsal. *L'Impromptu* features Molière's company
under their own names and ridicules the tragic actors of the Hôtel de Bourgone,
again under their true names. Replies were provided by Donneau de Visé in
Zelindre and *La Réponse à l'Impromptu de Versailles*, and by Montfleury *fils*,
son of the leading actor at the Hôtel de Bourgogne, in *L'Impromptu de l'Hôtel
de Conde*.

Actors and playwrights provide other kinds of writings as well, all of which
become grist to the historian's mill. Agnan Sarat (d. 1613) has left us *Le Legat
testamentaire du Prince des Sots*. The farce actors Bruscambille (Jean Des Lau-
riers), Tabarin (Antoine Giraud), and Gaultier-Garguille (Hughes Guéru) in their
various writings not only help us to understand something of the nature of their
performances, but they reflect as well on the audience before whom they performed, the relationship between performer and audience, and the general tenor
of the actors' lives. And Tristan l'Hermite's autobiographical romance, *Le Page
disgracié* (1642–43), records the dramatist's chequered career in the service of
the duc d'Orleans.

The most frequently cited work of fiction, however, is Paul Scarron's *Le Roman comique*, published in two parts in 1651 and 1657. Scarron was himself a
playwright and *salon* wit, and his account of the adventures and love affairs of
the members of a travelling troupe of actors has generally been accepted as a
realistic and valuable picture of the turbulent life and performances of provincial players in the seventeenth century. Nevertheless, *Le Roman comique*,
like Rojas' *El viaje entretenido* (discussed in Chapter 3), is a comic novel in
the picaresque tradition, and the conventions of the genre must be accounted
for in evaluating the work as evidence of theatrical life. Certainly Scarron's
novel follows tradition in its portrayal of the young man who falls in with an
acting troupe, the veteran players, and the comical dramatist. And Scarron, unlike Rojas, was never an actor; nor did he ever leave—nor crippled as he was,
could he leave—the confines of Paris. A historian's reading of *Le Roman comique* must be conditioned by these facts.

Travellers' Accounts

As usual, travellers provide us with some information, although their contribution appears to be less important for French theatre history than we might expect. We meet the young Thomas Platter again, who offers a description of Paris in 1599 and notes that Valleran's troupe was performing comedies in that year. Sir Philip Skippon visited France as well as Italy in the 1660s as did Edward, son of Sir Thomas Browne, but neither provides information of significance.

Descriptions of Paris

Finally, we turn to contemporary or near-contemporary descriptions of the French capital itself in search of information concerning the physical theatres and theatrical activity. Claude Malingre, in *Les Antiquités de la ville de Paris* (1640), records the dimensions of the *salle* in the Hôpital de la trinité and the offerings of the Confrérie de la Passion. Germaine Brice, whose *Description de la ville de Paris* went through many editions between 1684 and 1752, is also a useful reference. Perhaps of most importance, however, is a scholarly work by Henri Sauval (ca. 1620–ca. 1670). Although not published until 1724, *Histoire et recherches des antiquités de la ville de Paris* dates from a far earlier period and was evidently well known by 1655. Sauval was a learned man who was at home among learned friends, and his *Histoire* is the product of twenty years of research in Parisian archives. He is of course concerned with matters other than the theatre, but he offers descriptions of the Palais-Royal (11, 161–163) and the Petit Bourbon (II, 208–211); and his eleventh and twelfth books (II, 615–696) are concerned with costumes, fêtes and processions, spectacles and divertissements, ballets, tournaments, and acting troupes.

ARCHIVAL DOCUMENTS

Parisian archives and libraries have long furnished theatre historians with important manuscript material. Included is a vast miscellany of official, semi-official, and legal documents: royal decrees, acts and registers of the Parlement of Paris and the Council of State; leases, deeds, contracts, inventories; minutes and proceedings of the various royal academies; collections and inventories of material concerning court entertainments (including ballets), theatres, and acting troupes. The two great repositories are the Bibliothèque Nationale and the Archives Nationales, but the archives of the Comédie-Française, the Bibliothèque de l'Arsenal, and various departmental and municipal archives also house documents related to theatre. Some ideas of the volume of material held by these institutions, and of the incredible amount of patient searching necessary to winnow out pertinent information, can be inferred from the fact that the Minutier Central of the Archives Nationales alone contains better than 80 million documents, a figure rendered only sightly less intimidating by the realization that fewer than

18 million of them date from the seventeenth century. (For an early but still useful survey of theatrical material in the Archives Nationales, see Henri de Curzon, *Bibliographe Moderne* I, 52–83.)

While it is comforting to have some idea of the precise location of the original documents that scholars cite, few of us are likely in the first instance to search out the originals in the Bibliothèque Nationale or the Archives Nationales and we therefore depend upon published collections of archival material. Fortunately, as we have noted, historians of the French theatre have been particularly helpful in this regard. Not surprisingly, many collections are centred on the great French playwrights of the seventeenth century: Molière, Corneille, and Racine. Molière's career has been the subject of particular attention. The publishing of documents relating to Molière began in the nineteenth century with Eudore Soulié's *Recherches sur Molière et sa famille* (1863) and Emile Campardon's *Documents inédits sur J. B. Poquelin Molière* (1871) and was considerably augmented in the twentieth century by Madeleine Jurgens and Elizabeth Maxfield-Miller (1963) and by the two volumes of Georges Mongrédien's *Recueil des textes et des documents du XVIIe siècle relatifs à Molière* (1965). Mongrédien has also provided a similar volume on Corneille (1972); and Raymond Picard collected documents relating to Racine in *Corpus Racinianum* (1956). Deierkauf-Holsboer's *La Vie d'Alexandre Hardy* (1972) also includes a valuable collection of documents relating to that playwright.

Documents concerning actors have also been published. Again, Emile Campardon led the way in the nineteenth century with *Les Comédiens du roi de la troupe française pendant les deux derniers siècles* (1879) and *Les Comédiens du roi de la troupe italienne* (1880), both with the explanatory sub-titles, "Documents inédits recueillés aux archives nationales." These volumes, together with Jal's *Dictionnaire*, the *Histoire du théâtre française* of les frères Parfaict, and the works of Chappuzeau, Loret, Renaudot, and Tallement noted above, provide the main sources for Mongrédien's later work on actors of the seventeenth century, especially his *Dictionnaire biographique des comédiens français du XVIIᵉ siecle* (1961; *Supplément* by Jean Robert 1971). Besides birth and death records—which might of course be located anywhere in France—these works include warrants of royal pensions (nearly always annexed to an excerpt from the pensioner's baptism and a declaration written by him), *actes notaires* (marriage contracts, wills, and so on), and *procès-verbaux* (minutes of proceedings).

Finally, we turn to documents concerning the Hôtel de Bourgogne and the Théâtre du Marais, and when we do so we turn as well to the work of the remarkable Dutch theatre historian, S. Wilma Deierkauf-Holsboer. Her four volumes devoted to these two theatres seem destined to remain standard works of reference, and the more than one hundred and fifty documents included in the appendices to *Le Théâtre du Marais* (1954, 1958) and *Le Théâtre de l'Hôtel de Bourgogne* (1968–70) represent precious source material laboriously gathered from archives. Mme. Deierkauf-Holsboer pays special homage to legal documents. Writing of her work in the Archives Nationales since the first edition of *L'Histoire de la mise en scène* (1933), she points out in the revised edition of 1960:

We reported [in 1933] that we would not succeed in bringing more light to bear on the theatrical life of the seventeenth century than through the scrutiny of legal records [*minutes de notaires*], the only trustworthy manuscript sources. This difficult and long-term task has led to the discovery of hundreds of documents for the period we deal with here [1600–73] which provide us, among other things, with many details concerning theatres, their location, their structure, set design and set designers, the composition of acting troupes, and actors and actresses, preparations for the dramatic events, costumes, organization, etc. [p. 8]

Three inventories of documents and titles relating to the Hôtel de Bourgogne and another relating to the Théâtre du Marais are useful for reconstructing the history of the theatres. (See Deierkauf-Holsboer, *Hôtel de Bourgogne*, I, Appendix, no. 4, no. 18; also p. 8; and *Théâtre du Marais*, II, Appendix, no. 2.) The Hôtel de Bourgogne inventories for April 2, 1614, and March 31, 1639, are particularly important as adjunct guides to the *Collection of Principal Papers* (see above). The first provides brief descriptions of forty-seven documents relating to legal actions, seventy-six receipts, and twenty-two leases; the second, drawn up by lawyers, is a crucial guide to the history of the Hôtel de Bourgogne before 1597, when the Confrérie de la Passion gave up direct control of theatrical performances. From 1597, according to Deierkauf-Holsboer, the history of the theatre may be found in the *minutes de notaires*—the financial and administrative transactions of the companies: leases, *après-mort* inventories of actors, *actes d'association*, contracts for sets.

Leases

The details that leases provide include the names, given and family, of the leaser and the lessee; descriptions of the houses, the structures, and their locations; the amount of the rent and the method of payment, together with explanations for other charges and stipulations. And where information is scarce, such details can provide valuable clues to the conditions of performance. Deierkauf-Holsboer notes, for example, that a lease of March 25, 1598 (*Hôtel*, I, Appendix, no. 3), mentions "la grande salle" and "des loges" of the Hôtel de Bourgogne. A few years later, another lease, dated April 8, 1606 (*Hôtel*, I, Appendix, no. 8), refers to "la grande salle, théâtres et loges et la gallerye d'en haut, appelée le paradis." The plural "théâtres" suggests the possibility that there was more than one acting area in the Hôtel de Bourgogne, but since references to a *théâtre supérieure* are not consistent, it is also possible that this second stage was removable. (The contract for the new Marais of 1644 specifies a *théâtre supérieure*.) Otherwise, leases help us to trace the movements of acting troupes, their fortunes, and something of their internal organization.

Après-Mort Inventories

Among the documents printed by Deierkauf-Holsboer are several inventories taken of the possessions of actors after their deaths (for example *Marais*, I, Appendix, nos. 10–11; II, Appendix, no. 7). Not only do these inventories give some idea of the stage costumes and properties used by the actor, they also serve to counteract the impression of actors as impecunious vagabonds created by Scarron in *Le Roman comique*.

Actes d' Association

These contracts, more than a dozen of which are printed by Deierkauf-Holsboer in *Marais, Hôtel de Bourgogne*, and *Alexandre Hardy*, outline the legal constitution of an acting troupe for a determined period and stipulate the conditions under which the members of the enterprise were to work and receive remuneration. The discoveries the Dutch historian made for her study of Hardy are especially important for the light they shed on the activities of Hardy and Valleran de Comte during the early years of the seventeenth century. In one respect, however, these *actes d'association* are disappointing: With the exception of three contracts from the 1660s (*Marais*, II, Appendix, nos. 53, 61, 62), the *actes d'association* provide no information concerning the distribution of roles.

Contracts for Sets

A few documents in the Archives Nationales are concerned with set designs, but in general they offer less than what we might hope. Very few details concerning the décor itself can be derived from the contracts, and even information about the costs of sets and machines is scarce. The Marais contract with the designer Denis Buffequin in September 1660 for *La Toison d'Or* (*Marais*, II, Appendix, no. 44), for instance, specifies simply that the actors will provide the money necessary for all the lights that will shine on the machines. Another contract with Buffequin, this time, for a revival of *Andromède* in 1655 (*Marais*, II, Appendix, no. 1) is equally vague and compares unfavourably with the detailed description of the scenic effects for the original production published in *Andromède, Tragédie représentée avec les machines sur le théâtre Royal de Bourbon* (1650) (printed in Nagler, *Source Book*, pp. 167–172). Other contracts made in 1656 by the Comédiens du roi at the Hôtel de Bourgogne for a set for the lost *Astianax* (*Hôtel de Bourgogne*, II, Appendix, no. 11–12) inform us that the Bourgone actors by-passed the designer and dealt directly with the carpenter and painter.

PICTORIAL AND GRAPHIC EVIDENCE

The general impression we get from textbooks is that there is an unlimited amount of pictorial material relating to the French stage, and that what we are presented represents merely the tip of the iceberg. It is an impression confirmed by books such as Lucien Dubech's *Histoire générale illustrée du théâtre* (1932), the third volume of which contains numerous reproductions of engravings, sketches, and paintings representing the seventeenth-century theatre, and Sylvie Chevalley's *Album théâtre classique* (1970), which contains hundreds of examples of similar material. It is also true that we derive as well an impression of theatrical life that seems rich and detailed. While basically accurate, both impressions can also be misleading. A closer examination of this pictorial material reveals a predominance of portraits of playwrights, title-pages, illustrations from published plays, paintings based as much on the artist's imagination as on theatrical observation, and published engravings of scene designs—all of which we have come to realize need careful analysis and evaluation as evidence for theatre history. Consequently, the number of illustrations of central importance to the study of the French stage is drastically reduced, and the details concerning theatres and theatrical performance—the main concerns of theatre history—are both fewer and more difficult to establish than our original impression would suggest.

The Popular Theatre

The iconographic record of the popular theatre of French farce and Italian *commedia dell'arte* persists throughout the sixteenth and seventeenth centuries, although the amount of extant material naturally increases in the later period. Woodcuts accompanying the printed editions of farces such as *Pierre Patelin*, illustrated editions of Terence, engravings and pictures of the Italian comedy (after 1570)—all of these have been used in attempts to construct a picture of popular performance. We have touched on this before, but it is worth emphasizing yet again that book illustrations especially were intended mainly to decorate books, not to illustrate stages, that we are dealing with the art of painting or engraving, not with the art of the theatre. Nevertheless, the pictures tend to agree in their depiction of a simplified booth stage which is not at odds with what we might expect: a platform stage on barrels or trestles and a curtain behind. Such a stage is shown in a drawing now in the municipal library at Cambrai depicting a troupe of strolling players giving a performance in the country (Molinari, *Theatre through the Ages*, p. 171), and in the well-known painting of a Dutch fair by Pieter Balten (*Oxford Companion to the Theatre*, fig. 10). Such too is the stage depicted in a seventeenth-century engraving featuring the street show of the farceur Tabarin, who was entertaining Parisians about 1620 (Wiley, *Early Public Theatre in France*, fig. 10).

An important series of eight woodcuts in the National Library in Stockholm, Sweden, and in the Bibliothèque Nationale depicts scenes from the repertoire of the troupe of Agnan Sarat, who in 1578 leased the Hôtel de Bourgogne. (Some but not all of the woodcuts are printed in Wiley, fig. 4, and in Molinari, pp. 172–173.) The significance of the pictures lies in the mingling of French and Italian characters in the same dramatic episode, specifically, Agnan as a shepherd and Arlequin as a glass dealer. "Such a playlet," comments Wiley, "would intimate that Agnan was associated with the Italian actors. . . . Or it all might be a manifestation of the quirks of the artist's imagination" (p. 43). The two traditions are nonetheless again mixed in two versions of the same painting in the Musée de la Comédie-Française, dating from 1670. (See Dubech, *Histoire générale* III, 126; Molinari, *Theatre through the Ages*, p. 178.) Two earlier engravings by Pierre Mariette (Dubech, III, 129) and H. Liefrink (Dubech, III, 102) depict French farceurs in much the same manner as the *commedia* actors are depicted.

Pictures of individual French comic actors of the period are numerous. Among those most often reproduced are engravings of Turlupin, Gaultier Garguille, and Gros Guillaume by Abraham Bosse (Wiley, fig. 5–7); an engraving of Guillot-Gorju by Mariette (Wiley, fig. 8); representations of Jodelet, Gandolin, and Turlupin from the Collection Rondel in the Bibliothèque Nationale (Dubech, III, 137); and a famous depiction of Jodelet escaping from the burning Théâtre du Marais (Deierkauf-Holsboer, *Marais*, I, Plate V). It is true, as Mme. Deierkauf-Holsboer reminds us, that engravers of the period were not overly concerned with accuracy of representation, but it is equally true that their work does give us some idea of the comic actor's costumes and stage deportment.

This is especially true of the work of Abraham Bosse (1602–76), a disciple of Jacques Callot who produced almost 2,000 engravings illustrating the customs and social milieu of the France of Louis XIV. (André S. Blum catalogued 1,512 engravings in *L'Oeuvre gravée d'Abraham Bosse*.) While few of these engravings are devoted to theatrical subjects, many of them, particularly those of human figures, are "framed" and composed in the manner of a stage scene. We can see this theatrical composition, for instance, in *Mariage à la ville* and *Mariage à la compagne*, and in two engravings of a domestic battle (Blum, Plates 80–81). Bosse did engravings of *Captaine Fracasse* (Blum, Plate 44, no. 1415) and *L'Espagnol et son laquais* (Blum, Plate 44, no. 1071), both of which are strongly reminiscent of *commedia* figures. But the best known and most frequently reproduced of Bosse's theatrical engravings are *L'Hôtel de Bourgogne* (1634) and Troupe Royale (1635–36). The first (Blum, Plate 27; Dubech, III, 121) features Turlupin, Gaultier-Garguille, Gros-Guillaume, and a lady on stage, flanked by boxed "spectators"—an amused Frenchman and a startled Spaniard; it was later used for Scarron's *Roman comique* (1678). The second (Molinari, *Theatre through the Ages*, pp. 174–175; Deierkauf-Holsboer, *Marais*, I, Plate IV) shows us seven comedians: the Captain, the Lover, Turlupin, Guillot Gorju, Jodelet, Isabelle, and her father Jacquemin. Once again, the influence of the *commedia dell'arte* is apparent.

Theatres

Information concerning the locations and exteriors of theatres, their interior arrangements, and the nature of their stages can be derived from maps of Paris, architectural plans, and various engravings and sketches.

The earliest extant map of Paris to feature the Hôtel de Bourgogne is the Gomboust Plan of 1652 (reproduced in Wiley, *Early Public Theatre in France*, fig. 15), and the picture there given of a rectangular structure facing on the rue Mauconseil, with an extension northward to the rue Française, is confirmed in the Rochefort Map of 1676 (Wiley, fig. 11) and the Bullet Plan of 1707 (Wiley, figs. 14, 18, 19). The Gomboust and Bullet maps also show the Théâtre du Marais—Bullet in some detail. Since the Marais was originally a tennis court (a structure often used for dramatic performances), the location and especially the appearance of these *jeux de paume* are of considerable interest to theatre historians. The best evidence we have of the exterior appearance of a *jeu de paume* in the early seventeenth century is provided by the so-called Vellefaux drawing on parchment in the Archives Nationales, dating from about 1615 (Wiley, fig. 22). On it are depicted six *jeux de paume*, and accompanying the drawing is a blueprint of some of the lots and buildings of the district, allowing the calculation of dimensions. Finally, we have depicted in the Quesnel Map of 1609 the Foire Saint-Germain (Wiley, fig. 13). (An engraving of 1650—Wiley, fig. 12—shows the fair in detail, including a performance of some kind on a low canopied stage.) A full account of the maps is available in A. Bonnardot's *Etudes archeologiques sur les anciens plans de Paris* (1851).

Obvious starting points for the investigation of theatre architecture are books by contemporary architects or historians of architecture. Unfortunately, we have nothing useful from the seventeenth century; but two important works from the eighteenth century are available: Pierre-Jean Mariette's *L'Architecture française* (1727) and Jacques-François' Blondel's *L'Architecture française* (1752–56). Both include plans and elevations of the principal buildings of Paris and are particularly valuable for their drawings of the Salle des Machines, set up by Gaspare Vigarani in a wing of the Tuileries Palace in 1660. (See T. E. Lawrenson, *French Stage in the XVIIth Century*, figs. 88, 90; Izenour, *Theatre Design*, fig. 2.31.) Jacques Heuzey (*Revue d'Histoire du Théâtre* 6, 1954) discusses a sketch of the same theatre dated 1659–1662, preserved in the Archives Nationales. The fact that we are dealing with a royal palace explains, of course, why such material has survived and why later historians of architecture such as Mariette and Blondel were interested in it. In addition, in the Cabinet des Estampes of the Bibliothéque Nationale (Va 361 VII) is a collection of six plans, two of which are for the Salle des Ballets at Versailles (Lawrenson, figs. 93–94): The remaining four relate to unknown and anonymous projects. (Alfred Marie discusses the plans in *Revue d'Histoire du Théâtre*, 1951). Louis Battifol provides a brief description of an anonymous plan for the Palais-Cardinal preserved in the Cabinet des Estampes of the Bibliothèque Nationale (Va 231e), which shows a room eighteen metres by twenty metres by twelve metres high. The stage, he writes, is elevated two metres and is nine metres deep; the benches for spectators rose seven metres above the level of the audience. (See *Richelieu et Corneille*, p. 12.) Unfortunately, Battifol does not provide an illustration of the plan. The only other theatre for which plans survive is the Jeu de paume de l'Etoile, the last home of the Comédie Française in the seventeenth century, opened April 18, 1689. These plans, published by Nicole Bourdel in *Revue d'Histoire du Théâtre* (1955), were found in the Archives of the Comédie-Française among various memoires and legal documents and consist of the façade of the building, a cross-section of the auditorium, and plans of the first and third *loges*.

Engravings and sketches from a variety of sources provide important information concerning theatre interiors. The theatre in the Palais-Cardinal/Royal has been immortalized in a famous painting and an engraving based on the painting. The oil-on-canvas painting (reproduced by Molinari, *Theatre through the Ages*, pp. 188–189), depicts a performance before Cardinal Richelieu, Louis XIV, and Anne of Austria, none of whom is watching the stage. The engraving (Dubech, III, 228; Wiley, fig. 21; Lawrenson, fig. 87) has some of the scene reversed, but it differs more significantly in having the Cardinal replaced by a long-haired courtier. The printed edition of Jean Desmarets' *Mirame*, the play that opened the Palais-Cardinal in 1641, includes two pictures of the stage, one with the curtain open (Dubech, III, 237) and one with the curtain closed (Wiley, fig. 26). These illustrations were both folded in the middle of the volume, and the resulting crease line led Deierkauf-Holsboer into a rare error. She assumed in her *Histoire de la mise en scéne* that the curtain consisted of two halves which were drawn to reveal the scene. Wiley points out the error in *Early Public Theatres of France* (p. 198) and suggests that the curtain was of one piece and was raised or lowered by a roller. With this pictorial evidence must be compared as well Battifol's manuscript plan and the written description given by Henri Sauval in *Histoire et recherches des antiquités de la ville de Paris* (II, 161), where full details concerning this theatre in the Palais-Cardinal are provided.

Other palatial theatres have been similarly made familiar through oft-reproduced illustrations. A famous engraving from the *Ballet comique de la reine* depicts the Salle du Petit Bourbon in 1581. And the same court theatre is represented as well in a family of engravings in the Cabinet des Estampes of the Bibliothéque Nationale, executed to commemorate the meeting of the Estates General in 1614. (See, for example, the engraving reproduced in Dubech, III, 265.) The temporary theatres erected at Versailles after 1660 are illustrated in engravings done to commemorate elaborate festival productions such as the three-day extravaganza of 1664 titled *Pleasures of the Enchanted Island*, and also in a well-known engraving of Molière's *Malade Imaginaire* as it was performed at Versailles in 1674 (Dubech, III, 240).

The Hôtel de Bourgogne and the Théâtre du Marais are not so well documented pictorially. An illustration from Charles Hulpeau's *Jeu royal de la paume* (1632) provides an excellent view of the interior of a seventeenth-century tennis court (Dubech, III, 267; Wiley, fig. 17), the original structure of the Marais. And the frontispiece to Scudéry's *Comédie des comédiens* (1635) depicts an entrance to the Hôtel de Bourgogne (Dubech, III, 143; Wiley, fig. 16). Otherwise we are dependent upon a sketch and a subsequent engraving of the interior of an unidentified public theatre attributed variously to Abraham Bosse and François Chauveau. (The sketch is reproduced in Chevalley, *Album théâtre classique*, p. 4; the engraving in Wiley, fig. 20; Deierkauf-Holsboer, *Marais*, I, Plate XI; Dubech, III, 128.) Finally, besides the invaluable sketches of set designs, the *Mémoire de Mahelot* contains a rough drawing of a theatre interior which is difficult to interpret and seldom discussed. Presumably, it depicts the Hôtel de Bourgogne, but it does not seem to correspond to what we know about the interior of that theatre. For the time being, the drawing remains a puzzle.

Illustrations from Printed Plays

Seventeenth-century editions of French plays are often accompanied by illustrated frontispieces and by illustrations in the texts themselves. The extent to which these pictures can be relied upon as evidence for staging practice varies from case to case. Those of set designs accompanying editions of plays staged in the Italian manner can be evaluated like any other engravings of set designs, and within that context clearly can provide us with information. Other illustrations do in fact appear to be based on stage presentation, or at least on a conception of stage presentation not at variance with what we otherwise know. Those by Jérôme David in Jean Puget de la Serre's *Martyre de Sainte Catherine* (1643), for example, show the stage of the Hôtel de Bourgogne and give us an idea of how the *théâtre supérieure* might have been used. (See Lawrenson, *French Stage in the XVIIth Century*, figs. 57–58.) On the other hand, the prevalence of illustrations obviously based on the artist's conception of the scene and bearing no relationship at all to the stage ought to alert us to the fact that *all* illustrations of printed plays must be treated with scepticism. This is especially true of the many engravings included in editions of Corneille and Racine, which are common currency in popular histories and textbooks. While they undoubtedly have their own interest, they are only peripherally a part of the history of the theatre. As Lawrenson points out, "The engraver is here concerned with removing the picture from any scenic connotation and making it as impressive as possible. He is in fact illustrating the published work of literature and not the performance" (p. 114).

Exceptions to this generalization are the illustrations in editions of Molière, which do indeed appear to reflect the plays in performance. The way in which details from these engravings can profitably be used as evidence for stage history is illustrated by Susan Ellen Picinich in an article in *Theatre Survey* (1981). The author compares the ten engravings from six of the seven plays which feature the character Sganarelle—normally played by Molière himself—with the descriptions of the costumes in Molière's *après-mort* inventory. (For the inventory, see Jurgens and Maxfield-Miller, *Cent Ans de recherches sur Molière*, pp. 566–570.) Picinich concludes: "The engravings show the basic silhouette of the costume, while the inventory describes fabrics and colors, as well as accessories and trim. The engravings and descriptions clearly coincide" (XXII, 35).

The fact that Molière's characters live only on the stage as opposed to the independent historical life of most of Corneille and Racine's tragic characters may have helped to keep the engravers' imaginations bound to the theatre.

PERSPECTIVE THEORY AND SCENE DESIGN

Vitruvius' *De Re Architectura*, which played such an important role in the development of Italian theatrical practice, was equally well known in France. Jocandus' illustrated edition of Vitruvius was available early in the sixteenth century; Philander's edition and commentary were both available by mid-century; and a French translation by Jean Martin appeared in 1547. While this early spate of activity waned with the turn of the century, Vitruvius continued to be read and quoted throughout the seventeenth century, although Julien Mauclerc's *Traité de l'architecture suivant Vitruve* (1648) and Claude Perrault's *Les dix livres d'architecture de Vitruve* (1673, 1684) were the only new French editions of Vitruvius. In addition, Alberti's *De Re Aedifactoria*, based on Vitruvius, was translated into French by Jean Martin in 1553; and the first two books of Serlio's famous *Archittetura* (1545) were published in France in a bilingual edition.

The theory of perspective was similarly known and discussed in France, although writers seem to have been slow in realizing its significance for stage design. Jean Pelerin's *De artificiali perspectiva* was published in 1505, but as late as 1612 Salamon de Caus, in his *Perspective*, seems oblivious to any possible theatrical application of his theory. In fact, the first theorist to realize the theatrical possibilities of perspective design was Jean le Dubreuil, whose *Perspective pratique par un Parisien de la Compagnie de Jésus* appeared in three volumes between 1642 and 1649.

T. E. Lawrenson, who provides a thorough discussion of the theoretical background to theatre architecture and stage design in *French Stage in the XVIIth Century*, notes that the engravings of the Roman theatres that illustrate books on architecture in the sixteenth century are preoccupied in the main with decoration and proportion rather than function, and give no hint that the buildings they depict were in fact theatres. Lawrenson cites in particular Jacques Androuet Ducerceau's *Livre des édifices antiques romains* (1584), which includes engravings of the theatres of Marcellus, Lapideum, Balbus, Palatinum, and Pompeii (Lawrenson, figs. 33–35), none of which gives any sign of a stage. The theatres are conceived as houses, and pictures of interiors show the seats of the auditorium abutting directly onto the face wall of the *frons scaenae*. In fact, Lawrenson informs us, as influential as Vitruvian and perspective theory was on the French architectural establishment, it had little direct effect on French perspective stage design. Perspective scenery on the French stage was an Italian import, and even in court festivities and the ballet it was employed only on a limited basis before the middle of the seventeenth century. It is generally held, for instance, that the *Ballet de la délivrance de Renaud* (1617) was the first production in France to make use of angled wings and back shutters. And the *Mémoire de Mahelot* provides evidence that perspective did not reach the public stage until the 1630s.

Fortunately, there is plenty of pictorial evidence available for the student of stage design to trace its development in France, especially for court productions after 1581. Many of the designs are preserved in engravings executed to illustrate the *livrets* commemorating the performances and many of them have been reproduced in readily accessible publications, especially those concerned with the *ballet de cour*: Le Prunières, *Ballet de cour en France*; Christout, *Le Ballet de cour de Louis XIV*; McGowan, *L'Art du ballet de cour en France;* Beaumont, *Five Centuries of Ballet Design*. The principal repository of engravings is, as we might expect, the Bibliothéque Nationale in Paris. (See Henri Bouchot, *Catalogue de dessins relatifs à l'histoire du théâtre conservés au departement des Estampes de la Bibliothèque Nationale*, 1896.) But the largest single collection of theatrical sketches and drawings is to be found in the National Museum in Stockholm, Sweden. Here are twenty-five large folios containing 2,788 costume sketches and 1,233 drawings of stage and *fête* designs, acquired in 1742 from the estate of a former director of the Paris opera. While few of these drawings give any indication of the artist or the intended performance, it has been possible to identify some of them by collating them with engravings and drawings in the Bibliothèque Nationale and the Bibliothèque de 'Opéra, and by comparing them with stage-directions. A great many have proved to be studio works prepared by Jean Berain and his students and assistants, and copies of these exist in French collections as well. (The Stockholm collection is discussed by Agne Beijer in the *Gazette des Beaux Arts*, series 6, XXVIII, 1945.) In terms of sheer quantity, then, the number of drawings and engravings of scene designs from seventeenth-century France is impressive.

While the great age of French scene design really began with Torelli's French period (1645–61), other designers who were active during the first half of the century deserve at least honourable mention. We noted earlier the work of Balthasar de Beaujoyeulx for the production in 1581 of the *Ballet comique de la reine*. And we possess a working design by Tomaso Francini for the *Grand Ballet de la reine representant le soleil*, danced in the Petit Bourbon in 1621 (Oenslager, *Scene Design*, fig. 24). In addition, two nearly identical series of costume designs by Daniel Rabel for three ballets performed between 1625 and 1632 are preserved in the Cabinet des Dessins of the Louvre (32602–32693) and in the Cabinet des Estampes du Bibliothèque Nationale (Qb^3 Res.). Fifteen of these designs are also to be found in the Houghton Library at Harvard University. (Margaret McGowan reproduces eleven of the designs in *L'Art du ballet de cour*, Plates XVI-XXI.) But, as always, the main historical interest has centred on those designs associated with influential designers. And influential designers were those employed by Cardinal Mazarin, the widowed Queen Anne, and later Louis XIV: the Italians Giacomo Torelli, Gaspare Vigarani, and his son Carlo; and the French Jean Berain, who in 1674 succeeded Henri Gissey as "Dessinateur de la Chambre et du Cabinet du roi" and in 1682 succeeded Carlo Vigarani as principal designer for the court and the opera.

Torelli launched his Parisian career in 1645 at the Petit Bourbon with a production of *La Finta pazza*, the opera with which he had originally achieved fame at the Teatro Novissimo in 1641. Unlike its Venetian counter-part, the French production is documented in the published *libretto* by five engravings and an illustrated title-page (Bjürstrom, *Giacomo Torelli*, pp. 243–245), and in the printed description of the incorporated ballets by an engraved title-page and eighteen illustrations by Valerio Spada. Torelli supervised the set designs for *Orphée* (1647), although the actual designs were evidently executed by Charles Errard. Torelli was directly responsible for the machinery. The scenery was used again in 1650 for the performance of Corneille's *Andromède*, and six engravings by François Chauveau depict scenes and machines. (Oenslager reproduces a pen and ink drawing attributed to Errard and probably intended for *Orphée*, fig. 15 and Plate 3.) The manuscript of the *Ballet de la Nuit* (1653) is preserved in the Bibliothèque de l'Institute (ms. 1004) and includes 119 water-colour illustrations of the costumes. *Les Noces de Pelée et de Thetis* (1654) is particularly well documented pictorially. *Scene e machine preparate alle nozze di teti balletto* includes eleven engravings by Isaac Silvestre. And a manuscript in the Bibliothèque de l'Institute (ms. 1005) contains a set of seventy-three costume designs for the opera; variants of thirty-two of them are also to be found in the Bibliothèque Nationale, Collection Rothschild. Other drawings relating to the performance are in the Archives Nationales, the municipal library of Versailles, the Academy of Fine Arts in Stockholm, and other libraries in Rome, Vienna, and Paris.

An illustrated copy of the libretto for *Les Fêtes de Bacchus* (1651) is preserved in the Cabinet des Estampes of the Bibliothèque Nationale (P.d. 74. res.). It includes water-colour drawings of four sets and seventy-one costumes. They appear to have been painted after the performance and therefore may constitute a record of the sets and costumes rather than blueprints for them. It is sometimes assumed that Torelli was responsible for the designs.

Gaspare Vigarani (1586–1663) and his son Carlo (1622–1713) had less flamboyant and less easily documented careers. Gaspare had already achieved prominence in Modena before he was invited in 1659 to design the new theatre in the Tuileries palace. When he died a few years later, he was succeeded by his son Carlo, whose career seems to have been respectable but undistinguished. Father and son together prevailed at the French court for twenty years, but their work is little discussed by theatre historians.

Certainly, the Vigaranis were overshadowed by Jean I Berain (1637–1711), the French-born and -educated designer who served as "Dessinateur de la Chambre et du Cabinet du roi" for thirty years (1675–1705), during which time he supervised all the court entertainments and, after 1680, the opera and ballet as well. Scene and costume designs by Berain and his assistants Daniel Marot,

Jacques Rousseau, and Claude Gillot are scattered throughout Europe, but large collections are found in the Archives Nationales, the Bibliothèque de l'Opéra de Paris, and, as we have noted, in the National Museum in Stockhom. (See Weigert, *Jean I Berain*, for a descriptive catalogue of engravings.) Many of the costume sketches are counter proofs or studio drawings and were used as working drawings. Berain was undoubtedly the most influential designer of the last decades of the seventeenth century, and it is impossible to gain an appreciation of the theatrical celebrations and entertainments sponsored by Louis XIV without taking his artistic contribution into account.

REFERENCES

Arnaud, Charles. *Les Théories dramatiques au XVIIᵉ siècle: Etude sur la vie et les oeuvres de l'abbé d'Aubignac*. Paris, 1887.

Aubignac, François Hédelin, Abbé d'. *The Whole Art of the Stage*. New York, 1968. [1684]

Balzac, Jean Louis Guez de. *Les premières lettres*. Ed. H. Bibas and K.-T. Butler. 2 Vols. Paris, 1933.

Bapst, Germain. *Essai sur l'histoire du théâtre*. Paris, 1893.

Baschet, Arnaud. *Les Comédiens italiens à la cour de France sous Charles IX, Henri III, Henri IV et Louis XIII*. Paris, 1882.

Bassompierre, Maréchal de. *Journal de ma vie*. Ed. Marquis de Chanterac. 4 Vols. Paris, 1870–77.

Battifol, Louis. *Richelieu et Corneille*. Paris, 1936.

Beauchamps, Pierre-François Godard de. *Recherches sur les théâtres de France, depuis l'année onze cent soixants un jusqu'à présent*. 3 Vols. Paris, 1735.

Beaumont, Cyril W. *Five Centuries of Ballet Design*. London and New York, 1939.

Beijer, Agne. "XVI-XVIII Century Theatrical Designs at the National Museum." *Gazette des Beaux Arts*, series 6, XXVIII (1945), 213–236.

Bibliothèque de théâtre français. Dresden, 1768.

Bjürstrom, Per. *Giacomo Torelli and Baroque Stage Design*. Rev. ed. Stockholm, 1962.

Blum, André. *L'Oeuvre gravée d'Abraham Bosse*. Paris, 1924.

Bonnardot, A. *Etudes archéologiques sur les anciens plans de Paris des XVIᵉ XVIIᵉ, et XVIIIᵉ siècles*. Paris, 1851.

Bouchot, Henri. *Catalogue de dessins relatifs à l'histoire du théâtre conservés au département des Estampes de la Bibliothèque Nationale*. Paris, 1896.

Bourdel, Nicole. "L'Etablissement et la construction de l'Hôtel des comédians Français ru des Fosses-Saint-Germain-des-Prés (Ancienne Comédie) 1687–1690." *Revue d'Histoire du Théâtre*, (1955) 145–172.

Brantôme, Pierre de Bourdeilles, abbé de. *Mémoires de Messire Pierre de Bourdeille, seigneur de Brantôme*. Leiden, 1665–66.

Brereton, Geoffrey. *French Comic Drama from the Sixteenth to the Eighteenth Century*. London, 1977.

———. *French Tragic Drama in the Sixteenth and Seventeenth Centuries*. London, 1973.

Brice, Germain. *Description de la ville de Paris et de tout ce qu'elle contient de plus remarquable*. Ed. Pierre Codet. Paris and Geneva, 1971. [Reproduction of 9th edition of 1752.]

Brockett, Oscar G. *History of the Theatre*. 3d ed. Boston, 1977.

Brown, Howard Mayer. *Music in the French Secular Theatre, 1400–1550*. Cambridge, Massachusetts, 1963.

Browne, Edward. *A Journal of a Visit to Paris in the Year 1664*. Ed. Geoffrey Keynes. London, 1923.

Bussy-Rabutin, Roger de. *Correspondence*. Ed. L. Lalanne. 6 Vols. Paris, 1858–59.

Campardon, Emile. *Les Comédiens du roi de la troupe française pendant les deux derniers siècles. Documents inédits recueillés aux archives nationales*. Paris, 1879.

———. *Les Comédiens du roi de la troupe italienne pendant les deux derniers siècles. Documents inédits recueillés aux archives nationales*. 2 Vols. Paris, 1880.

———. *Documents inédits sur J. B. Poquelin Molière*. Paris, 1871.

———. *Les Spectacles de la foire. Documents inédites recueillés aux archives nationales*. 2 Vols. Paris, 1877.

Caula, G. A., ed. *Balet comique de la royne*. [Facsimile.] Turin, 1962.

Celler, Ludovic [Louis Leclercq]. *Les Décors, les costumes et la mise en scène au XVIIe siècle 1615–1680*. Paris, 1869.

———. *Les Origines de l'opéra et le ballet de la reine (1581)*. Paris, 1868.

Champion, P.H.J.B. *Histoire poetique du XVe siècle*. 2 Vols. Paris, 1923.

Chapelain, Jean. *Lettres*. Ed. P. Tamizey de Larroque. 2 Vols. Paris, 1880–83.

———. *Opuscules critiques*. Ed. A. C. Hunter. Paris, 1936.

Chappuzeau, Samuel. *Théâtre français*. Ed. Georges Monval. Paris, 1875.

Chevalley, Sylvie, ed. *Album théâtre classique: La Vie théâtrale sous Louis XIII et Louis XIV*. Paris, 1970.

Choisy, François-Timoléon, Abbé de. *Mémoires*. Ed. M. de Lescure. Paris, 1888.

Christout, Marie-Françoise. *Le Ballet de cour de Louis XIV*. Paris, 1967.

Cohen, Selma Jeanne, ed. *Dance as a Theatre Art: Source Readings in Dance History from 1581 to the Present*. New York, 1974.

Corneille, Pierre. *Writings on the Theatre*. Ed. H. T. Barnwell. Oxford, 1965.

Curzon, Henri de. "Etat sommaire des pièces et documents concernant le théâtre et la musique conservés aux Archives nationales à Paris." *Bibliographe moderne* I (1899), 52–53.

Dangeau, Phillippe de. *Journal*. Ed. Eudore Soulié et al. 19 Vols. Paris, 1854–60.

Deierkauf-Holsboer, S. Wilma. *L'Histoire de la mise en scène dans le théâtre français à Paris de 1600 à 1673*. Paris, 1933; rev. 1960.

———. *Le Théâtre de l'Hôtel de Bourgogne*. 2 Vols. Paris, 1968–70.

———. *Le Théâtre du Marais*. 2 Vols. Paris, 1954–1958.

———. *La Vie d'Alexandre Hardy: Poète du Rois 1572–1632*. Paris, 1947; rev. 1972.

Droz, Eugénie, and H. Lewicka, eds. *Le Recueil Trepperel*. Vol. II: *Les Farces*. Paris, 1961.

Dubech, Lucien. *Histoire générale illustrée du théâtre*. 5 Vols. Paris, 1932.

Dumanoir, Guillaume. *Le Mariage de la musique avec la danse (1664)*. Ed. J. Gallay. Paris, 1870.

Fournel, V. *Les Contemporaires de Molière*. 3 Vols. Paris, 1863–75.

Fransen, J. "Documents inédits de l'Hôtel de Bourgogne." *Revue d'Histoire Littéraire de la France* 27 (1927), 321–355.

Gasté, Armand. *La Querelle du Cid: Pièces et Pamphlets publiés d'aprés les originaux*. Geneva, 1970. [1898]

Gautier-Garguille. *Chansons*. Ed. E. Fournier. Paris, 1858.

Gilbert, Allan H., ed. *Literary Criticism: Plato to Dryden*. Detroit, 1962. [1940]

Griffiths, Richard. *The Dramatic Technique of Antoine de Montchrestien: Rhetoric and Style in French Renaissance Tragedy*. Oxford, 1970.

Hawkins, Frederick William. *Annals of the French Stage from Its Origin to the Death of Racine*. 2 Vols. London, 1884.

Héroard, Jean. *Journal sur l'enfance et la jeunesse de Louis XIII (1601–28)*. Ed. E. Soulié and E. de Barthélmey. 2 Vols. Paris, 1868.

Heuzey, Jacques. "Notes sur un dessin représentant la Salle des Machines aux XVIIᵉ siècle." *Revue d'Histoire du Théâtre 6 (1954), 60-67*.

Hodges, C. Walter. *The Globe Restored*. 2d ed. London, 1968.

Hubert, A. *Le Registre d'Hubert 1672–1673*. Ed. Sylvie Chevalley. In *Revue d'Histoire du Théâtre*, 25 (1973), 1–195.

Jal, Auguste. *Dictionnaire critique de biographie et d'histoire*. Paris, 1867; 2d ed. 1872.

Jeffrey, Brian. *French Renaissance Comedy 1552–1630*. Oxford, 1969.

Jurgens, Madeleine, and Elizabeth Maxfield-Miller. *Cent Ans de recherches sur Molière, sur sa famille et sur les comédiens de sa troupe*. Paris, 1963.

Lacroix, Paul. *Ballets et mascarades de cour de Henri III à Louis XIV*. 6 Vols. Geneva, 1868–70.

———. ed. *Notes et documents sur l'histoire des théâtres de Paris*. Paris, 1880.

La Grange [Charles Varlet]. *Le Registre de La Grange 1659–85*. Ed. B. E. and G. P. Young. 2 Vols. Paris, 1947.

———. *Registre de la Grange (1659–1685)*. [Facsimile.] Notes by Sylvie Chevalley. Paris, 1973.

Lancaster, Henry Carrington. *The Comédie Française, 1680–1701: Plays, Actors, Spectators, Finances*. Baltimore, 1941.

———. *A History of French Dramatic Literature in the Seventeenth Century*. 5 Parts in 9 Vols. Baltimore, 1929–42.

———, ed. *Le Mémoire de Mahelot, Laurent et d'autres décorateurs de l'Hôtel de Bourgogne et de la Comédie Française au XVIIᵉ siécle*. Paris, 1920.

Lauze, François de. *Apologie de la danse* Tr. Jean Wildeblood. New York, 1952.

Lawrenson, T. E. *The French Stage in the XVIIth Century: A Study in the Advent of the Italian Order*. Manchester, 1957.

Lawton, H. W. *Handbook of French Renaissance Dramatic Theory*. Manchester, 1949.

Lebègue, Raymond. "Tableau de la comédie française de la Renaissance." *Bibliothèque d'Humanisme et Renaissance* VIII (1946), 278–344.

L'Estoile, Pierre de. *Mémoires-journaux*. Ed. G. Brunet *et al*. 12 Vols. Paris, 1875–96.

Lesure, François. "Le Recueil de Ballets de Michel Henry." In *Les Fêtes de la Renaissance*, vol. I. Ed. Jean Jacquot. Paris, 1956.

Loret, Jean. *La Muze historique 1650–1665*. Ed. Ch. L. Livel. 4 Vols. Paris, 1857–78.

Lough, John. *Paris Theatre Audiences in the Seventeenth and Eighteenth Centuries*. London, 1957.

———. *Seventeenth-Century French Drama: The Background*. Oxford, 1979.

McGowan, Margaret M. *L'Art du ballet de cour en France 1581–1643*. Paris, 1963.

Maintenon, Françoise d'Aubigné, Marquise de. *Correspondence générale de Madame de Maintenon*. Ed. T. Lavallée. 4 Vols. Paris, 1865–66.

Malherbe, François de. *Oeuvres*. Ed. L. LaLanne. 5 Vols. Paris, 1862–69.

Malingre, Claude. *Les Antiquités de la ville de Paris*. Paris, 1640.

Marie, Alfred. "Les Théâtres du château de Versailles." *Revue d'Histoire du Théâtre* 3 (1951), 133–52.

Marolles, Michel de. *Les Mémoires de Michel de Marolles, Abbé de Villeloin.* 2 Vols. Paris, 1656.

Mélèse, Pierre. *Répertoire analytique des documents contemporains d'information et de critique concernant le théâtre à Paris sous Louis XIV (1659–1713).* Paris, 1934.

———. *Le Théâtre et le public à Paris sous Louis XIV (1659–1713).* Paris, 1934.

Ménestrier, Claude-François. *L'Autel de Lyon consacré à Louys Auguste et placé dans le temple de la gloire.* Lyons, 1658.

———. *Des Ballets anciens et modernes selon les régles du théâtre.* Paris, 1682.

———. *Des Représentations en musique anciennes et modernes.* Paris, 1681.

Michaud, J. F., and J.J.F. Poujoulat, eds. *Nouvelle Collection des mémoires pour servir à l'histoire de France.* 34 Vols. Paris, 1836–39.

Molinari, Cesare. *Theatre though the Ages.* Tr. Colin Hamer. London, 1975.

Mongrédien, Georges. *Dictionnaire biographique des comédiens français du XVIIe siécle.* Paris, 1961.

———. *Les Grands Comédiens du XVIIe siècle.* Paris, 1927.

———. *Recueil des textes et des documents du XVIIe siécle relatifs à Corneille.* Paris, 1972.

———. *Recueil des textes et des documents du XVIIc siècle relatifs à Molière.* 2 Vols. Paris, 1965.

———, and Jean Robert. *Supplément au Dictionnaire biographique des comédiens français du XVIIe siècle.* Paris, 1971.

Nagler, A. M. ed. *A Source Book in Theatrical History.* New York, 1959.[1952]

Nicoll, Allardyce. *Stuart Masques and the Renaissance Stage.* London, 1938.

Oenslager, Donald. *Stage Design: Four Centuries of Scenic Invention.* New York, 1975.

Oxford Companion to the Theatre. Ed. Phyllis Hartnoll. 2d ed. Oxford, 1957.

Parfaict, Claude and Françoise. *L'Histoire du théâtre français depuis son origine jusqu'à présent.* Paris, 1735–49.

Philips, Henry. *The Theatre and Its Critics in Seventeenth-Century France.* Oxford, 1980.

Picard, Raymond. *Corpus Racinianum.* Paris, 1956.

Picinich, Susan Ellen. "Moliére's Costumes as Sganarelle," *Theatre Survey* XXII (1981), 35–50.

Platter, Thomas. *Beschreibung der Reisen Durch Frankreich, Spanien, England und Die Niederlande 1595–1600.* Ed. Rut Keiser. 2 Vols. Basel and Stuttgart, 1965.

Pougin, Arthur. *Dictionnaire historique et pittoresque du théâtre.* Paris, 1885.

Prunières, H. *Le Ballet de cour en France avant Benserade et Lully.* Paris, 1913.

Pure, Abbé Michel de. *Idées des spectacles anciens et nouveaux.* Paris, 1668.

Racan, Honorat de Bueil, Seigneur de. *Oeuvres complètes.* Ed. T. de Latour. 2 Vols. Paris, 1857.

Renaudot, Theophraste. *Recueil des gazettes, nouvelles, relations et autres choses mémorables de toute l'année.* 21 Vols. Paris, 1633–53.

Rigal, Eugéne. *Alexandre Hardy et le théâtre français à la fin du XVIe et au commencement du XVIIe siècle.* Paris, 1889.

———. *Le Théâtre français avant la période classique.* Geneva, 1969 [1901]

Royer, Alphonse. *Histoire universelle du théâtre.* 6 Vols. Paris, 1869–78.

Saint-Evrémond, Charles de Saint-Denis. *Lettres.* Ed. C. Giraud. Vol. III: *Oeuvres de Saint-Evrémond.* Paris, 1865.

Saint-Simon, duc de. *Mémoires.* Ed. A. de Boislisle. 43 Vols. Paris, 1879–1930.

Saisselin, Rémy G. *The Rule of Reason and the Ruses of the Heart: A Philosophical Dictionary of Classical French Criticism, Critics, and Aesthetic Issues*. Cleveland and London, 1970.

Sauval, Henri. *Histoire et recherches des antiquités de la ville de Paris*. 3 Vols. Paris, 1724.

Scarron, Paul. *Le Roman comique*. Ed. E. Magne. Paris, 1937.[1651–57]

Sévigné, Marie de Rabutin Chantal, Marquise de. *Lettres*. Ed. E. Gerard-Gailly. 3 Vols. Paris, 1953–57.

Silin, Charles. *Benserade and His Ballets de Cour*. Baltimore, 1940.

Skippon, Philip. *An Account of a Journey Made through Part of the Low Countries, Germany, Italy and France*. In *A Collection of Voyages and Travels*, Vol. VI. London, 1732.

Soulié, Eudore. *Recherches sur Moliére et sa famille*. Paris, 1863.

Stone, Donald, Jr. *French Humanist Tragedy*. Manchester, 1974.

Tabarin. *Oeuvres complètes*. Ed. Gustave Aventin. 2 Vols. Paris, 1858.

Tabourot, Jehan [Thoinot Arbeau]. *Orchésographie*. Tr. Cyril W. Beaumont. London, 1925.[1589]

————. *Orchésographie*. Tr. Mary Stewart Evans. New York, 1948.[1589]

Tallemant des Réaux, Gédéon. *Historiettes*. Ed. Georges Mongrédien. 8 Vols. Paris, 1932–34.

Tassin, Nicolas. *Les Plans et profils de toutes les principales villes et lieux considérables de France*. Paris, 1634.

Tristan l'Hermite. *Le Page disgracié*. A. Dietrich. Paris, 1898.[1643]

Urbain, C., and E. Levesque. *L'Eglise et le théâtre*. Paris, 1930.

Villa, Nicole. *Le XVIIᵉ Siècle vu par Abraham Bosse, graveur du roy*. Paris, 1973.

Weigert, Roger-Armand. *Jean I Berain, Dessinateur de la Chambre et du Cabinet du Roi (1640–1711)*. 2 Vols. Paris, 1937.

Wiley, W. L. *The Early Public Theatre in France*. Cambridge, Massachusetts, 1960.

FESTIVAL AND PAGEANTRY

INTRODUCTION

The activities of Renaissance princes usually included under the headings of "festival" or "*fête*" or "pageantry" are often difficult to define in precise terms, and their relationship to theatre remains uncertain. We have had occasion to refer in earlier chapters to the tournaments and entries, disguisings, mummings, and *entrements* that were features of the medieval period; and to the *intermezzi*, masques, and *ballets de cour* that developed as courtly entertainments in the Renaissance. To these we may add processions, progresses, water spectacles, fireworks displays, *mascarades, divertissements, carnivale*, and a multitude of other, more specialized terms and activities. Nor were these activities strictly aristocratic. Civic officials and guilds often were responsible for the details (although a noble personage may have provided the occasion). Ordinary citizens participated, if only as members of an audience, in royal entries. Prelates greeted rulers and officiated at investitures and coronations. Above all, these were political events, intended in general to aggrandize the prince and in particular instances to further a specific political aim. Catherine de'Medici pursued her policies in late sixteenth-century France through her courtly "magnificences"; and the celebrated meeting between Henry VIII and Francis I on the Field of Cloth of Gold in 1520 was an unsuccessful but magnificent exercise in diplomacy. Conceiving of these occasions in terms of political function has provided a most useful approach to the study of Renaissance festival and pageantry.

Whether the forms of pageantry are truly theatrical or merely para-theatrical, the study of *fête* and entry has earned a belated recognition in the larger field of theatre history, and consideration of its relationship to the study of the regular or literary theatre is increasingly taken as part of the theatre historian's job. Pageantry, like the mystery, was part of the medieval heritage of the Renaissance, and the images and emblematic devices that had served a civilization for 1,000 years were unlikely to be swept away by rediscovered or newly invented techniques and forms, however learned. Glynne Wickham's reply to those who had objected to the inclusion of the tournament and pageant theatre in his discussion of the medieval stage, while concerned specifically with the English theatre, is equally applicable to the Renaissance theatre in general: "My answer is that Pageantry is itself the quintessence of emblematic art, as anyone acquainted with Heraldry can confirm; to deny it a place in the early history of English drama guarantees failure to understand the subsequent development of both the drama and the methods of performance" (*Early English Stages*, II.i, 209).

GUIDES AND SURVEYS

In his *Italian Civic Pageantry in the High Renaissance* (1979), the American scholar Bonner Mitchell points to the "very rich material of cultural history" represented by the evidence for civic celebrations, but he laments the undeveloped state of the study of such material as a separate discipline. He notes the lack of permanent organizations and specialized journals and the paucity of adequate bibliographies. Only a few *fêtes* have received systematic detailed study. The territory is nonetheless not entirely uncharted, and in fact the student coming to it for the first time may come to the conclusion that there are plenty of maps. The most convenient bibliographical list for the royal entries of Europe is that provided by George Kernodle in *From Art to Theatre* (pp. 226–238). We are otherwise dependent upon more specialized lists and descriptions of accounts of entries and festivals, usually devoted to a single country.

Italy

Bonner Mitchell's work, noted above, is a descriptive bibliography of sixty-five selected entries and festivals in eighteen Italian cities between 1494 and 1549. Mitchell provides summaries of the festivals and descriptions of the printed sources. Other recent biblioqraphies and studies include Giovanna Maria Bertelà and Annamaria Petrioli Tofani's *Feste e apparati Medicei* (1969) and A. M. Nagler's *Theatre Festivals of the Medici* (1964) on Florentine celebrations; Franco Mancini's *Feste ed apparati civili e religiosi in Napoli* (1968) for Naples; M. Fagiolo Dell'Arco and S. Carandini's *L'effimero barocco* (1977–78) for Rome; Mercedes Viale Ferrero's *Feste delle madame reali di Savoia* (1965), an introduction to the *fêtes* of Savoy during the first half of the seventeenth century.

Spain and Charles V

Still the most useful bibliography of *relaciones* of royal entries in Spain is J. Alenda y Mira's *Relaciones de solemnidades y fiestas públicas de Espana*, published in 1903. Alenda y Mira lists accounts of 1,550 entries through the seventeenth century, including entries outside Spain in which any of the Hapsburgs, who ruled Spain 1516–1700, were involved. And the most important Hapsburg in the first half of the sixteenth century was undoubtedly Charles V, who held the concurrent titles of King of Spain (1516–56) and Holy Roman Emperor (1519–56). Charles employed the ceremonial progress as a political weapon. The peripatetic emperor made triumphal journeys nineteen times to Germany and the Low Countries, and another nineteen times to Italy, Spain, France, and England. The significance of Charles' entries for students of Renaissance pageantry is indicated by Roy Strong: ". . . The revival of empire represented in the figure of the Emperor Charles V enables Renaissance humanists and artists to apply to a living individual the whole rediscovered repertory of classical antiquity" (*Splendor at Court*, p. 81). An entire volume of *Les Fêtes de la Renaissance*, edited by Jean Jacquot under the auspices of the Centre National de la Recherche Scientifique (1960), is devoted to ceremonies associated with the emperor. Jacquot's own contribution, "Panorame des fêtes et cérémonies du Regne" (pp. 413–491), is especially useful.

Low Countries

Some of the richest and most lavishly illustrated material deriving from royal entries was produced in Holland and Belgium to commemorate visits by princes and power brokers ranging from the Emperor Charles V to Leicester of England to Archduke Ferdinand of Spain (whose entry into Ghent in 1635 was supervised by Rubens) to William of Orange (whose entry into The Hague in 1691 was one of the most publicized in the Netherlands). An illustrated survey (in Dutch) of royal entries in the southern Low Countries from 1515 to 1635 is provided by I. Von Roeder-Baumbach and H. G. Evers (1943). A later, chronologically arranged bibliography of books and pamphlets describing entries and funeral ceremonies is John Landwehr's *Splendid Ceremonies* (1971).

France

The festivals and pageantry of France have the honour of being the subject of the earliest published collections of descriptions, those of Théodore Godefroy: *Le Cérémonial de France* (1619) and *Le Cérémonial françois* (1649). The latter is particularly important. An early modern bibliography by Paul Le Vager lists a dozen manuscript accounts and 142 accounts printed before 1600 (*Les Entrées solonnelles à Paris*, 1896). Josèphe Chartrou's *Les Entrées solonnelles et triomphales à la Renaissance*, which appeared in 1928, remains the standard account of the Italian influence on the French triumph. In *Les Plaisirs et les fêtes* (1944), Emile Magne treats the royal entries of 1614, 1616, and 1629; court entertainments under Louis XIII; the marriage and 1660 entry of Louis XIV; and the three "fétes de Versailles" of 1664, 1668, and 1674—but his analysis consists principally of description. The most comprehensive survey of French pageantry, however, is that of Gabriel Mourey, whose *Livre des fêtes françaises* was published in 1930. Mourey attempts to assemble or deal with the most important of the numerous documents concerning the French *fête* from the entry of Isabelle of Bavaria in Paris in 1389 to the time of Napoleon. The work is illustrated, and Mourey pays particular attention to paintings, engravings, and tapestries, both as art in their own right and as historical documents "as precise as [they are] precious." He goes further when treating the pageantry of the Renaissance, citing as analogues in a common tradition of emblematic presentation various works of strictly figurative art: the woodcuts illustrating editions of Petrarch's *Trionfi*; Andrea Mantegna's *Triumph of Caesar* (1484), a set of nine canvases featuring triumphal arches; Albrecht Dürer's engravings of the attendants of the Emperor Maximillian. (Although Mourey does not draw attention to it specifically, Dürer also designed a large triumphal arch for the Emperor, covered with historical and allegorical detail. The design was executed as a woodcut; otherwise, both arch and triumph were imaginary.) Finally, Bernard Guenée and Françoise Lehoux reprint extracts from the primary sources for royal entries of the fourteenth and fifteenth centuries in *Les Entrées royales françaises* (1968).

Perhaps the best known, certainly the most discussed, festivals of France were those arranged by Catherine de'Medici, widow of Henri II (accidentally killed in a tilt in 1558) and a major political force in France until her death in 1589. "The history of festivals at the Valois court in the second half of the sixteenth century," writes Strong, "is so closely bound up with her that they can almost be written in biographical terms" (*Splendor at Court*, p. 121). Catherine's "magnificences" consisted typically of a series of *fêtes* spread over several days and featuring chivalric spectacle, music, and song within a dramatic framework, with pageant cars, water shows, feasting, singing, and dancing evolving into a symbolic whole. (The culmination of the process was probably the celebration of a royal wedding in 1581, which included the famous *Ballet comique de la reine*.) Besides the 1581 celebration, festivals were mounted at Chenonceau (1563) and Fontainebleau (1564), at Paris in 1572 for the wedding of Catherine's daughter to the King of Navarre (the occasion of the infamous St. Bartholomew Day Massacre), and in 1573 for the visit of the Polish ambassadors. In addition there was a ceremonial progress through France 1564–66 and a triumphal entry into Paris of Charles IX and Elisabeth of Austria in 1571. (Victor E. Graham and W. McAllister Johnson provide detailed studies and transcripts of the crucial documents for the progress and the entry in *Royal Tour of France by Charles IX and Catherine de'Medici*, 1979, and *Paris Entries of Charles IX and Elisabeth of Austria 1571*, 1974.) These festivals are documented pictorially in half a dozen drawings by Antoine Caron and in the Valois Tapestries (discussed below).

England

Serious examination of the progresses of Queen Elizabeth and James I began in the late eighteenth century. The first two volumes of John Nichols' *Progresses and Public Processions of Queen Elizabeth* were published in 1788; a third volume appeared in 1807. Most copies of these first editions were destroyed by fire, and Nichols provided a new edition in 1823. In 1828 he added four volumes devoted to the progresses and festivities of James I. Nichols' interests were antiquarian rather than historical or analytic, and he includes little attempt at reconstruction or analysis of the materials he lists and prints. Still, there has been no more recent collection of the basic documents and Nichols' work can still be profitably consulted. A more descriptive survey is provided by Robert Withington in *English Pageantry* (1918–26). More detailed descriptive analyses are found in David M. Bergeron's *English Civic Pageantry* (1971), together with a consideration of historical developments, production techniques, and themes. Sydney Anglo's *Spectacle, Pageantry and Early Tudor Policy* (1969) surveys English festivals from Henry VII to the coronation of Queen Elizabeth in 1559, and interprets them in terms of an on-going political process.

A feature peculiar to English pageantry was the Lord Mayor's Show, which had its beginnings in the mid-sixteenth century and by the early years of the seventeenth century had substantially replaced the royal entry and procession in London. The published descriptive texts are the work of well-known playwrights. The first printed pamphlet, containing only speeches, was George Peele's *Device of the Pageant Borne before Wolstan Dixi* (1585), but all the subsequent "texts" of Lord Mayors' Shows (twenty-nine of them) contain both text and description, and are the work of only seven pageant-dramatists. Again, antiquarian interest prompted the early collection of materials: F. W. Fairholt's *History of Lord Mayors' Pageants* appeared in 1843. Withington and Bergeron provide later surveys.

THE EVIDENCE

The official nature of most civic and royal pageantry ensured that records of one sort or another were kept by authorities, and that the archives of state, municipality, and guild—the organizations involved in entries and festivals—can yield pertinent information concerning preparations and expenses. Some of this material has been published, and we have had occasion to refer to it in previous chapters; but some of it remains in manuscript form, and unless scholars have made a particular search for documentation on a particular pageant, most of us are likely to remain ignorant of its existence. The on-going labours of N. D. Shergold and J. E. Varey in Spanish archives has thrown light on festivals as well as on the regular theatre. Varey, for example, has reconstructed the festivities of 1636 organized in Madrid to celebrate, among other things, the birthday of the heir apparent. And he was able to do so principally on the basis of documents discovered in the Municipal Archives of Madrid. These, together with the *Relacion* by Andrés Sánchez de Esejo, constitute the evidence for the pageantry. (See *Renaissance Drama* n.s. I, 253–282.) Similarly, Graham and Johnson in 1974 published for the first time a complete record of the accounts in the Bibliothèque Nationale concerning the preparations for the 1571 entry of Charles IX and Elisabeth of Austria (*Paris Entries*, Appendix IV).

Although English coronation processions and royal entries into London were arranged by the Mayor and Corporation of the city, trade guilds could be called upon to provide particular pageants; and indeed, they seem to have had almost total responsibility for the Lord Mayors' Shows between 1635 and 1640. The main sources of information, therefore, are the Corporation of London Records and the records of the Livery Companies of London. Some of the relevant material from the former is cited and printed in Nichols' volumes on the progresses of Elizabeth and James I and in Withington's *English Pageantry*, but the documents pertaining to the theatre and pageantry have not been systematically collected and published. The records of the Livery Companies have fared better: The Malone Society published *A Calendar of Dramatic Records in the Books of the Livery Companies of London 1485–1640* in 1954 and a similar *Calendar* for the Clothworkers' Company in 1959.

Such records exist in archives and public depositories throughout Europe, but as we have witnessed time and again, such institutions yield their treasures only to patient and painstaking search. We would all prefer published documentation, neatly catalogued and indexed, even computerized. But until the millenium arrives, we shall have to content ourselves with the untidy process of piecemeal publication, supplemented by occasional forays into archives ourselves.

The principal evidence for most tournaments, entries, and festivals, however, consists of written descriptions—usually in print, sometimes in manuscript—of the event and the iconographic artifacts, the texts of speeches and inscriptions, and the pictorial record itself. These are not easily distinguishable categories. Descriptions range from incomplete or fragmentary observations buried in letters, diaries, and memoires to accounts by chroniclers and historians to pamphlets produced for distribution hot on the heels of the event to carefully prepared festival-books or official records, painstakingly produced and lavishly illustrated. The "texts" were usually incorporated into the official accounts, but the poetry involved might well be preserved in separate collections as well. And the pictorial record includes engravings accompanying the published festival-book or official description, oil paintings, tapestries, and occasional drawings. As we would expect, the most complete and elaborate documentation dates in general from the late sixteenth and the seventeenth centuries, when on the Continent at least the commemorative volume became an *objet d'art* in its own right, designed to preserve in permanent form the message of the passing pageant that inspired it.

Contemporary or near-contemporary chroniclers and historians are among the first to be consulted for information concerning the activities of the great and powerful. They are especially valuable for pageantry of the sixteenth century and earlier. In England, the accounts of Robert Fabyan (1516), Edward Hall (1542), Richard Grafton (1568), Raphael Holinshed (1577), and John Stow (1580 seq.) provide information surrounding various ceremonies and entries of importance to the political chronicler, and even in those instances where little detailed description is offered they help to provide a context for the interpretation of the pageant's symbolism. In France, the earlier chronicles of Froissart and

Enguerrand de Monstrelet were supplemented by François de Belleforest's *Histoire des neuf roys Charles de France* (1568). (In addition, Bonner Mitchell has drawn attention to some little-noticed wood-cuts illustrating the entries of Charles VIII of France into Florence, Rome, and Siena in 1494 in a copy of *Le Vergier d'honneur* by André de la Vigne, would-be official historian of the king, preserved in the Bibliothèque Nationale.) In Spain, the *Crónica* of R. Muntaner (1562) includes information concerning festivities associated with royal visits, coronations, peace pacts, and so on. Gaspare Bugati's *Historia universale* (1570) provides eyewitness accounts of some Italian festivals; but the best known Italian historian of the sixteenth century (with the exception of Machiavelli) was Francesco Guicciardini, whose *Storia d'Italia* can profitably be consulted for information concerning the years 1492–1532.

The Emperor Charles V and his many progresses throughout Europe are especially well documented by historians in several languages. Jean de Vandenesse's *Journal des voyages de Charles-Quint de 1514 à 1551* (1552) offers some unfortunately sparse accounts, as does Guillaume de Montoiche's *Voyage et expédition de Charles-Quint au pays de Tunis* (1535). (Both Vandenesse and Montoiche are available in a *Collection de voyages*, edited by Louis Prosper Gachard.) On the other hand, very detailed accounts—in fact the chief accounts—of Charles' entries into Bologna, Genoa, and Mantua in 1529–30 are provided by a manuscript, *Cronaca del soggiorno di Carlo V in Italia*, by Luigi Gonzaga (edited by Giacinto Romano, 1892). The most comprehensive treatment of the Emperor's entries among historians, however, is the *Crónica del Emperador Carlos V* by Alonso de Santa Cruz, described by Bonner Mitchell as "the would-be Spanish historiographer of the emperor." Santa Cruz, drawing on detailed contemporary sources, often is able to provide full accounts of the entries he discusses, including the texts of the inscriptions (in Spanish translation), descriptions of the *apparati*, and explanations of historical and mythological allusions.

Santa Cruz is also a principal source of information concerning the tour of Italy, Germany, and the Low Countries by Charles' son Philip in 1548–49. A work devoted exclusively to that tour, however, is Juan Christoval Calvete de Estrella's *El felicissimo viaje del muy alto y muy poderoso Principe Don Philippo* (1552). (The work is available in a nineteenth-century French translation, *Le Très-Heureux Voyage*, as well as in a modern Spanish edition.) Philip's later trip to England is chronicled by A. Munoz in *Viaje de Felipe II a Inglaterra* (1554).

While these and many other histories and chronicles contribute to our overall picture of princes and pageantry, less formal but sometimes more detailed descriptions of Renaissance pageants are to be found in diaries, letters, and memoirs. Again, our examples are highly selective and intended to be representative rather than comprehensive. Many of the diarists and letter-writers we have discussed in other contexts: Jean Héroard, Pierre de l'Estoile, Henry Machym, Marino Sanudo. But diaries kept by two Papal masters of ceremonies, Biagio

Martinelli (Biagio da Cesena) and Paride de' Grassi, offer insiders' points of view on Roman entries in the early sixteenth century. (See Bonner Mitchell, *Italian Civic Pageantry*.) François Rabelais discusses preparations for the entry of Charles V into Rome in 1536 and provides a full account of the tournament held at Rome in March 1549 to celebrate the birth of Henri II's second son. Marguerite de Valois, daughter of Catherine de'Medici, left an account in her *Mémoires* (published 1628) of the Bayonne entry of 1565. The *Recueil d'aucuns discours* (published 1665) by Pierre de Bourdeilles de Brantôme also provides a lively picture of the Valois court in the last half of the sixteenth century.

Most references in diaries and letters to royal and civic celebrations are brief, however, and even when combined with contemporary historical accounts are rarely adequate for a full reconstruction of the pageants. As the sixteenth century wore on, these occasional and haphazard accounts began to be supplemented by descriptive pamphlets, offered to the public almost contemporaneously with the events they purported to record; indeed, they were sometimes published before the event and thereby served as programmes to allow viewers to follow and understand what they were seeing. (This seems to have been true, for instance, of the London Lord Mayors' Shows.) Many were anonymous and others are by otherwise unknown writers; few would be considered worthy of the pageants they commemorate. They differ from the descriptions in diaries and histories mainly in their increasing numbers and by the fact that their regular production is testimony to a growing concern for a permanent written record of otherwise passing shows. And the glory of those shows, contributed to by the leading artists and writers of the time, ultimately demanded that official festival-books be printed, often under the supervision of the pageant's devisors and the artists who had designed the statues, pictures, and triumphal arches. It is very difficult to distinguish in absolute terms between pamphlets and festival-books. Bonner Mitchell refers to "semi-official reports" and points to an account in a letter of 1513 as an early example of a festival-book, or *livret*. What we can be sure of is that we have crossed a divide between simple record of event and published "art" when we find the festival-book appearing later—even years later—than the pageant it records, and illustrated by numerous engravings by well-known artists. (On occasion, as in the instance of the entries of Pope Clement VII and the Emperor Charles V into Bologna in 1529–30, series of woodcuts or engravings were published separately.)

Illustrated festival- or pageant-books were actually a Continental phenomenon. With the exception of Stephen Harrison's *Arches of Triumph erected in honour of K. James I* (1604), no pictorial record accompanies the published descriptions of English pageants. In Europe, on the other hand, illuminated manuscripts in the medieval manner continued to be produced as presentation copies into the sixteenth century, and woodcuts and engravings are common in festival-books from an early date. Evidently the earliest set of illustrations known in the history of French pageantry are the paintings of the seven pageants making up the entry of Mary Tudor into Paris in 1514. The pictures and a detailed account of the pageantry by Pierre Gringoire are preserved in a manuscript in the British Library (Cotton ms. Vespasian B.II). (The manuscript was edited in 1934 by Charles Read Baskervill.) The book by Rémy Dupuys describing the entry of Charles V into Bruges in 1515 is illustrated by thirty-three nearly full-page woodcuts. By the last quarter of the century copperplate engravings had replaced woodcuts, but the number of illustrations had not diminished: A book describing an Antwerp-Brussels pageant of 1594 includes thirty-three copper-plate engravings; that commemorating the funeral in 1622 of the Archduke of Austria is illustrated by sixty-four double-leaf engravings; and the books cele-brating the entry of William of Orange into The Hague in 1691 by a total of at least sixty etchings. With a few exceptions, the published pictorial record for Italian and French pageantry is not great before about 1550, but the second half of the sixteenth century and the seventeenth century saw the art of the engraver flourish. (A particularly attractive series of etchings in colour illustrate the book describing a *sbarra*, or tournament, in the courtyard of the Pitti Palace in Flor-ence in 1579 in honour of the marriage of Francesco de'Medici and Bianca Cappello. See Nagler, *Theatre Festivals of the Medici*, figs. 27–40.) Spanish festival-books, or *relaciones*, seem to have been the least likely to contain il-lustrations.

We should note that the woodcuts or engravings are not simply indications of the manner of performance or the nature of the playing places; they are to a large extent reproductions in another medium of the art and artifacts that carried the burden of the symbolic meaning of the pageants. But the woodcuts and en-gravings published as parts of commemorative volumes do not constitute the whole of the available pictorial record. Some drawings of *apparati* do exist, although they are rare (especially for the sixteenth century), badly scattered, and their publication erratic. Two chiaroscuro canvases and three preparatory drawings (two or them by the painter Andrea del Sarto), associated with char-iots used in a Florentine carnival parade of 1513, are reproduced by John Shearman in the *Burlington Magazine* (1962). Four drawings by Antonio da Sangallo of an archway for the entry of Charles V into Rome in 1536 are pre-served in the Uffizi Gallery. Some drawings of *apparati* in the so-called Siena Sketchbook, commonly attributed to Baldassare Peruzzi and also housed in the Uffizi, have proved well-nigh impossible to identify with any particular entry. Two of the preparatory drawings by Polidoro da Caravaggio, charged with the preparation of the *apparati* for Charles V's entry into Messina in 1535, are re-produced by Strong in *Splendor at Court* (figs. 72–73). Strong also reproduces two drawings of the festival at Binche in honour of the visit of Charles and Philip in 1549 (figs. 64, 85). And so it goes: an untidy record at best, one that has yet to be completed and the evidence fully incorporated into the description and analysis of Renaissance pageantry.

Compared to continental Europe, the pictorial record of English pageantry is meagre indeed. In fact, what is here discussed constitutes almost all of it:

a. A drawing in the State Museum in Berlin has been attributed to Hans Holbein and is associated with the entry of Anne Boleyn in 1533 (Strong, *Splendor at Court*, fig. 6).

b. A wall painting depicting the procession of Edward VI from the Tower of Westminster once adorned Cowdray House in Sussex. The original was destroyed by fire in 1793, but the Society of Antiquaries published an engraving of it in 1787, and there exists a water-colour copy of it as well. Sydney Anglo expresses disappointment in it, since it depicts only scaffolding, stages for spectators, and tapestry decoration, and nothing of the event itself (*Spectacle, Pageantry and Early Tudor Policy*, p. 283n.)

c. Jean Puget de la Serre's *Histoire de l'entrée de la Reyne Mère dans la Grande Bretaigne*, published in London in 1639, contains illustrations of the colourful procession in honour of King Charles' mother-in-law, Marie de'Medici, and thus almost qualifies as an English illustrated pageant-book.

d. Stephen Harrison's *Arches of Triumph* (1604) contains a series of engravings of arches for the procession of James I through London to his coronation. (See Bergeron, *English Civic Pageanty*, Plates 2–8.)

e. A set of manuscript drawings in the possession of the Fishmongers' Company depicts pageants for Anthony Munday's *Chrysanaleia: The Golden Fishing*, the Lord Mayor's Show for 1616. (They are reproduced in Bergeron, *English Civic Pageantry*, Plates 9–12.) Bergeron considers these drawings comparable in value to Harrison's engravings. It is conceded that the drawings are international in style, an indication that continental practice was not confined to the continent.

f. An eyewitness account of Thomas Dekker's Lord Mayor's Show of 1629 by Abram Booth, secretary to a delegation of the Netherlands East India Company in London at the time, preserved in a manuscript at the University of Utrecht, includes sketches of six pageant devices. (See Malone Society *Collections* V, Plates I-VI.)

And that is pretty much that.

There are two extended pictorial records of pageants which have received particular attention, both because of what they tell us about the pageants and because of their considerable artistic merit. One is the Tournament Roll of Westminster, prepared to record the tournament held in 1511 to celebrate the birth of a son to Henry VIII, and the other is the Valois Tapestries, depicting the magnificences of Catherine de'Medici. While they are in fact masterpieces in their own rights, from the point of view of the historian of the theatre and pageantry, they undoubtedly should be considered as part of a single tradition of pictorial narrative, often executed in tapestries but including as well some of the long series of woodcuts and engravings that adorn many of the published festival-books.

The Great Tournament Roll of Westminster, the "greatest treasure of the College of Arms," is a magnificently executed pictorial narrative on a parchment roll eighteen metres long by over thirty-seven centimetres wide. On it are depicted three separate scenes: the entry into the lists of a procession which

includes four Knight Challengers; a view of the tilt itself, with Challengers at
one end and Answerers at the other, the combat between the King and An-
swerer watched by the Queen, who with members of the court is shown within
a gallery; and the procession returning from the lists after the event. The roll is
reproduced slightly larger than half-size in the second volume of Sydney Anglo's *Great Tournament Roll of Westminster* (1968). Costs prohibited the entire
reproduction in colour, but the few membranes so reproduced give some idea
of the glory of the original. Anglo points out that the roll has a three-fold
significance:

. . . It is a document recording the magnificence of a prince striving for recognition as
a European potentate; it is a record of a form of court spectacle which had been evolving
throughout the history of the tournament in Europe; and, within that class of tournament
it records specifically the feats of arms held by Henry VIII at Westminster in February
1511. [I, xi]

He also notes the desirability of viewing the roll in the general tradition of
"narrative strip," a form that included tapestries, paintings, and the illustrations to René d'Anjou's *Livre de tournois* (I, 74–82).

Anglo also suggests that the famous Valois Tapestries be considered in relation to this tradition. These eight very large hangings, ranging in size from
3.55 metres to 4.03 metres in height and from 3.28 metres to 6.7 metres in
width, are housed in the Uffizi Gallery in Florence. Seven of them have festivals for their subjects: a tournament in a romantic allegorical setting; a tilt in
masquerade dress; a water-*fête*; a combat at barriers; a water combat in costume; a land combat in fancy dress; and what appears to be an early *ballet de
cour*. The last tapestry depicts a journey. The tapestries are reproduced in Plates
I-VIII of *The Valois Tapestries* by Frances Yates, who provides a complete discussion and analysis. "To pass in front of the Valois Tapestries," writes Yates,
"is to have been present at a series of magnificences at the French court" (p.
51). But whether we are dealing with representative or typical scenes or with
illustrations depicting specific festivals which can be documented from other
sources as well is another matter. It was not until 1927 that it was noted that
two of the tapestries correspond with the known descriptions of the Bayonne
festivals of 1565, and that another corresponds with an entertainment for the
visit of the Polish ambassadors in 1573. The problem of identification of the
scenes with particular *fêtes* is complicated by the fact that there is a time gap
between the events depicted in the backgrounds, which appear to have taken
place during the reign of Charles IX, and the figures in the foregrounds, where
Charles is conspicuous by his absence. Moreover, the provenance and history
of the tapestries are murky. Although they were certainly woven in Flanders,
we have no direct evidence concerning exactly when they were done, by whom,
or for whom. It seems likely that they came to Florence with Catherine
de'Medici's granddaughter, Christine of Lorraine, when she married Ferdinand

I in 1589. But until something about the process of their purpose, design, and manufacture could be determined, whatever the Valois Tapestries might be able to tell us was doubtful.

A breakthrough came in the 1950s, when it was discovered that a series of drawings attributed to Antoine Caron, which are scattered throughout various collections in Edinburgh, London, Paris, and New York, resembled in subject matter the scenes in six of the Valois Tapestries. These drawings differ from other drawings of festivals in presenting panoramas of the scenes rather than isolated segments. Specifically, they represent the following: a water combat, a water festival, a tilt, a garden festival, a tournament of Virtue and Love, and a journey. (The drawings are reproduced in Yates, Plates IX-XII.) While the correspondence with the tapestry scenes is not perfect, it has been determined that the drawings precede the tapestries in time and were likely sources for the latter. What is more, it is unlikely that either Caron or the maker of the tapestries was present at any of the events shown. Caron depended on the written descriptions of the festival pageantry. And the artist responsible for the tapestries consulted these same accounts as well as Caron's drawings. The artistic license that allowed the insertion of foreground figures later in date than the occasion depicted behind them also allowed an indoor performance to be depicted as an outdoor one. Like all theatre iconography, the Caron drawings and the Valois Tapestries must be carefully interpreted; but they do provide precious pictorial testimony concerning the magnificences of Catherine de'Medici between 1564 and 1573, particularly those at Fontainebleau (1564) and Bayonne (1565), and those for the Polish ambassadors (1573).

REFERENCES

Alenda y Mira, J. *Relaciones de solemnidades y fiestas públicas de España*. Madrid, 1903.
Anglo, Sydney. *The Great Tournament Roll of Westminister*. 2 Vols. Oxford, 1968.
———. "The London Pageants for the Reception of Katherine of Aragon: November 1501." *Journal of the Warburg and Courtland Institutes* XXVI (1963), 53–89.
———. *Spectacle, Pageantry and Early Tudor Policy*. London, 1969.
Baskerville, Charles Read, ed. *Pierre Gringoire's Pageants for the Entry of Mary Tudor into Paris*. Chicago, 1934.
Bergeron, David M. "The Emblematic Nature of English Civic Pageantry." *Renaissance Drama* n.s. I (1968), 167–198.
———. *English Civic Pageantry 1558–1642*. Columbia, South Carolina 1971.
———. *Twentieth-Century Criticism of English Masques, Pageants, and Entertainments: 1558–1642*. San Antonio, 1972.
———. "Venetian State Papers and English Civic Pageantry." *Renaissance Quarterly* XXIII (1970), 37–47.
Bertelà, Giovanna Maria, and Annamaria Petrioli Tofani. *Feste e apparati Medicei da Cosimo I a Cosimo II*. Florence, 1969.

Calvete de Estrella, Juan Christoval. *El felicissimo viaje del muy alto y muy poderoso Principe Don Philippo*. Ed. Miguel Artigas. Sociedat de Bibliófilos Españōles. Madrid, 1930. [1552]

———. *Le Très-Heureux Voyage*. Tr. J. Petit. Publications de la Sociétè des Bibliophiles de Belgique. 5 Vols. Brussels, 1873–84.

Chartrou, Josèphe. *Les Entrées solennelles et triomphales à la Renaissance (1484–1551)*. Paris, 1928

Dell'Arco, M. Fagiolo, and Silvia Carandini. *L'effimero barocco: Strutture della festa nella Roma del '600*. 2 Vols. Rome, 1977–78.

Fairholt, F. W. *History of Lord Mayors' Pageants*. Percy Society Publications, vol. X. 2 Vols. London, 1943.

Gachard, Louis Prosper, ed. *Collection de voyages des soverains des Pays-Bas*. 4 Vols. Brussels, 1874–82.

Gervartius, Casper, and Peter Paul Rubens. *Pompa Introitus Ferdinandi Austriaci Hispaniarum Infantis, etc. in Urbem Antverpium*. Antwerp, 1642. [1971 Facsimile.]

Godefroy, Théodore. *Le Cérémonial de France*. Paris, 1619.

———. *Le Cérémonial françois*. 2 Vols. Paris, 1649.

Gonzaga, Luigi. *Cronaca del soggiorno di Carlo V in Italia (dal 26 luglio al 25 aprile 1530), documento di storia italiana estratto da un codice della Regia Biblioteca Universitaria di Pavia*. Ed. Giacinto Romano. Milan, 1892.

Graham, Victor E., and W. McAllister Johnson. *The Paris Entries of Charles IX and Elisabeth of Austria 1571*. Toronto, 1974.

———. *The Royal Tour of France by Charles IX and Catherine de'Medici: Festivals and Entries, 1564–66*. Toronto, 1979.

Griffin, Alice V. *Pageantry on the Shakespearean Stage*. New Haven, 1951.

Guenée, Bernard, and Françoise Lehoux. *Les Entrées royales françaises de 1328 à 1515*. Paris, 1968.

Hall, Edward. *Union of the Two Noble and Illustrate Families of Lancaster and York*. Ed. H. Ellis. London, 1809.

Holinshed, Raphael. *Chronicles of England, Scotland and Ireland*. 6 Vols. New York, 1965. [1807–8]

Jacquot, Jean, ed. *Les Fêtes de la Renaissance*. 3 Vols. Paris, 1956–75.

Kernodle, George R. *From Art to Theatre: Form and Convention in the Renaissance*. Chicago, 1944.

Landwehr, John. *Splendid Ceremonies: Stage Entries and Royal Funerals in the Low Countries, 1515–1791: A Bibliography*. Nieuwkoop and Leiden, 1971.

Lecoq, Anne-Marie. "La Città Festeggiante: les fêtes publiques au XVe et XVIe siècles." *La Revue de l'Art*, no. 33 (1976), 83–100.

Le Vager, Paul. *Les Entrées solennelles à Paris des Rois et Reines de France, des souverains et princes étranges, ambassadeurs, etc*. Paris, 1876.

Magne, Emile. *Les Plaisirs et les fêtes en France au XVIIe siècle*. Geneva, 1944.

Malone Society. *Collections III: A Calendar of Dramatic Records in the Books of the Livery Companies of London 1485–1640*. Ed. Jean Robertson and D. J. Gordon. Oxford, 1954.

———. *Collections V: A Calendar of the Dramatic Records in the Books of the London Clothworkers' Company*. Ed. F. P. Wilson. Oxford, 1959.

Mancini, Franco. *Feste ed apparati civili e religiosi in Napoli dal viceregno alla capitale*. Naples, 1968.

Minor, Andrew C., and Bonner Mitchell, eds. *A Renaissance Entertainment: Festivities for the Marriage of Cosimo I, Duke of Florence in 1539*. Columbia, Missouri, 1968.

Mitchell, Bonner. *Italian Civic Pageantry in the High Renaissance: A Descriptive Bibliography of Triumphal Entries and Selected Other Festivals for State Occasions*. Florence, 1979.

Mourey, Gabriel. *Le Livre des fêtes françaises*. Paris, 1930.

Nagler, A. M. *Theatre Festivals of the Medici 1539–1637*. New Haven and London, 1964.

Nichols, J. G., ed. *The Fishmongers Pageant on Lord Mayor's Day 1616 Devised by Anthony Munday*. London, 1844.

Nichols, John. *The Progresses, Processions, and Magnificent Festivities of King James the First*. 4 Vols. London, 1828.

———. *The Progresses and Public Processions of Queen Elizabeth*. 3 Vols. London, 1823.

Petrolio, Annamaria. *Mostra di disegni vasariani. Carri trionfali e costumi per la genealogie degli dei (1565)*. Florence, 1966.

Russell, Joycelyne C. *The Field of Cloth of Gold: Men and Manners in 1520*. London, 1969.

Santa Cruz, Alonso de. *Cronica del Emperador Carolos V compuesta por Alonso de Santa Cruz su cosmografo major*. Ed. D. Ricardo Beltran y Rozpide and Don Antonio Blasquez y Delgado-Aguilera. 5 Vols. Madrid, 1920–25.

Sayle, R.T.D. *Lord Mayors' Pageants of the Merchant Taylors' Company in the 15th, 16th and 17th Centuries*. London, 1931.

Shearman, John. "Pontorno and Andrea del Sarto, 1513." *Burlington Magazine* CIV (1962), 478–483.

Stow, John. *Annales, or, A General Chronicle of England*. Continuation by Edmond Howes. London, 1615, 1631.

Strong, Roy. *Splendor at Court*. Boston, 1973.

———, and J. A. Van Dorsten. *Leicester's Triumph*. Leiden and London, 1964.

Tani, Gino. "Le Comte d'Aglié et le ballet de cour en Italie." In *Les Fêtes de la Renaissance*. Ed. Jean Jacquot. Vol. I. (Paris, 1956).

Van de Velde, Carl, and Hans Vlieghe. *Stadsvier ingente Gent in 1635 voor de Blijde Intrede van Kardinal-Infant*. Ghent, 1969.

Varey, J. E. "Calderón, Cosme Lotti, Velazquez, and the Madrid Festivities of 1636–1637." *Renaissance Drama* n.s. I (1968), 253–282.

Viale Ferrero, Mercedes. *Feste delle madame reali di Savoia*. Turin, 1965.

Von Roeder-Baumbach, I., and H. G. Evers. *Versieringen bij Blijde Inkomsten gebruikt inde Zuidelijke Nederlanden gedurende de 16de en 17de e euw*. Antwerp, 1943.

Wickham, Glynne. *Early English Stages 1300–1660*. 3 Vols. in 4. London, 1959–81.

Withington, Robert. *English Pageantry: An Historical Outline*. 2 Vols. New York, 1963. [1918–26]

Yates, Frances A. *The Valois Tapestries*. London, 1959.

INDEX

About the Author

RONALD W. VINCE is Associate Professor of English and a member of the Instructional Committee on Dramatic Arts at McMaster University, Canada. He has published articles in *English Studies, Essays in Theatre, Walt Whitman Review,* and *Studies in English Literature.*